ANOTHER WORD FROM ARLOTT

ANOTHER WORD FROM ARLOTT

A further collection of John Arlott's broadcasts, cricket commentaries and writings
selected by
DAVID RAYVERN ALLEN

PELHAM BOOKS

First published in Great Britain by
Pelham Books Ltd
44 Bedford Square
London WC1B 3DP
1985

British Library Cataloguing in Publication Data

Allen, David Rayvern
Another word from Arlott.
1. Cricket
I. Title
796.35′8′0924 GV917

ISBN 0 7207 1620 9

Printed and bound in Great Britain by
Butler & Tanner Ltd, Frome and London

Contents

Acknowledgements

For every article printed or programme transmitted there are perhaps, at a conservative estimate, twenty people whose contribution is not immediately apparent. The service areas of publishing and broadcasting are full of anonymous heroes and heroines. Who recalls the photographic researcher who has pursued a precious print beyond any reasonable expectation or the tape engineer whose dexterous marriage of a dozen or so rough cuts manufactures a small miracle of time and motion? At the end of the day the dedication and skills of these and their like remain largely unsung. Let us clear our throats for them now.

John is the first to recognize those who have helped on his journey through the years and he joins in saluting an eminent cast all of whom have, in different ways, added to these pages: Harry Altham, Sam Aukland, Trevor Bailey, Ronnie Barker, Mike Barnard, Sydney Barnes, Denzil Batchelor, Mervyn Burden, Neville Cardus, Michael Carey, Brian Close, Learie Constantine, Ronnie Corbett, Ted Dexter, Desmond Eagar, Alan Gibson, Jim Gray, Charlie Griffith, Wesley Hall, Leo Harrison, Jack Hobbs, Henry Horton, Len Hutton, Colin Ingleby-Mackenzie, David Jacobs, Charles Kortright, Tony Lewis, Danny Livingstone, Roy Marshall, Wilfred Rhodes, Peter Sainsbury, George Scott, Derek Shackleton, Philip Sharpe, E. J. 'Tiger' Smith, Ernest Stockton, Jack Walsh, Alan Wassell, Moray Watson, David White, Anona Winn, Wilfred Wooller, Frank Worrell and Norman Yardley. The pity is, a quarter of them have departed.

Grateful thanks to the BBC for permission to transcribe

a few of John's many broadcasts, Terry Jones and Michael Palin for a section of their Cricket Commentator's sketch, to Dennis Stevens for the articles from *Hampshire – the County Magazine,* to Christopher Martin-Jenkins for pieces that originally appeared in *The Cricketer,* to Richard Boston for the essay on Louis MacNeice in *Vole,* to Imogen Grosberg for her poem 'On his Seventieth Birthday' and to *The Listener, The Spectator, The Guardian* and *The Times* similarly for other offerings.

I am indebted also to Geoffrey Copinger, Geoffrey Whitelock, Stephen Green and Tony Winder for their help in providing material and to Muriel Gascoin and Clare Ford for their assistance in polishing the draft publication.

A special thought for John himself. His words on tape and in print are measureless in quantity and quality; the inspiration they kindle knows no frontier. His continued support and gentle suggestion on the way to preparing this volume has not only been valued as such but utterly invaluable in kind.

DAVID RAYVERN ALLEN

Picture Credits

The photographs in this book are reproduced by kind permission of Allsport Photographic Ltd (page 5); BBC Hulton Picture Library (pages 3, 23, 30, 37, 41, 46, 57, 69, 98, 117, 119, 122, 195, 208, 243, 244, 245, 258, 260); *Bournemouth Evening Echo* (pages 144, 147); *The Cricketer* (page 294); Patrick Eagar (pages 129, 255); *Hampshire – The County Magazine* (page 215); Rev. D. H. R. Jones (page 149); The Mansell Collection Ltd (page 47); Nottinghamshire County Cricket Club (page 77); S & G Agency Ltd (pages 72, 221, 270, 291); Times Newspapers Ltd (page 179); *Yorkshire Post* (page 25); Winchester Tourist Office (pages 8, 10).

INTRODUCTION

Applause.

ANNOUNCER: And now over to the Oval for the cricket.

RONNIE CORBETT *as John Arlott:* Thank you very much. Well, in fact, we're not at the Oval, as you can see, because unfortunately bad light closed play early and we popped round here to the Almumbo restaurant for a quick bite.... Here's a really wonderful example of a very accurate slow waiter (*audience laugh*) coming in – this lovely lazy action and he's about to hand me the menu and you'll notice he's bending as he does so – thank you very much indeed. (*laughter*) Richie, did you notice, by the way, that he happens to be a left-hander, did you notice?

RONNIE BARKER *as Richie Benaud:* Yes John, I did notice. I did notice that....

MORAY WATSON *as Peter West:* I notice also, that the minestrone and the chicken risotto are back on the menu again. What d'you make of that, John?

RONNIE CORBETT *as John Arlott:* Well, I'm very pleased to see the minestrone back on the menu. You see, it's the sort of thing this meal really needed. Pleased to see they've dropped the suet pudding, pleased to see that and frankly, I'm quite amazed to see that chicken risotto getting a second chance. (*laughter*)

RONNIE BARKER *as Richie Benaud:* I think it's very easy to under-estimate the rissotto, you could fare a lot worse. Of course, there is the question of the runs to be considered. (*laughter*)

(*Part of a Cricket Commentators sketch written by Terry Jones and Michael Palin for* The Two Ronnies *BBC Television, 1976.*)

In his time, John has had the pleasure, or perhaps otherwise, of hearing his voice parodied by a host of professional and amateur performers, and none will be short of examples to quote. A random selection bridges Jonathan Miller and Peter Cavanagh who were early opportunists on stage, a number of Carroll Levis 'discoveries' who 'did Arlott' as their set piece on television and radio soon after he had made an impact with the listening public, and more recently, writer and commentator, Christopher Martin-Jenkins, who has delighted audiences at cricket dinners with a memorable impression developed, no doubt, from close observation at the adjoining 'mike'. The mimicry is not confined to these shores. A few years ago author and broadcaster, Tony Cozier, remarked that, 'in the West Indies Arlott is better known than most of the England players. Whenever a school match is in progress, you'll always find young boys sitting under trees giving ball to ball commentaries imitating him.' Indeed, at one period during the fifties, it was virtually impossible to travel on the railway around Britain without thinking that one had heard those familiar tones. The station announcers at several mainline termini, and in particular one at Nottingham Midland, modelled their tannoy delivery in kind. The actual owner of 'the voice' is quietly amused: 'If they ask me, I'll do the best impression yet.'

In one sense then, it would seem extraordinary to find that at the beginning of his broadcasting career John was given to doubts about the sound of his voice, 'later described as a passport to fame.' The occasion during a rehearsal, when actor Valentine Dyall realized he was trying to change his accent and threatened to 'personally cut out his tongue' if he did so, is well documented. Less known is the instance when he returned to Hampshire after a lengthy period working away. John wandered into a field just by his parents' home in Basingstoke and began chatting to some haymakers. Inquired one, 'What be this 'ere Lunnon talk you'm puttin' on then?'

When, however, memory stirs the voices of wireless in the forties, it is easy to realize that John had, as a relative

A signing session at Bristol during the match between Gloucestershire and the New Zealand tourists in August, 1949

newcomer, found himself in a faintly hostile land of self-contained and somewhat mannered 'Oxford'. His accent or dialect, call it what you will, was often, in those days, inaccurately described as West Country, Somerset or Gloucester; sometimes, acceptably, as Hampshire; rarely, precisely, as Basingstoke.

The voice was marginally less distinctive then than it is now, though of course, still instantly distinguishable. Therefore, in the context of the time, his doubts become thoroughly understandable. The eventual breakthrough and acceptance of regional accents in broadcasting on a wide scale did not occur until the 1960s.

Doubts of a different sort had been expressed by his father when he joined the BBC after leaving the Police Force. 'It seems an insecure sort of place to me,' he said, as John prepared to leave Lodge Road, Southampton, for shared digs with composer Constant Lambert and painter/designer/sculptor Michael Ayrton and his wife in All Souls Place, lying just off the port bow of the broadcasting battleship in London, W.1. His unease was quickly dispelled though, as his son made chances to work in many areas of radio and the press, and eventually television from 1949.

Apparent immediately was a remarkable ability as a communicator, especially in unscripted programmes. If, before World War II, 'Teddy' Wakelam and Howard Marshall had pioneered the act of commentary, there is no doubt that, after it, John transformed that act into an art form. In an article for *The Listener* in 1975, writer and journalist Brian Glanville recalled his awakening to the voice 'rich and orotund, southern and rural, pregnant with images of the countryside' and also analysed the method:

> What seems to me to make Arlott the best cricket commentator and perhaps the best sports commentator I have ever heard is the way he combines manner with matter. There have been, and are, commentators with splendid voices but no feeling for words and little for the game on which they commentate. There are others who know their subject inside out, may well have excelled as players, but come over the air as dull dogs, with unattractive voices and no style. Arlott, it seems to me, has all three positive attributes.

In the same way as a listener can be beguiled by 'the voice' so can a reader be captured by the written word. Once, in an interview, John reasoned that, 'doing BBC commentary actually helps me write my article at the end of the day.'

Although, as a natural commentator, happenings went in through the eyes and out through the mouth with subsequent almost total non-recollection, John found that: 'it acts as a filter, heightens your experience and provides you with what the drama theorists call "dominance".' An advantage for the majority reading the commentaries in the forthcoming pages is that they will be able to 'hear' the lines as spoken, even though changes of inflection ('the very meat of broadcast prose') are virtually impossible to convey when put on paper.

Any proposed rounded anthology of Arlott, though, is

Time to reflect, having discarded headphones after a commentary stint.

bound to reflect the amazing range of interest. Cricket, of course, is recurrent throughout the book as is poetry, the inspiration for which, sadly, eventually became denuded by a demanding work-pattern. Topographical tours in verse, trips to Europe with the *Evening News*, historical surveys of Hampshire, outings to diverse sports, adventures with wine and food, flirtations with politics, engagements with controversial issues, each has found a place and been part of the canon. It is only a part. John's collecting enthusiasms are multifarious and chapters could just as easily have been devoted to articles on engraved glass, *Vanity Fair* cartoons, cigarette cards, Japanese colour block prints or Himalayan herbs.

Above all, John is a connoisseur of human nature and takes pleasure in life. And so, his view takes in both the

A greetings card sent by illustrator Royman Browne to John in November, 1953.

personalities and the product in the market place. He is, in Alderney, but twelve minutes flight from France: 'When planes are right, you can go to Cherbourg on a Thursday market day, have a splendid meal and buy anything French you want: shop in the market, wonderful choice whether its flowers, seeds, vegetables, fruit; it's superb and it's the size of a football pitch and the cheese market next to it, butter, Normandy butter, oh, it's a splendid place to go to.'

His appreciation is manifest in his work. We are fortunate who are able to share it.

I

Hampshire – My Home County

Is it too fanciful to imagine Alderney as an island fortress off the Hampshire coast? Certainly for most, realistic access is only by way of the county airports at Eastleigh and Hurn and since John has joined the dozen or so ex-Hampshire residents now living on Alderney, the link and passenger traffic has become greater. Before discovering the peace of the Channel Isles, Hampshire's famous son (some thirty years ago) took the listening public on a whistle-stop tour of his native county.

Hampshire – My Home County

Hampshire is home to me, and, more than that, it was for years my world. My parents' families lived there for generations – my father's people in the north of the county, my mother's in the New Forest – and I myself had never been out of the county for more than a fortnight until I was thirty.

So much seems to me to go on there, so much, and such a variety of things, that I can think of no broad generalization which will give you the shape of it in a single sentence. You might say it is a county of chalk hills, because the North Downs, the South Downs, and the Berkshire Downs run into it. But then it is also a county of forests, the New Forest, Bere Forest.

You might say it is a county of villages – and many of them remain unspoilt – but what of Portsmouth, Southampton, and Bournemouth? Say, if you will, that it is a maritime county with that major naval base, one of the

Winchester Cathedral.

greatest civil ports in the world, and a large and healthy seaside resort – but inland lies the great Army centre of Aldershot and the lovely city of Winchester.

Say, if you like, that it is an agricultural county, because its hogs, sheep, strawberries, and dairy lands are famous – but what of the industries springing up all through it, especially round Southampton?

Let me say, rather, that it is the old England. Of course, it is older than that. Stone Age and Bronze Age men left their traces all over the county, and the Brythons, from whom Britain takes its name, built their camps along the Downs. The Romans established themselves at Winchester, Portchester, Silchester, and the villas in a dozen other places.

But for the Saxons, Hampshire was the core of the Kingdom of Wessex, and the Saxon, English, and eventually British nations sprang from the capital hub of Winchester.

HAMPSHIRE CAESARS

You could not ask stronger evidence of the roots of the Roman Empire about these parts than in the name Julius Caesar, which still crops up: one of that name, from near the Surrey border, was an outstanding cricketer a hundred years ago; and Julius Caesar was the name of a boy I was at school with.

My father, and his father before him, and his forebears for years were born at Silchester. One of the first trips I remember was to the house where my father was born: a thatched cottage with a yew tree in front of it – they call the yew 'the Hampshire weed' – and he and I took my son to Silchester, too, to see that house.

Now away south, with one of Hampshire's several fine straight Roman roads to take us through Basingstoke – now twice the size it was when I was a boy, with its motor, chemical and leather works, its foundry and atomic energy plant – down to Winchester.

Winchester is still for me the loveliest city in the world,

dominated by the great cathedral – of old, its nave was the longest in Europe except for St Peter's in Rome – with its peaceful and beautiful close, and the gentle buildings of William of Wykeham's great school, the houses and shops of every period in the past thousand years standing cheek-by-jowl in the complete harmony that speaks unhurried growth.

Climb the steep St Catherine's Hill, as Winchester schoolboys used to have to do every morning before breakfast: you look down on a city whose beauty and variety will charm away whole hours of just staring across the water-meadows to that pattern of warm and mellow age.

There is the great hospital of St Cross where, after war-time rationing, the wayfarer may again claim the traditional dole of bread and a horn of ale from the monks.

South-east we go by way of Gilbert White's peacefully immortal Selborne and of Hambledon, where if cricket did not begin, at least one hundred and fifty years ago the

St Cross.

first great cricket club grew and played, a team that might play, and often defeat, the rest of England for a wager of 500 guineas and often as much again in side-bets.

And now into Portsmouth. As we come in, let us pause just over the crest of Portsdown and look down on the harbour and city, set out like a geography demonstration of inlets, bays, peninsulas and islands. Then, down and over the single bridge by which every vehicle must enter and leave.

A perfect place to police, you would say, and certainly, by means of a check on the bridge, it used to be claimed that no car could be stolen and taken out of Portsmouth. But once this happened, and there were enquiries, recriminations, doubts, even disbelief, until it was found that the thieves had driven the car into a warehouse and into a pantechnicon there, and the pantechnicon with the stolen car in it was waved, naturally enough, through the check-point across the causeway to the mainland.

Portsmouth and Southsea are the twin towns of Portsea Island, naval base and seaside resort. You may look over Nelson's flagship, the *Victory* or the latest battleship, listen to the concert parties, or, if you turn to sport, there is the United Services ground, housing good top-class club and Services rugby and cricket, as well as county cricket.

'POMPEY CHIMES'

At Fratton Park through autumn, winter and spring, you may watch the flourishing first division club Portsmouth – Pompey – whose supporters urge them on with a song that, in their travels, they have made familiar on every football ground of England, to the tune of 'Pompey Chimes'.

Then, with the line of the Isle of Wight on the horizon, we turn away west, through the strawberry fields of Botley, to Southampton, with its modern civic centre standing up out of the flatness after the bombing of the last war, with its miles of docks, terminal point of the great liners.

Along the west side of Southampton Water lies the New Forest, the royal hunting forest which saw the death of William Rufus in Canterton Glen. Rufus Stone, near Cadnam, marks the spot, with, nearby, the inn called the 'Sir William Tyrrell', named for the man who killed the King.

The New Forest is a haunt of the naturalist, for some of the rarest of British flowers, butterflies, and moths are to be found there; nowhere else in England is there woodland in such prodigality, such room for the rambler, the camper, the rider.

And so we go on by way of Buckler's Hard, where many of Nelson's ships were built of New Forest oak, by Beaulieu and ancient Christchurch with its great Priory to Bournemouth, with its pines and its relaxing air.

Still much is left to be said of Hampshire, some of it, perhaps, in the lovely evocative names of its villages: Kingsclere, Beaulieu, Godsfield, Bishop's Waltham, Otterbourne, Queen Bower, Rowland's Castle, Greywell, Waggoner's Wells – names and places of the county which is the old England, the first England.

BBC Eastern Service, April 1956

2

RIPLEY *v.* NEW ZEALAND SERVICES

John auditioned as a broadcaster at the instigation of John Betjeman. Betjeman had enjoyed reading several of the young Arlott's poems and mentioned his name to Geoffrey Grigson, a *producer in the BBC's West of England Service at Bristol.*

'Grigson thought I had the voice to make a good broadcaster and he wanted me to do a series of Sunday night postscripts which at the time J.B. Priestley was doing. So I put in four or five scripts and they were absolute rubbish – I had no idea about script-writing at all – a year or two later when I knew what script-writing was about I could see what rubbish they were –'

Grigson obviously did not share that opinion for in January of 1945 he wrote to the Assistant Director of Talks: 'I enclose the only copy of a draft script by John Arlott on the Hambledon Cricket Club. It seems to me a very much better script than his earlier one and I feel that he showed with that first script that he was a potentially very good broadcaster indeed. May I have your verdict and the script back.'

The verdict must have been favourable as the broadcast of 'The Hampshire Giants' took place in the spring. At that stage in his career, still employed by the Police Force and not yet an established member of the BBC staff, John was anxious to accumulate as much broadcasting experience as he could. A further chance soon arrived, in June of 1945, with the sirens of war barely silent, a village chemist in Surrey decided to palliate the pain of recent events in the most agreeable way possible. He organized a cricket match;*

* Reprinted in *A Word from Arlott.*

the BBC sent Detective-sergeant Arlott to investigate. All he remembers now of the occasion is visiting a local pub run by two elderly spinsters who, 'with a sense of shock, served me drink'.

ANNOUNCER: This is London calling in the Pacific Service of the BBC. The speaker today is John Arlott – a young policeman from Hampshire, whose great interests are cricket and writing. He is going to talk about cricket in the village of Ripley in Surrey, where yesterday a New Zealand Services team met the Ripley Cricket Club on the village green.

JOHN ARLOTT: I have been to see the New Zealand Services XI play cricket against Ripley on Ripley village green, down in Surrey. On a village green. Now the English village green is a sacred place – sacred to the people of the village and to their fairs and their games – most of all, sacred to their cricket. It is true that football is played there in the winter, but then the carefully mown cricket square is roped off to save it from damage by footballers' boots. Village cricket has been the subject of many jokes, but it was on the village greens of England that the game of cricket was born and bred – and it was a great game before it left them. A village club, Hambledon, in my native Hampshire was, from 1770 to 1785, the greatest single club that cricket has even known – only of a great team could Nyren have written, as he wrote of Hambledon after naming the club's eleven best players: 'No eleven in all England could have stood against these men, and I think they might have beaten any two-and-twenty.'

Ripley isn't a big village, even today its population is only about 1,500, but its village green, bounded by a row of elms on one side and by the village street on the other, is an ideal setting for cricket, real cricket – the game which is not associated with the Stop Press or great concrete grandstands.

And today all Ripley turned out to greet us, even the Vicar came on from his morning service to say Grace for us at lunch, and almost half the population must have been there.

Bombs in the blitz and fly-bo bombs in 1944 dropped in the village, some of them even on the green, but, as one local cricketer put it: 'Thank Heaven they didn't hit the pitch.'

Well, we started at twelve for 11.30, the New Zealanders batting first, and batting on a wicket as true as mower and roller could make it. Stewart Dempster and F/O Clive Geary of Otago went in first, and Ripley opening bowlers were Shorter and Geoff Pinnock. Geoff Pinnock's family has played for Ripley for three generations, and he straight away gave the village boys reason to shout by bowling Geary for a duck. Then Sergeant Vincent came and went before we realized he had arrived. After that there was a stand of 33 by Stewart Dempster and Roger Blunt, and both of them looked likely to stay all day until Blunt mis-hit a gift of a full toss straight into fine-leg's hands. Then a Ripley visitor, Kerville, an Australian from the Carlton Club, Victoria who was the next bowler, bowled Dempster with what looked very much like a shooter. And then the rot set in, Corporal George Sage from Auckland, 14; F/O John Elliott also from Auckland, not out 12; they did their best, but the rest of the batsmen, out of practice, did not look very impressive; the wicket was of varying pace, and in the end, New Zealand were all out for 82 - Kerville 5 for 13.

Then it was Ripley's turn. Their other star visitor, Peter Sunnucks, from Kent, and Manning, a local public schoolboy, were their first pair, and Dumbleton soon bowled Manning for 3. But then Sunnucks was joined by Hugh Lindo, the star local batsman, and a typical village cricket batsman. Many years of village cricket had taught him not to judge any ball until it had bounced and with a judicious series of half-cock defensive shots and pushes behind gully off his back foot, he helped Sunnucks to put on 42 runs before the Kent man was bowled by Dumbleton for 30. His was the best innings of the day, careful and chanceless, and all the time, Freddy Badcock, who had travelled all night with Blunt and Dempster to play in the match, was, despite his tiredness, bowling away from one end as steadily as ever. A quick run-out at 64 and that was the crisis of the game. Roger Blunt put himself on to bowl, the wicket was crumbling and his leg break was turning like a striking snake and raising little puffs of dust. Lindo caught and bowled Blunt 15, 67 for 4. Fred Pullen, the local captain, put a powerful if rather uncertain bat to the bowling for a few minutes. Then Pullen caught Vincent bowled Blunt, 12 – 76 for 5. Jelly – yes, that really was his name – hung a hopeless bat at a googly and did not appear a bit surprised when he looked round to find his middle stump had gone – 76 for 6. But the next two batsmen, Doe and Marsh seemed to have no nerves at all. Blunt spun and flighted the ball, Badcock was as steady as the Rock of Gibraltar at the other end, but Doe and Marsh were still there at 84 for 6 and Ripley won – Blunt 4 for 21.

So that was Ripley, with the flags round the marquee, a real New Zealand flag amongst them, some cheerful careless cricket after tea with the game won and lost – strawberries and ice cream, salad and beer and deck chairs, shooters, googlies and the frantic arguments of small boys: 'You told me Fishlock was going to play.' 'So he is.' 'No he ain't.' And the New Zealanders laughing and not worrying about losing.

So the great men of cricket have come again to Ripley. And why Ripley? Well, there's history about Ripley cricket. There was *recorded* cricket at Ripley more than a hundred and seventy years ago – when the players used to wear top-hats, knee-breeches and stockings, and they bowled underhand. But that was no childish game. John Wells tore off a finger-nail against his shoe-buckle in fielding a ball; Hambledon played All-England for £500 a side; Brown of Brighton, the fast underhand bowler who needed three long-stops as well as a wicket-keeper, beat all four of them and killed a dog on the boundary. In those days the wicket was two upright stumps a foot high, with a 2ft stump laid across them and a hole dug underneath. To complete a run the batsman had to ground his bat in this hole; while, to run him out, the fieldman had to put the ball in the hole before the bat reached it – you can imagine the agony of the 'close thing' as William Ward, a cricketer of the time, wrote: 'Many severe injuries of the hands were the consequences of this regulation.' But I want you to remember the size of the wicket, 1ft high and 2ft wide, nothing in between – I shall return to this business of the wicket because it is part of the story of Ripley.

It was from Ripley that the great Lumpy came. Lumpy was the best bowler in England after Harris of Hambledon, and was the only bowler the Hambledon batsmen feared. His name was not really Lumpy, of course; according to his gravestone in Walton-on-Thames churchyard not far away, it was Edward Stevens, but, as the careful, mathematically-minded editor of *Lillywhite's Scores and Biographies* says: 'The compiler of this book has (contrary to his usual custom) not inserted his real name in the matches in which he appears, because he was so much better known by that of "Lumpy".'

We know quite a lot about this great man of the old cricket, and since his native Ripley is our subject we shall recall some of his history. In his young days he was said to have been 'a bit of a smuggler', but Nyren says that he was an honest man. However, the standing of smuggling in England in those days was such that the two statements are not necessarily contradictory. He was thirty-seven before the dates of any of the great matches of which we have records, but even by those incomplete records he was a giant of the game.

Now remember we're talking about the eighteenth century. Well, in those days it was the rule for the visiting team to select the spot where the wickets should be pitched, and this job was usually done by their star bowler. Harris of Hambledon always used to select rising ground against which to bowl, so that his deliveries would 'get up' and as you will appreciate that would tend to keep runs down and to cause the batsmen to hit catches. But Lumpy would throw away all other advantages and select ground that sloped away, for it was his delight to bowl out his opponents with shooters – as the old poet wrote of him:

Honest Lumpy did allow
He ne'er could bowl but o'er a brow.

Once in 1775 when Lumpy was playing for five of All-England against five of Hambledon he was bowling when John Small came in, last man for Hambledon with fourteen runs wanted to win. Small got the runs, but three times balls from Lumpy passed through that gap in the wicket that I told you. Even his opponents thought it not quite fair (though that did not prevent them from taking their £200 in stake money) and we can guess that Lumpy was not backward in drawing attention to his bad luck. So because Lumpy was beaten by that 2ft by 1ft hollow wicket, eventually and after a lot of argument in 1779 the number of stumps for the game of cricket was changed to three; they were made higher and brought so close together that the ball couldn't pass between them – in other words the wicket as we know it today.

And Lumpy was remembered at Hambledon – he was remembered there for a long time. In the 'Waterloo Arms' at Barn Green which is near Hambledon, there used to be a painting of him dancing with a jug of ale clasped in his hand. Well, ale and cricket used to go hand in hand, but even at that old Lumpy seems to have been a pretty eccentric old character.

Lumpy was Lord Tankerville's man; that is, he was a member of his lordship's household and played cricket for him whenever he was wanted. His patron seems to have had great faith in him and, besides the many match-stakes that he won, Lord Tankerville once made, and won, a wager of £100 that Lumpy could bowl and hit a feather placed on the pitch once in four balls. For a fairly fast bowler this was a remarkable degree of accuracy and, linked with the staying power that enabled him to bowl day-long without losing his effectiveness, made him an automatic choice for any great team of his time.

Pycroft, in his book *The Cricket Field* poetically summing up the great players of the past, calls on Lumpy first, of all the opponents of Hambledon, in these words: 'Come forth! thou pride of Surrey! thou Prince of the ancient bowlers! thou man of iron nerve, never-failing eye! Come forth Lumpy! Come forth from the well-filled cellar and well-stored larder of thy first and greatest patron the Earl of Tankerville!' ... Hm, so that was where Lumpy spent the time.

And today, at Ripley where the village green hasn't changed a scrap since he bowled there one hundred and seventy years ago, it wasn't difficult to conjure up the old man, short, fat and round-shouldered and looking anxiously for a slope of the ground on which to bowl his shooters in the coming match, when there'd be 3,000 countrymen from the county round to cheer him. And afterwards, for him, there would be great rounds of beef and terrific apple pies washed down with flagons of ale (and ale was ale then) over at the 'Talbot', the pub across the way. And, in the evening, there would be Tom Leer and Sueter singing glees accompanied by John Small on his fiddle.

And that was more or less how it was for us today, and although you won't believe me, as the New Zealanders drove away, the little boys who stopped their game on the old green to wave to them were playing cricket with a two-stump wicket with a bar laid across the top – the annoying thing about that story is that it's true – perhaps it's too true to be acceptable.

But of those old days of cricket, and I suppose cricket as it was today, well, what we felt was said by Nyren one hundred and fifty, years ago, when writing in his old age:

I have been there, and still would go
T'was like a little Heaven here below.

BBC Pacific Service, 'As I see it',
June 1945

3

English County Cricket Prospects, 1946

By 1946 John had taken a post as literary programmes producer in the BBC Overseas Service. He had already written and narrated a number of successful cricket features and with Arthur Russell, who was in charge of actuality programmes in the same department, had now begun commentating for the Eastern Service. Officially, it was felt that, 'with his West Country accent, he was a "natural" in giving a real atmosphere of green fields and white flannels' to his commentaries. Unofficially, of course, the BBC were never quite sure about regional accents until a number of years later.

Be that as it may, John was rapidly building an enviable reputation as a gifted broadcaster even in those early weeks of first-class cricket's restoration.

ANNOUNCER: The first peacetime cricket season has now begun and India's visiting team has already given an excellent account of itself. John Arlott surveys the season's prospects, and deplores the fact that so many of our first-class cricketers should have lost their lives in the war.

JOHN ARLOTT: Of English cricket in 1946, I am tempted to say that it is a season in which I speak of prospects only to think of problems.

Many of the English counties are in considerable difficulty. Grounds, pavilions, and stands have been bombed, finances are at a low ebb, and support in the new season is as yet problematical – though I think it reasonable to be optimistic about good attendances.

This year, India has sent us a team which was strong

enough to defeat the Australian side that had won two Test matches in England last year. And, during the season, we shall have to find a team to face the Australians in Australia next winter.

The major problem for English cricket in 1946 – the state of the game here, which makes all prophecy for the season more uncertain than ever before – is this: for six years there has been no real first-class cricket in England. There have been Test matches, inter-Service matches, and other games, but there has been no real first-class cricket, despite the great names recorded in the war-time games.

'I shall be catching those in June,' says the first-class cricketer when he misses a difficult catch early in the season; 'I shall be catching those in June.' And there is much truth in that old and rather ironic saying. The best cricket is played by men playing regularly day in, day out, week after week. Only under such intense conditions does the difficult catch become a reflex action, the long innings, or the long spell of accurate bowling, become possible without trace of relaxation.

Under war-time conditions, when gifted cricketers came from their Service units and the factories to play holiday cricket, some great reputations were maintained and some new reputations made; but these will not stand against the searching test of the first three months of county cricket played with the old concentration and intensity.

Out of this testing, England has to find her new Test team to face the strong side that India has sent against us. If we look at the last English touring side to visit Australia – the side of 1936–7 – we shall find that it does not contain the name of any one man, unless it be Hardstaff, of whom we may not find ourselves having to say that he is past his best. We must face the fact that G.O. Allen, Hammond, Ames, Fishlock, Worthington, Copson, are now middle-aged men – but R.S. Modi and Abdul Hafeez are only twenty-one. Hammond has been appointed captain of the English Test team, and has been co-opted to the selection committee for the three matches against India.

In Australia, next winter, we shall be meeting a team of young men – men with their greatest triumphs yet before them. There is no cricketer in England under thirty years of age, except Denis Compton, of whom

In pensive mood.

one could say with confidence that he was Test-match choice this year.

The first three months of this season will show men with great cricket names past their best, show many of them unable to make good the six years away from concentrated cricket. It will show some of the young men, hailed on their appearance in war-time cricket as prodigies, as no more than average players. Those first three months, with our Test match opponents from India among us, and the Tests themselves hard upon us, will be the testing time.

Out of this testing, England has to find a team to face the strongest side India has sent to us. Not only have we to select a team, but we have – if we are to face the future seasons with confidence – to discover new bowlers.

If I spoke of nothing else, this talk would not be long enough for me to tell you of all the cricketers who gave their lives in this war. They were our friends, and we shall remember them. I speak here of Hedley Verity and Kenneth Farnes, not to compare their sacrifice with that of their fellows, but because they are germane to my argument. Had there been no war, we should have expected Farnes and Verity still to be of our outstanding Test match bowlers.

Farnes promised to be one of the truly great fast bowlers, and Verity, in 1939, showed no signs of weakening under the great burden that was thrust upon him. Now, they will play no more, and we have no certain sight of their successors. A fast bowler and a slow left-arm bowler are essential to any properly balanced side. Neither of the two outstanding left-arm bowlers in England looks good enough to take Verity's place in Test cricket – Paine of Warwickshire, because he does not spin the ball enough, and James Langridge of Sussex, because he lacks Verity's power of penetration on a good wicket.

Of the pre-war fast bowlers, Nichols of Essex has retired from first-class cricket, Larwood is long gone

Hedley Verity, the great Yorkshire and England left-arm spinner.

from representative games, and Copson and H.D. Read, who, sound as they were, lacked the spark of greatness, are past the age of promise. It is, in fact, doubtful if there is a really good fast bowler in England. This lack of fast bowlers – forty years ago there was a real fast bowler in every county team in England – is thrown into stronger relief by the lack of good fast-medium bowlers to open the bowling.

There is no Maurice Tate in English cricket today, and of the best who bowled in his style – the brothers Alfred and George Pope of Derbyshire, and Jim Smith of Middlesex – have left county cricket for Northern League cricket; and Perks of Worcester and Pollard of

Lancashire, like the left-hander of the same speed, Voce, are still in the Forces, and are not likely to be available for the season. It appears that England has only two real hopes of dismissing the Indian side cheaply in Test matches – and those are, first, the discovery of a great fast bowler and, secondly, English wickets.

Green, usually damp, and far more responsive to spin than the Indian matting wickets, these English pitches may enable such leg-break-cum-googly bowlers as Wilkinson of Lancashire and Wright of Kent to master the younger Indian batsmen.

War-time cricket revealed three promising bowlers, any one of whom may prove a discovery. T.E. Bailey, a Dulwich schoolboy, and then a Royal Marine officer, sometimes bowled quite fast, but he is still young and not so robust as the classic fast bowlers. If he increases in strength and stamina, and continues to develop his present impressively flowing action, he may be the fast bowler that English cricket is waiting for. A.V. Bedser, one of the Bedser twins, who will play for Surrey, has given signs of promise, but has had no proper testing. Another Marine, A.W.H. Mallett, looks to be an effective medium-pace bowler.

Several other young bowlers showed considerable promise immediately before the war, and we shall watch them with interest this season – such men as Nutter of Lancashire, Godfrey and Dean of Hampshire, Jenkins of Worcester, Robinson of Yorkshire, and P.F. Judge of Glamorgan, who has bowled very well in India.

Neither is there any dearth of good batsmen; in fact, it may prove extremely difficult to choose between the many brilliant batsmen available. Fishlock and Hammond may well come to the test of the new season with confidence. Hutton is said to be fit again – Hutton, who stood, in 1939, in the line of Shrewsbury and Sutcliffe. All or any of the first four Middlesex batsmen might be chosen for England.

Hardstaff and Simpson of Nottinghamshire have had good practice, and scored many runs in India, and must be seriously considered – Simpson may yet prove a great batting discovery. Oldfield of Lancashire, Dollery of Warwickshire, Halliday of Yorkshire, and Harrison of Hampshire, are all possible choices, possible future giants of cricket. If neither Ames nor Griffith should keep wicket for England, there is C.R. Maxwell, formerly of Nottingham. There are wicket-keepers and to spare in the country.

Our visitors come to us from India with a great reputation – let there be no doubt that we face them with respect. Unless England finds a great fast bowler, or a spin bowler on one side or the other rises to greater heights than has ever been reached before, it seems that the Test matches may well be drawn between two such powerful batting sides.

The Indian team's tour opened, in the traditional way, at Worcester, where Bradman played his great first innings in England. It was at Worcester that I last saw the Nawab of Pataudi, who knows the ground and the people so well. One hot August day in 1938 I fielded out while he made a superb century against my native Hampshire. For him it will have been like coming home. For his team, we hope that we may make England seem like a home to them, and that they will redeem their high promise.

English county cricket has begun again with enthusiasm, and will be the richer for the presence here of C.B. Clarke, the West Indies' spin bowler, and the New Zealander Martin Donnelly. At the moment, Yorkshire, Lancashire, and Middlesex look to be the strongest counties, the Middlesex batting looks almost ponderous.

But beyond the match results of this season we shall be watching the search for England's new Test men. After the last war, we chose too many of the settled men, who were past their best, and we paid the penalty for that lack of foresight. Above all, we shall be watching the search for new bowlers. And, behind the great matches, the town and factory and village and school teams will be returning once more to their neglected and grass-grown pitches, where they will be training the great names of a generation to come.

And in this first peacetime cricket season, thousands of people will once again play the game with an unmixed delight, and thousands more will watch it with the old enthusiasm, and cricket critics will continue to say that the players of this generation are not the men that their fathers were – but they are.

BBC Eastern Service, May 1946

4

THE SEASON'S PROSPECTS, 1947

In 1947 John was on the road once more. Before setting off he surveyed the season's prospects for the programme One Man's Horizon.

On April 28 I shall pack my bag again and go to Worcester, and, on April 29, the English cricket season will start there with the match between Worcester and South Africa. Yet, only a fortnight ago I read that the Worcester cricket ground was flooded; the Severn, which conspires with the cathedral to set the ground against so handsome a background, had overflowed its banks and the entire cricket ground was under water. But in four weeks' time we hope the water will have gone down and cricket will start.

But I don't feel that I've been away from cricket since last season ended. There's been so much cricket in the newspapers; I shall have some more to say about that in a minute. In our papers we watched the sad story of the English Test side in Australia, seeking the paper eagerly first thing in the morning, as the news came through from the other side of the world, to find out how we'd done. We regarded the State matches with a certain amount of complacency – couldn't really exhibit the anxiety over them that we've done over the Test matches.

And there's been news too from India – that colossal stand by Vijay Hazare and Gul Mohammed in a recent match, and that was somehow rather more for me than figures in the record book.

There's a picture of Hazare with all his watchful care, concentrating on every ball, suspecting – I always used to

Vijay Hazare bowling during the Indian tour of 1946.

think – greater subtlety in the bowling than there was, but suddenly picking on the loose ball, and crashing it away to mid-wicket on the leg side, or slashing it down wide of cover's left hand. At the other end Gul Mohammed – there's a temptation to call him a small man because he isn't very tall, but you've only to be near him to appreciate the colossal strength of his body to know that if you call Gul Mohammed a small man, you yourself are an extremely unperceptive man.

Gul Mohammed at the other end really enjoying himself, with that terrific square slash of his that sends the ball down past third man. Someone must have been bowling a little too short outside the off stump. He was a cricketer to take his chances, and his chances often got him out, but when he came off, he was magnificent to watch. No one in English cricket last year I think hit the ball quite so hard on the off side as Gul did when he was set and the bowling was coming through quick on a true wicket, outside his off stump. So cricket in the papers has kept us going, and I like to think that cricket in the papers was at the back of the Home Secretary's mind when he decided not to enforce his mid-week sport ban on cricket. We know that there was one very powerful argument that could be adduced, and that was, that cricket crowds aren't really large. The size of our grounds here makes it certain that few more than 30,000 people will see even a Test match, and of course, week after week, 20 or 30 first-class soccer clubs will hope to have bigger crowds than that.

No – the cricket crowds aren't very big, but I like to think that the Home Secretary thought that behind those rather small crowds at the county games, the relatively small crowds of the Test matches, there was a vast army of people who followed cricket in the newspapers, who turned as eagerly as I've always done to the cricket pages in the morning to see how their favourite county's done, how their favourite players had done and just what was likely to happen the next day: who look rather gloomily at the newspapers when a previous day had been one of rain and all the play had been rained off, but who liked to follow their cricket if necessary, at second hand, year in year out and that he remembered them and let cricket go on.

So cricket will start at Worcester, in that lovely setting with all its old memories – its memories of Root who swung a ball more than one could believe any man could do, whose deliveries started on the line of the off stump, and suddenly darted away as if Root had them on a string, swung outside the batsman's legs, and if he touched the ball it was up in that suicide crowd of short legs gathered to take catches. The wicket-keeper standing back well outside the leg stump, and Root untidily – hair blowing a bit, shirt sleeves flapping – rushing up, hour after hour, it seemed, as if he never grew tired, keeping the batsmen perpetually watching his in-swingers which still swung after the shine had gone off the ball – the first of the really great in-swing leg-trap attacks. Worcester has its memories of, year after year, the touring side starting there – of Bradman and Headley opening their triumphant seasons there, of the Indians last year, going out in the bitter cold wind to field after putting Worcester in, and hammering their way through a match which they so narrowly lost and which they almost gloriously won. Memories too of Reg Perks – the fast bowler who for years has borne a burden far too great for any one man, as Worcester's fast-medium bowler.

And on from Worcester, I hope to see a lot of England: Test matches in the smoke haze of Sheffield; Nottingham where the pavilion faces into the sun – most of the first-class pavilions face north so that you can't both sit in the pavilion and sit in the sun. But on the roof at Nottingham where the BBC commentary box is, the sun on a hot day blazes down all day long. You absorb the sun, you absorb the cricket, and it's with a sigh that you go into the commentary box to tell people about the match.

My strangest memory of Nottingham, perhaps, is seeing two county cricket matches on a day for three days – of going to Chesterfield to watch Derby and India and then by fast car from Chesterfield to the commentary point installed for the Nottinghamshire and Worcester match at Trent Bridge and describing Derbyshire playing India while I watched Nottinghamshire play Worcestershire – which wasn't always easy. Two or three of my friends in the field, and a great yearning on my part to cheer when they took a wicket – even though I might be telling a rather sad story from Chesterfield. I hope it was not a dual-personality broadcast.

There will be cricket under the threat of rain at Manchester and the comedian's joke is true for me there; it always does seem to rain when I go to Manchester. Cricket under the haze of smoke at Leeds – all those Test match grounds have their particular atmosphere; there's that impish, cockney, sparrow-haunted griminess of the Oval, it couldn't be anywhere else but South London with the clang of the trams outside and the great flats overlooking the ground.

Cricket, too, in the stately dignity of Lord's, that prosperous Victorian pavilion and the modern sweep of the great white concrete stand that includes the score box; there will be cricket for me, too, I hope, at Taunton, where you go across the bridge over the river into the grounds and find a stall immediately inside selling cockles – unique as refreshment at a cricket ground. Perhaps I'll get down to Wales again, I hope I shall, perhaps to Ebbw Vale or Swansea where they play their cricket among the chimneys and the coal mines and the Welsh crowd, in its twenty-odd years of first-class cricket (Glamorgan's the junior first-class county), have come to know the game as well as any crowd in England and to comment on it in their high Welsh voices – and for so many years every time that John Clay hit a pad in Wales, 3,000 Welshmen joined with him in the appeal; but John Clay won't be playing any first-class cricket this year, and that means that a great idol of my youth has gone. Ever since Glamorgan started to play first-class cricket John Clay has played for them; first of all as a young fast bowler, and took his hundred wickets as a fast bowler, later as a leg-break bowler, took a hundred wickets as a leg-break bowler and then for many years as one of the two best off-break bowlers in the world, a man who could spin the ball to a blind length all day long. Who played cricket with good humour, carefully and conscientiously and well. He was never very keen you know to play in Test matches; he used to think that younger men should be given a chance. He played for Glamorgan I think from a sense of duty; I know he did last year. Maurice Turnbull is dead, Turnbull, one of the greatest of all schoolboy cricketers – the man who came to Glamorgan for cricket as a sixteen-year-old schoolboy and against the then magnificent attack of Lancashire with its Test match bowlers, Ted MacDonald and Dick Tyldesley, scored 60 runs. Years afterwards he led Glamorgan to the real peak of its cricket. Maurice Turnbull knew that no side can play good cricket if it doesn't field well, that no side can ever hope to succeed in first-class cricket unless its fielding is superb, and he built up in the Glamorgan side a legacy of good fielding. It was exciting to watch Glamorgan in the field because every man was on his toes and every man held his catches, you didn't stay in that side if you couldn't hold them; that was Maurice Turnbull's legacy. John Clay was his friend and I think regarded himself as Turnbull's cricket executor. He watched over the thing that Turnbull had left and he saw that it was safe and that it was going to pay its dividend, and now he's gone from first-class cricket and he brings that wise head and that kindly good temper of his to the selection of our Test match side, there's no man, I'm sure, that anyone in England would sooner see appointed a selector.

John Clay's won't be the only missing face from English cricket this year; Maurice Leyland's gone, a man with the most powerful forearms I ever saw, the man who dug England out of hole after hole in Test matches by that dogged Yorkshire defence of his and the great hammer stroke of those mighty forearms that sent the ball down on the off-side before the fieldsman could move to it. Leyland has retired from county cricket, and Wally Hammond, it seems, will play very little cricket in the future. Some of us might perhaps have preferred to see him go out in a great flourish of trumpets to finish as England's Test match captain and then go from cricket forever, but he tells us that when business claims and the fibrositis which has worried him so much in Australia will allow, he'll play first-class cricket again for Gloucestershire. And perhaps it's not a good thing for him to go out now, because if he comes back, though rarely, we know that the younger generation will see him, and you can't mistake that stamp of greatness about Hammond. He may not be in his best form, but you only have to see him play a few cover drives to know that there is something great. It's a greatness that other players can't achieve by scoring hundreds or two hundreds of runs. There's a majesty about Hammond at the crease that tells you he is a great cricketer. Everyone who likes cricket should have the chance of seeing him and the man who doesn't perceive his greatness has no eyes for cricket.

I wonder if the old men are right – the old men tell us that this is going to be a baking summer, and they speak of 1921, and then I, instead of thinking of the droughts, as perhaps I should, of the scorched-up crops, think of Gregory and MacDonald, those two great Australian fast bowlers sweeping through English cricket in 1921 with no batsman in the country except perhaps Lord Tennyson and Philip Mead of my native Hampshire, and Frank Woolley of Kent, really able to stand against them. And I wonder if it will happen this year, and then I think a little sadly that we haven't any fast bowlers, that everyone says we have no fast bowlers. There's Pritchard of Warwick, but Pritchard's a New Zealander, he can't play for England in the Tests, but he will show us some good fast bowling. And then I think I'm not going to be pessimistic about it – that English cricket has always supplied its own needs, that cricket is so deep in the country; there's such a feel for the game, on much lower levels than county cricket, that we shall get these men again. We shall find the great fast bowlers, maybe Aspinall of Yorkshire; maybe Godfrey from Hampshire; it may be Peter Judge from Glamorgan; it may be someone of whom neither you nor I have ever heard, but the fast bowler will come, the great English bowlers will come, and once again, I think, English cricket will work out its solution in its own institution, and – my summer on the road? Yes, I shall enjoy it as much as ever.

BBC 'One Man's Horizon', March 1947

5

THREE AUSTRALIAN TESTS, 1948

The tourists for the 1948 season were the all-conquering Australians. One of the few times during the Test series when England had the ascendancy was at Old Trafford, when an undefeated Compton century helped them to 363 in the first innings. The Aussie opening batsman, Sidney Barnes, had received a fierce blow in the ribs from a pull by Dick Pollard when fielding at short-leg and had been stretchered off to hospital by four policemen. During Australia's reply, to everyone's surprise Barnes came in to bat and stayed at the crease for half-an-hour. John picks up the commentary:

Australia 140 for 5. Back comes the ball to Bedser again. Barnes there patting the wicket, going down patting that spot where Hassett was tapping yesterday, and bending now he's – oh dear – he's gone down on his knees, I think he's in very considerable pain. This is so extremely sad, it must've taken all the courage in the world to come out and bat after the blow Barnes had yesterday. And Chester's now calling someone out of the pavilion to look after him, a small boy down at long leg takes the opportunity to go onto the field and ask Denis Compton for his autograph. There's a little crowd of players round Barnes now. He's obviously batted every stroke he's played this morning in pain. Takes somehow what gilt there is off England's good position at the moment, to see so good an Australian batsman just not really fit to bat.

The first day of the next Test at Leeds saw Hutton and Washbrook make a century opening stand for England. Eventually Umpire Frank Chester indicated that the new ball was about to be taken.

Sidney Barnes facing Trevor Bailey during the Australians and Essex match at Southend in 1948. Barnes scored 79 in a 145 opening partnership with Bill Brown that took only 95 minutes.

... shows it with a warning and paternal air to Hutton. And Lindwall seizes it and he's just going to bowl with a new ball now from the grandstand end. Goes through the Lindwall bout of physical jerks. The shirt is now comfortably loose and it fills with wind as he comes up now from the grandstand end. Bowls the first ball to Hutton. A magnificent out swinger. (*Applause.*) Hit for 4. Now that was hit on the half volley by Hutton for 4, and a difficult ball it was to cope with. Over its last two yards it went eight inches. It went off the line of the middle and off, clean outside the offstump. And Hutton right over it hit it firmly past the somnolent Toshack at point, for 4 runs.

And now here comes Lindwall again to Hutton. (*Gasp from crowd.*) And that was a magnificent in-swinger –

(*applause*) – that bowled him off his pad. (*Lengthy applause.*) Well that was another magnificent ball. It's got rid of Hutton and he's out, bowled Lindwall 81. Hutton bowled Lindwall 81, England are 168 for 1.

Later, in the same innings:

Washbrook firmly to Hassett. Hassett quickly threatens to throw the wicket down. Neat pick-up. No run. Not pleasant this business of paper bowling across the wicket when you're 99 not out. Quite enough on the mind already.

Now up comes Toshack. Bowls to Washbrook. Washbrook plays a not very decisive shot, along the line of his leg stump and three men there to pick up a rather gentle stroke. In good Australian fashion, the noose of the field tight round him now as he struggles for his 100. And Toshack a nasty man to complete your 100 against.

Here he is, bowls to Washbrook. (*Shout and applause.*) Washbrook off the inside edge. (*Applause.*) England 189 for 1, Washbrook not out 100. His first 100 against Australia in England ... made in three hours forty minutes with sixteen fours.

In the last Test at the Oval, England were completely outclassed and lost by an innings and 149 runs. John wrapped up the match:

Bill Johnston's bowling and nothing in a way could be more fitting if Johnston was to take the last wicket of this series. The most improved bowler of the series and a man I think of whom we shall hear much in the future. Probably always will be a greater bowler in England than Australia, a greater humidity of our atmosphere makes him very dangerous indeed.

Now here he comes, from the Vauxhall end and he bowls to Hollies and Hollies swings him hard and high, everyone's stolen stumps and Morris has caught him. (*Excited shout and applause.*) It took an awful long time to come down. Every stump was out of the ground, every bail was in a player's pocket before Arthur Morris made that catch and England are all out 188. Barnes has got a stump, neither Young nor Hollies has, and now yes, there's a small boy who wants their autographs, he's being removed by two policemen, a policeman and an official. Umpire Davies has got a stump, Loxton's got a bail and now in almost complete silence these two batsmen – Jack Young not out 3, and Eric Hollies nought, caught Morris bowled Johnston, come back into the pavilion and the fifth Test and the England/Australia series of 1948 is all over. Australia retain the Ashes, win the series by four Tests to none. The first time, I believe, that that's ever been done and now the players are back in the pavilion and the crowd is coming out of its seats round towards, on one side at least, round towards the pavilion.

Eventually, the victorious Australians and vanquished Englishmen appeared on the balcony and took their final bows:

... people sitting along the roof of the grandstand to the left and here's the Don (*cheers and applause*), Norman Yardley, Barnes, 'Shrimp' Leveson-Gower, Keith Johnson, the Australian manager, two BBC engineers climbing across with an effects mike. (*Three cheers from crowd.*) Three cheers for the Don who's waving down to the crowd from the balcony – with Sidney Barnes's camera hard on him. Lindsay Hassett (*applause*), Don Tallon (*applause*), Ian Johnson (*applause*). Camera man. Billy Brown (*applause*) – Neil Harvey, that specially loud cheer, still in his shirt sleeves, they caught him changing. Big Bill Johnston still in complete whites, looking shyer and more ill-at-ease than I've seen him all the tour. Arthur Morris, 196 in this game brought out by the Don himself (*applause*). Sam Loxton, who's instantly bolted back into the dressing-room. They're calling for Sidney Barnes ... (*Three cheers from crowd.*)

BBC Light Programme, 1948

6

Terrors of the Commentary Box

Some might be surprised to find that cricket commentary is not all fizz and frolics. There are times of tremor and stress.

The best cricket commentary stories have, sadly, been flogged to death – the report of the Middlesex match, in the days of John Warr's captaincy, which began with 'Warr's declared': the off-spinner who had 'three short legs, a long leg and no slip': the Australian commentator who, giving the score in Australian fashion said that Australia were 'four for 142', understood by a staggered English listener as '441 for two'.

Brian Johnston, too, has coined some rich efforts but, even if they were not his copyright, he has squeezed them fairly thoroughly dry by now.

Commentators' terrors are usually those of urgency: a moment, and an informant to ask, and all would be well: but that is not always possible. The most dangerous moments are when commentator and scorer both look down at the score-sheet at the same moment as something *happens*. They both look up to see the result but not the events that led up to it. Ideally that should never happen: but it does: and it calls for some rapid and inventive stalling while the evidence is gathered.

BAFFLED BY NEW CAPS

My coldest horror occurred at the start of my first Test commentary – England *v.* India, at Lord's in 1946. The England innings began in the minute I came on the air. A

Concentrating on the job in the open air at Bristol.

commentator comes to know his subjects – as, indeed, most of us know people at a distance – by their *shape* – of head and body. But the Indians' new sweaters and caps had been delivered that very day and, bafflingly – a new cap will effectively disguise a thoroughly familiar player against automatic recognition at first sight – they had not taken the shape of their wearers. The close fieldsmen, all in identical new caps and sweaters, crouched down in a ring round the bat with their backs to me. Mercifully, no catch went to hand and my decision to call each fieldsman by the name of the man who *should* have been in that position seemed to work.

In those early post-war days, commentators, as a rule, had no scorer or 'number two' at matches other than Tests and, on a dim afternoon at Edinburgh – Scotland *v.* India, 1946 – while I was trying to cram all the back details of the day's play into a brief, late afternoon, overseas broadcast, *and* keep my own scorecard up to date, Sarwate took two Scottish wickets with consecutive balls – or *were* they consecutive? *was* there a ball in between? The field was not brought up as if for a hat-trick ball: was it or not? Which was worse, to miss a hat trick or to announce one which was not? I took a chance – hat-trick ball – down went Hodge's middle stump and it seemed an hour before the fieldsmen went up to shake hands with Sarwate to confirm the hat-trick.

THE BEDSER PUZZLE

Alec Bedser taking his twin, Eric's place as opening batsman when Surrey had 10 minutes to bat at the end of a day: Ken Barrington or Colin Cowdrey 'walking' for a bump ball 'catch'. 'Counting' an over at a crucial state of a game, saying 'here comes the last ball' and then the bowler going back for another (that *has* been known to be an umpire's error): failing to hear the shout of 'no ball' through the glass of the commentary-box window and then, automatically, following the ball and missing the umpire's arm-signal: faced with a player (Sir Leonard Hutton) given out for 'obstruction of the field' in a Test: Don Ward of Glamorgan 'called' by the square leg umpire – for too many fieldsmen on the leg side: all easy with hindsight, not simple, *on the instant*, in the absence of two-way radio with the umpire.

Not complaints, though: only terrors – which, perhaps, heighten the pleasures.

Don Bates' Benefit Year, 1968

7

The Old Man

In his introduction to a radio feature on the centenary of the birth of W.G. Grace, which at the time, 1948, was the most technically demanding and intricate programme ever broadcast by the BBC that had been devoted to a single cricketer, John wrote:

He was a great batsman and a magnificent strategic bowler – yet his personality was such that it is remembered by those who played with him to the exclusion of his actual performances. He was an 'eminent Victorian', yet he was also as boyish and simple a medical practitioner as might be found in all the West Country. Cricket made him much money – yet it could never repay the service it had of him.

The making of a programme on Grace demanded more than a recital of facts, it had to have as its aim the production of an impression – for Grace produced in those who knew him a feeling, an impact – not a blur of statistics. Simple as he may have been by comparison with some men, his character was, nevertheless, many-sided. Therefore it would be fatal to produce a portrait of a 'type' or even of a man who began and ended in his cricket.

I had to have first-hand evidence from the best sources. Hence, in the preparation of the programme I met many men who had known and played with W.G. Although it was expressed in different ways and although it sprang from different causes, the reaction to W.G. common to all these men was that of affection. W.G. was loved for the man he was, not for the runs he made. That affection had to be reflected . . .

The Old Man

A tribute to W.G. Grace, born at Downend 18 July 1848, on the occasion of his centenary.

Cast:

John Arlott	Narrator
Preston Lockwood	W.G. Grace
Phyllis Smale	Mrs Grace & Servant
George Holloway	Reader & Bishop of Hereford
Robert Bashford	Westcountry Voice & E.S. Carter
Myles Rudge	Young Man, First Voice, Clifton & Umpire
Lewis Gedge	First Yorkshire Voice, Allen Hill, Third Voice & Townsend
Edward Lee	Second Yorkshire Voice & Lockwood
Hedley Goodall	Second Voice, Jem Mace, Anxious Man & Croome
Alan McGilvray	Murdoch
S.D. Kumar	Ranji
Tom Harrison	Tom Emmett
Paul Rogers	Studd, I.D. Walker & 'Fun'

and the recorded voices of W.S.A. Brown, J.B. Hobbs, C.B. Fry, C.J. Kortright, Arthur Paish and C.J. Barnett.

ANNOUNCER: This is the West of England Home Service. W.G. Grace of Gloucestershire – the immortal W.G. – was born exactly one hundred years ago today. As our tribute to the greatest of cricketers we present *The Old Man*, a centenary programme written and introduced by John Arlott.

(*Slight dog barking, fade behind*)

MRS GRACE: The Chestnuts, Downend, Gloucestershire. May 1st 1858.

(*Fade up sound of bat on ball, barking of dogs and boys voices, laughing, shouting.*) (*Cross fade to bat on ball again.*)

FIRST BOY'S VOICE: Cross-batted into the shrubbery again, Teddy.

2ND BOY'S VOICE: Never mind – the dogs will find it if Mary can't.

1ST VOICE: That was a good length ball – a good job for you Mother didn't see you hit across it.

2ND VOICE: Mother? – she's in the parlour writing letters. She can't see . . . (*Fade.*)

(*Cross fade to*)

MRS GRACE: (*reading*) To Mr George Parr, Secretary
The All-England Eleven,
Trent Bridge Ground,
Nottingham.

Dear Sir,
I have heard that you are wishful of including young cricketers of promise in your All-England Eleven during the coming season. You may be interested to know that my third son, Edward Mills Grace, who plays for the West Gloucestershire, has the makings of a fine player. He has scored several hundreds and is a fast round-arm bowler and a safe catch at point.

I have a younger son, William Gilbert Grace, growing up and not yet old enough for great matches, but one day he will be a better batsman than any of his brothers because his back play is sounder than theirs.

Yours truly,

MARTHA GRACE

NARRATOR: 'He will be a better batsman than his brothers' – how right W.G. Grace's mother was. But even she, I think, would have been surprised to look twenty years on into Victorian England and to read this notice at the gate of a crowded county field.

MALE COUNTRY VOICE: Cricket Match – Admission 3d. If Dr W.G. Grace plays admission 6d.

NARRATOR: Why was cricket with W.G. threepence more? Because he was not only the greatest cricketer of

W. G. trying to look casual.

the age, but one of the greatest men of his age – because he was a character – and because he was a character who had achieved feats unheard of before in his chosen field. Just turn the pages of Lillywhite, Wisden, *Scores and Biographies* –

READER: July, 1864 – W.G. Grace – not yet sixteen, scores 170 out of a total of 356 for South Wales against the Gentlemen of Sussex at Hove. Forty-four years afterwards he plays his last innings in first-class cricket for London Country. In first-class cricket between 1864 and 1908 – forty-four years – he scored 54,896 runs with 126 centuries – at an average of 39.55 – and took 2,876 wickets at less than 18 runs a piece. In *all* cricket – between 1860 – on the day after his twelfth birthday – and July 25th 1914 when he was sixty-six – he made 80,000 runs and took 7,000 wickets. For the Gentlemen

The Gloucestershire side in 1877 that beat England by 5 wickets at the Oval. *Back row L to R*: W. O. Moberly, W. Fairbanks, G. F. Grace, F. G. Monkland, W. R. Gilbert, W. Midwinter. *Front row L to R*: Capt H. B. Kingscote, F. Townsend, R. F. Miles, W. G. Grace, E. M. Grace. The umpire in plain clothes is C. K. Pullin.

against the Players he scored 6,000 runs at an average of 42.

NARRATOR: It would be easy to produce for you yet more bewildering figures, but you can find the statistics in any good cricket reference book – and his figures may be beaten without detracting one scrap from the greatness of W.G.: I am concerned with greatness, not with damned dots. Dr William Gilbert Grace has dropped out of sight below the horizon of today, and I want to bring before you the evidence of those who saw W.G. plain – who saw a greatness that figures can never express. I want to call to the bar of your judgement great cricketers still with us – men who knew and played with Grace – and I want to do as the Reverend James Mitford, one of the earliest great writers on cricket, did – to conjure out of their pavilions men long since dismissed for the last time. But I will take no dramatic liberties – I shall offer you only reliable evidence.

Now, there are two essentials for greatness – the man and the occasion – if these two fuse the flame is unmistakable and it was recognized – as one great cricketer and man may recognize another – by Prince Kumar Shri Ranjitsingh – Ranji of the golden age of English batting – who said –

INDIAN VOICE: There is one great landmark that separates the old batting from the new – the appearance of Dr W.G. Grace in the cricket world. He revolutionized batting. He turned it from an accomplishment into a science. Before W.G. batsmen were of two kinds – a batsman played a forward game or he played a back game.

Each player, too, seems to have made a speciality of some particular stroke. What W.G. did was to unite in his mighty self all the good points of all the good players, and to make utility the criterion of style. He founded the modern theory of batting by making forward- and back-play of equal importance, relying neither on the one nor on the other, but on both. Any cricketer who thinks for a moment can see the enormous change W.G. introduced into the game. I hold him to be, not only the finest player born or unborn, but the maker of modern batting. He turned the old one-stringed instrument into a many-chorded lyre. And, in addition, he made his execution equal his invention. All of us now have the instrument, but we lack his execution. It is not that we do not know, but that we cannot perform. Before W.G., batsmen did not know what could be made of batting. The development of bowling has been natural and gradual; each great bowler has added his quota. W.G. discovered batting; he turned its many narrow straight channels into one great winding river. Those who nowadays try to follow in his footsteps may or may not get within measurable distance of him, but it was he who pioneered and made the road. Where a great man has led many can go afterwards, but the honour is his who found and cut the path. The theory of modern batting is in all essentials the result of W.G.'s thinking and working on the game.

NARRATOR: 'The finest player born or unborn' – the champion – yet loved by all kinds and conditions of men. W.G. was accepted not only as a performer, as innovator, but as a man. In his early cricketing days an old enthusiast brought him Alfred Mynn's pads as the rightful successor of the lion of Kent – yet Grace played like a boy with children. He handled a cricket team with the hand of a master yet he was teased by the young players to whom his cricketing word was law – and he took their teasing with a laugh and a glass of champagne – in such a man kindliness and manliness go together. Look back through the smoke of two world wars to any one of a thousand English fields and see there a tall man with a ringed red and yellow MCC cap perched on his head – a huge black beard falling across his barrel chest – and cricket bat looking like a toy in his hand – there is the Gloucestershire countryman of pure country strain who served as captain so faithfully and so well the Gloucester club which his father had just mooted and done so much to found; who, without a moment of unfaithfulness to himself, became known to millions; who carved thousands of runs out of half a century of bowlers; who tricked out hundreds of batsmen – and – through the smoke of sixty years, he says –

DR GRACE: What are you at there, boy – reading a book? – wearing your eyes out eh? – you don't catch me at that –

NARRATOR: No, he saved his eyes for Wisden, books on whist, an occasional medical reference book and, above all, cricket – *his* wisdom came of native shrewdness – remember the most famous of all the W.G. stories –

DR GRACE: Now, me lad, you're new to us – where do you bat?

YOUNG MAN: Well, Doctor, I don't mind, but I may say I've never made a duck in my life.

DR GRACE: What, never made a blob in your life – what? what? never made a blob? Then last's your place – Ye've not been playing long enough – he, heh, heh – last's your place.

NARRATOR: The old man was careful about the batting order of his sides. He worked it out very cannily and according to the state of the game – and he always said to his batsmen 'You *come* in at such a wicket down,' never 'You go in': to the Old Man, the other batsmen came in to him. Once – in a North against South match at Scarborough – he was well dug in at lunch on the third day –

1ST YORKSHIRE VOICE: If we can get the old 'un out we'd catch the early train tonight.

2ND YORKSHIRE VOICE: Little hope of that – unless we can fill him with champagne at lunch.

1ST VOICE: Let's try it.

(*Fade down and fade to dining-room noises with laughter of W.G. Grace.*)

2ND VOICE: Here's a bottle of special for you, Doctor.

DR GRACE: No ye don't – shan't have it, shan't have it – but you keep it cool – I'll have it at five o'clock – heh, heh, heh.

NARRATOR: And he did – still not out – and they didn't

catch their train. Bowlers could hardly disturb W.G. at his greatest – remember that almost legendary ball from Ernest Jones the Australian fast-bowler that went through the Doctor's beard for leg-byes.

(*Thump of feet in bowler's run up, bounce of ball and zipp.*)

DR GRACE: Eh? Run up, run up, Jacker, that's leg-byes.

(*Thump of feet three seconds.*)

What the hangment are ye at Jonah? eh? What are ye at?

(*Fade to closed acoustic then* –)

(*Ruminatively*) Ah, Jones, yes, that feller who bowled through my beard, yes, he was fast, I'd say he was fast all right – d'ye know – sometimes I don't like to remember how many generations of bowlers I've played against – in the sixties there was Tarrant – and Tinley and Jackson – and then, after them there was Alfred Shaw and Martin MacIntyre – and in the late seventies, Ulyett and Allen Hill and Tom Emmett and Freeman and A.G. Steel then, in the eighties Peate and C.T. Studd and then Lohmann and Briggs and Attewell and Peel, yes, there was always new ones – J.T. Hearne and Sam Woods and Mold – he hurt most of all because he threw – and Spofforth – there was a bowler for you – control – he could control his length and his break better than any – and Tom Richardson and Walter Mead and Kortright and Lockwood and Rhodes – Hirst – yes I am the survivor of eight generations of bowlers –

NARRATOR: Yet he knew his cricket *naturally* – one day there was an argument in the pavilion.

1ST VOICE: Well how do you play Shaw's off-break?

2ND VOICE: You must go out to him – then he can't turn enough to beat the bat.

3RD VOICE: I always play him back – you'll be stumped if you go down the wicket to him – I've tried going out – and the half-cock – he breaks too sharp for anything but the back shot.

1ST VOICE: Here comes Doctor Grace – he can play him – let's ask him.

2ND VOICE: What's the way to play Shaw's off-break Doctor?

W. G. GRACE: I think you ought to put the bat against the ball.

NARRATOR: Yes, it was as natural as that: it had to be on the wickets he played on. And on such wickets, too – and here we turn for our evidence not to a cricketer, but to a man famous in another sport – Jem Mace – bare-fist champion of England and first boxing champion of England and America – the champion who came back and won –

JEM MACE: (*Norfolk voice*) I'd sooner stand up to Tom Sayers for ten rounds than keep wicket on this Lord's wicket the way it is today.

NARRATOR: Yes, he was the master batsman of them all – but he could bowl too – and loved it – once when he was playing for the Gentlemen of the South captained by I.D. Walker, he had been bowling for a long time and no wickets had fallen when Walker came up to him –

I. D. WALKER: They've collared us all right W.G. – who shall I put on now?

DR GRACE: I tell you what – I'll go on at the other end.

I. D. WALKER: (*in stupefied tone*) I believe you will, too –

(*Fade out and instantly up to*)

(*Six comfortably paced but heavy strides and grunt from Grace, then thump of ball on pad* –)

DR GRACE: (*grunt*) Heh's thet – heh's thet? – He's right in front – a straight ball – he's out – what did I tell you – I can fool 'em.

NARRATOR: Yes, the Doctor was shrewd. And he had a genuine native humour, too – he spoke with the tongue of his native Gloucestershire where he was brought up and educated. His voice was high for a big man – but not so high as his brother E.M's. I recall that Fred Barratt the old Notts fast bowler, another tall man with high shoulders and a round chest, had the same type of tenor voice – his voice too came as a shock from so big a man. There have been men who were called great largely because of the things they said – because of their speeches – if this was so of W.G., it was not so in the usual way. His best known speeches are those of his Canadian and United States tour of 1872 – which I want you to hear, if you will, in full –

READER: Montreal, August 22nd, 1872 –

(Fade up banqueting noises and above them –)

DR GRACE: Gentlemen, I beg to thank you for the honour you have done me. I never saw better bowling than I have seen today and I hope to see as good wherever I go.

(Applause.)

READER: Ottawa – August 28th, 1872.

(Fade up banqueting noises and above them –)

DR GRACE: Gentlemen. I beg to thank you for the honour you have done me. I never saw a better ground than I saw today and I hope to see as good wherever I go.

(Applause.)

READER: Toronto, September 4th, 1872.

(Fade up banqueting noises and above them –)

DR GRACE: Mr Chairman and gentlemen. I beg to thank you for the honour you have done me. I never saw better good fellows than I saw today and I hope to see as good wherever I go.

(Applause.)

READER: London Ontario, September 12th, 1872.

(Fade up banqueting noises and above them –)

DR GRACE: Ladies and Gentlemen. I beg to thank you for the honour you have done me. I never saw prettier ladies than I have seen today and I hope to see as pretty wherever I go.

NARRATOR: Oh, Doctor.

DR GRACE: Heh, heh, heh.

NARRATOR: But W.G. could always say the right thing when he wanted to – who but W.G. would have come up to A.P. Lucas's father after he and A.P. had just made a long stand together and said –

DR GRACE: How d'ye do Mr Lucas – I have just been batting with the second best bat in England.

NARRATOR: You see there was never any doubt, for forty years who was the best.

But most men are well spoken of by their friends – it is the rank of Tuscany whose evidence builds the case – and now there materializes out of the smoke of Sheffield the one and only Tom Emmett – that Yorkshire man of Yorkshiremen – who mixed wides with unplayable balls, and cricket with a shrewd tongue — E.S. Carter, the old time Surrey amateur in talking to him.

CARTER: What do you think of this young Grace who's making so many runs Tom?

EMMETT: Happen he'll make runs enough off'n bowlers i' the South, but let him come up to Sheffield against me and George Freeman and we'll show thee summut.

READER: South versus North, July 6th, 1869. South all out 173. W.G. Grace 122 – with Emmett and Freeman bowling.

CARTER: Well, Tom, you've had W.G. Grace at Sheffield what do you think of him now?

EMMETT: Mr Carter, a' call yon Grace a nonesuch – he ought to be made play wi' a littler bat.

READER: May 1870. MCC versus Yorkshire at Lord's on a sticky wicket.

NARRATOR: Remember it, Doctor?

DR GRACE: Yes, I should say that was the finest innings I ever played.

NARRATOR: And do you remember it, shade of Tom Emmett?

EMMETT: I do – me and George Freeman have said time and again it were wonderful doctor weren't killed outright or scared of bowling for the rest of his days. Ah think o' his pluck when I see one of these young fellows nowadays scared if a ball hits him on the hand. He should have seen our expresses flying about the doctor's ribs and head in that game. Why, a don't think there were a square inch of sound flesh on the Owd Un's body when he done that innings.

READER: 1876 – Grace 344 for MCC against Kent, next game, 177 versus Notts – and the next match is

Gloucester versus Yorks at Cheltenham –

EMMETT: As sooth as ma neame's Tom Emmett I'll shoot that big doctor afoor he gets oondred ageanst oos –

READER: Gloucester versus Yorkshire at Cheltenham 1876. W.G. Grace 318 – and when he was 270 not out:

LOCKWOOD: (*Yorkshire voice*) Have another shy at the big 'un Allen.

ALLEN HILL: None for me – a'm finished, wi 'um.

EMMETT: Why doesn't tha' make 'un bowl – tha's captain.

ALLEN HILL: Why doesn't tha' bowl thyself Tom – tha's frightened.

EMMETT: Give me t'ball.

UMPIRE'S VOICE: (*distant*) Wide.

EMMETT: Dang it all it's Grace before meat, Grace afterwards and Grace all day and I've a feeling there'll be Grace tomorrow.

NARRATOR: And there was. The ranks of Tuscany. It was Grace who stood up to the great cricket of the early Australian sides and W.L. Murdoch, the greatest batsman of nineteenth-century Australian cricket, who said:

MURDOCH: (*Australian voice*) What do I think of W.G.? Why, that I have never seen his like and never shall. I tell you my opinion, which is that W.G. should never be put underground. When he dies his body ought to be embalmed and permanently exhibited in the British Museum as the colossal cricketer of all time.

NARRATOR: And, on the subject of great cricketers, the next witness I should like to call is Jack Hobbs. The batting of Jack Hobbs was like a confirmation of Grace's batting. All the strokes to all bowling – W.G.'s 100th hundred was made against Somerset – and Jack Hobbs made his 127th hundred to beat the old man's record also against Somerset – remember, Jack?

J.B. HOBBS: (*Insert recording*)

I can remember very clearly the day I scored my 127th century and beat W.G.'s record of 126, and though it may seem strange to you, I can tell you that I remember just as clearly W.G. scoring his hundredth century. I remember all the excitement of reading the papers when it happened. I was only a boy at the time away at Cambridge where we didn't see a lot of first-class cricket and we were brought up on W.G.

ARLOTT: Brought up on him? – and you played with him didn't you?

J.B. HOBBS: Yes, I played my first game for Surrey against the Gentlemen of England, captained by W.G. by the way, and that was the first time I came into contact with him. I remember that Mr Alcock the Surrey Secretary took me into his office afterwards and congratulated me on my score and said he was pleased with the way I had played W.G.'s slow bowling. W.G. he said was very artful at getting out youngsters. He was the greatest personality I have ever met on a cricket field. (*Cut.*) I have beaten some of W.G.'s figures and there may never be a greater run-getter than Don Bradman, but there will never be a greater cricketing personality than W.G. The Doctor left his stamp on cricket so deep that no one can ever blot it out. Some of us will be remembered in the years to come because our names are here and there in the record books, but we shall not be remembered as W.G. is remembered. And I can tell you this, everyone who played with or came into contact with him just loved the Doctor – 'The Old Man' they fondly called him, and it was their firm opinion that no other cricketer was in the same class. I am proud that I saw him and played in a match with him and am grateful to him for creating and leaving behind him the art of batting. He set a standard high as the stars and we who have followed have been better players because we hitched our wagon to his star. (*End*)

NARRATOR: But perhaps batsmen have a fellow feeling for W.G. – so shall we turn to the ranks of Tuscany again? – to the fast bowlers, Grace's classical opponents – to the man said to be the fastest of them all? Yes, C.J. Kortright, there's another great name – name? –

Mr C. J. Kortright 'cutting a dash' in straw boater.

more than a name – a man now approaching eighty who lives in Brentwood with great gusto and his memory full of cricket history. So my next witness is C. J. Kortright of Essex.

Well, Mr Kortright, no one's better qualified than you are to tell me how W.G. played fast bowling. Will you tell me?

KORTRIGHT: I'd say he was one of the outstanding men who knew how to do it without hesitation. He played it in a very different style to what is the style nowadays. He would come out and with his huge reach, he would smother the length ball and anything the least bit over-tossed he would hit hard past me. That is why I had to keep a man in the deep always, because I was inclined to over-toss in those days. But he was a master at it – he knew what to do exactly. Never hesitated and it was very hard to get the ball past him. I remember that occasion when he took a priceless 130 at Leyton. The old man made me look simple as dirt. He, well, he – that ball outside the off-stump – he wasn't attempting to hit it with his bat, but he was punching it with his thick felt gloves through the slips, and I was bowling fairly fast then. He was punching me with his hands down the slips to third man and everyone was very much surprised at that.

ARLOTT: Yes I am sure. And now will you take me back fifty years from July 18th, 1948 to July 1898 – W.G.'s Jubilee Match at Lord's. Do you remember that Gents *v.* Players game?

KORTRIGHT: I do very much indeed. Yes, I had the great honour of playing in that match. Well it was the hottest day on record and that is when the horses were all lying down in the street in the cabs. Well that was the occasion when the old man lost the toss and we went out. Sir Stanley and I started off the bowling to Bobby Abel and Arthur Shrewsbury, and for half an hour there was no run and I kept on, and the old man was most encouraging. 'Well Korty,' he said, 'want to come off?' So I said, 'Well, I can keep on,' and so he kept me on and I went from 12.0 to 2.0 without a break. Well I was pretty warm after that.

ARLOTT: Yes I expect you were. But now can we go on to the Gentlemen's second innings, the fourth innings of that game when they were playing to save the match.

KORTRIGHT: We had a very powerful batting side, but those length bowlers simply trundled our batsmen out till it came to number eleven and I was number eleven. Well, that was at twenty minutes to six. As I passed him going up the Nursery End the old man, who had gone in late because he was lame, he had got a bruised heel and he went in about number seven or eight, he says, 'Korty,' he says, 'Don't be nervous, play your usual game,' and I said, 'Alright Doc, I'll do my best.' So I looked at the time, twenty to six; well we managed to jog along till 6.30 when having stuck it out that length I gave a sigh of relief thinking it was all over. Then to my chagrin (that's a good word) I found we had to go on to 7.

We managed to stick it out till five minutes to seven when Arthur Shrewsbury put on Bill Lockwood – a deadly bowler with that nasty slow ball which I never knew how to treat and I knew it had got to come and – first two balls I stopped – the old man said, 'Well played, well played,' and then number three came – that horrible slow thing which he bowled so awfully well and I suppose I had a fit of inferiority complex and gave a half-hearted flick at it and it went somewhere out in the cover-point district where Scofie Haigh was fielding and he made a running catch of it and that was that. All over. And I failed by three minutes or three balls to save the old man's Jubilee Match. (*End*)

NARRATOR: Thank you – that did take me back. Now some more important evidence from the last century – Grace was an amateur cricketer in a day when the relationship between amateur and professional *could* be difficult. So I found Arthur Paish who was a young professional under W.G. fifty years ago – Arthur lives now near Gloucester and still comes to watch county cricket there. Do you remember the first time you saw W.G., Arthur?

ARTHUR PAISH: '86 – about '86, at Cheltenham College. I was quite a little chap about eight years old, and I got into the match, incidentally, by finding out one railing wider than another in the College ground, got in there and from that day onward until W.G. left Gloucestershire I don't think I missed seeing him play in Cheltenham district.

ARLOTT: And can you remember when you first played under him?

PAISH: I first played under W.G. in 1898. I was playing at Marlborough College and he sent me a telegram to play against Lancashire at Gloucester. Eventually I arrived on the ground and old Jack Board, our wicket-keeper, took me and introduced me to him. He put his arm over my shoulder and he said: 'Well my boy, the best of luck to you, and you are not afraid to bowl to a man who has just made 300 are you?' – I said 'No Sir.' That was Frank Sugg that had just come up from Taunton. I made 300 or just about that. Old W.G. nursed me up and the old man was very good to me. He kept himself remarkably fit and he expected every one of us to do the same. W.G. was one of the best of the pros. – one of the best friends the pros. had and if there was anything to be got out of the fame of earning money, and putting them in the way of earning money at the time, he always did so. People think that because he used to talk very loud and that sort of thing, that he was a bit of a martinet, but he was not, he would tell you what he thought of you and that sort of thing if you made a mistake, but he would come and catch hold of your arm the next minute and everything was forgotten.

ARLOTT: And how was he playing in those days – what was his batting like for instance?

PAISH: It didn't matter what bowling he had – slow or fast. There was no messing about – he let the fast bowlers have it at his age just as well as he did years and years before. He could play fast bowling beautifully. And the wickets then for fast bowlers were not so good as they are today and we had bowlers like Lockwood, Richardson and Kortright and the old man used to master the lot of them, and always putting the bat at the ball. I never wish to play under a better man. (*End*)

NARRATOR: 'Always putting the bat at the ball' – Gloucestershire – that's a tradition that is still alive – in another man who has opened the innings for Gloucestershire and for England – Charlie Barnett – and here he is:

C.J. BARNETT: I never saw W.G. Grace, but I know almost to an inch and a wrinkle what he looked like because you cannot be born and bred in Gloucestershire without seeing pictures of him on walls, or in books, wherever there is interest in cricket, and even where they hardly know a bat from a ball they are still proud of him. I know, too, the things he said and how he said them because you could not grow up in this county in my day without countless men telling you of W.G. and what he did and what he said. You cannot go in first for Gloucester and be unconscious of a tradition – all the time you remember that there is a standard set by a man who loved Gloucestershire and loved cricket. He played hard for both and almost made both – and he always put bat to ball – he always attacked. As a Gloucestershire man I'll be content if we pass on that tradition to those who come after us.

NARRATOR: And now I want to call upon the shade of a doubly qualified witness – A.C.M. Croome – who played much with W.G. for Gloucestershire and who was subsequently famous as a critic of the game. Croome's evidence, too, is of a man, not specifically of a cricket player, when he says:

A.C.M. CROOME: In all human probability it is due to W.G. Grace that I have survived to remember him for he saved my life at Manchester in 1887. While I was fielding I ran into the railings in front of the Old Trafford pavilion and fell onto one of the spikes which made a deep wound in my throat. They had to send out for needle and thread to stitch me up – for nearly half an hour before the materials came W.G. held the edges of the wound together. It was of vital importance that the wounded part should be kept absolutely still. I should have known if there had been any twitching of the great finger and thumb for I was conscious most of the time and my neck and face nerves were severely bruised. All that half-hour his hand never shook. It would have been a remarkable feat of endurance under any circumstances, but the old man had been fielding out for over four hundred runs and had taken his full share of the bowling. There are two reasons for telling you this. One is obvious, the other is its evidence of W.G.'s amazing stamina.

NARRATOR: Croome was one of Grace's team in the match at Clifton College played there on a perfect wicket – perfect for hundreds of runs – and he was looking at the wicket when Grace and the opposing skipper came out to toss.

DR GRACE: You call –

OTHER VOICE: Heads.

DR GRACE: (*after pause*) I've got yer, I've got yer, its tails.

OTHER VOICE: Damn.

DR GRACE: I don't know so much about damn – there's a rise in the ground there and that chucker of yours might be nasty off it – I suppose we'd better bat though or these boys of mine will be grumbling about the old man.

NARRATOR: At the end of the day W.G. Grace was still batting –

DR GRACE: Heh, heh, heh, and that fast bowler still bowling from the wrong end – bowling from the wrong end all day – and the only player he's got rid of is his own wicket-keeper off that ridge that's too short and too wide to worry anyone.

NARRATOR: But Croome knew his man as a man.

CROOME: W.G. was always guided by the spirit rather

than the letter: wasn't it W.G. who allowed the Surrey reserve wicket-keeper to take Steadman's place at the Oval when Steadman was injured in the first few overs of the match? And if he hadn't Walter Read would have had to keep wicket and he would not only have let byes but would have to bat afterwards with sore hands – a double advantage for Gloucester – but not the sort of advantage W.G. wanted to take.

NARRATOR: Another witness from beyond this world is the great C.T. Studd – probably the greatest cricketer of even that great family of cricketers – C.T. Studd of Cambridge University, Middlesex and England.

C.T. STUDD: Everyone who bowled against W.G. knew that it wasn't enough to bowl a good ball everytime, but that he had to bowl his best ball or look silly. I remember Fred Morley bowling his best on a sticky wicket in a Gents and Players match at Lord's – Fred was making her talk Chinese – one ball would bump shoulder high and the next one shoot. Old W.G. played a whole over of shooters from Fred, and when the umpire called over the whole pavilion rose in cheers as though he had made a century. W.G.'s prose made Fred's poetry look piffle, but each of those balls might have meant a wicket if it had not been Grace batting there.

Grace was a great man to have on your side – such a full-blooded optimist. There are times when it seems to a bowler hopeless to think of getting a batsman out or stopping his hitting – those times never came to W.G. But he was a much better bowler than he looked from the pavilion and he was always so cock-sure he could get you out that you had to strengthen your own opinion that he wouldn't – or else he would.

And I don't fancy many people ever saw him miss a catch – but then the ball could hardly miss his pair of hands – and it looked like a pea in a top hat when it got inside.

His eye was about the finest there ever was –

NARRATOR: And then Studd said something that has

been said nowhere else – and no score card, no book of records, no book of history, not even a photograph or a painting will tell you this –

STUDD: It was worth going a long journey just to look into W.G.'s eyes.

NARRATOR: Before 1870 Dr W.G. Grace was established as the greatest batsman in the world: in 1871 he made 2,739 runs at an average of 78.9; the next best batsman of the season was Richard Daft with 565 runs at an average of 37; only one other batsman scored 1000 runs – and that was Jupp who had nine more innings than the Doctor; and the magazine *Fun* in 1873 produced this passage:

READER: 'The Society for the Improvement of Things in General and the Diffusion of Perfect Equality, at a meeting to be held shortly, will submit the following propositions:

That W.G. Grace shall owe a couple of hundred or so before batting – these to be reckoned against his side should he not wipe them off.

That his shoe spikes shall be turned inwards.

That he shall be declared out whenever the umpire likes.

That he shall always be the eleventh player.

That he shall not be allowed to play at all.'

(*Fade up sound of bat on ball and sharp roar of applause.*)

WEST COUNTRY VOICE: (*over*) Old Grace another four – and that's another.

(*Applause higher louder and fade to silence. Knocker. Door opens.*)

ANXIOUS MAN'S VOICE: My Jimmy got a fearful stomach ache – is Dr Grace in?

SERVANT'S VOICE: In? Course he's in – don't you know he been in since four o'clock yesterday, scored 200 he has.

(*Fade and mix up applause, sound of bat on ball.*)

NARRATOR: Year after year he carried the Gentlemen on his shoulders in the only real period of amateur dominance. In 1882, however, the press could begin to suggest that the great man was now past his best. Then, in May 1895, rising forty-seven, heavier than ever and with his knee troubling him – then came greatness: a champion came back – the inviolable rule of sport shattered by a man greater than that fallible humanity for whom rules are made.

READER: May 9th, 10th and 11th, 1895. For MCC and Ground versus Sussex. W.G. Grace 13, and 103.

May 13th and 14th for MCC versus Yorkshire at Lord's. W.G. Grace 18, and 25.

May 16th, 17th and 18th, for Gloucestershire versus Somerset. W.G. Grace 288.

NARRATOR: He had never made a century on the Bristol ground before. His 288 was the third best score he had ever made in first-class cricket and this was his hundredth hundred in first-class cricket. Let us turn to C.L. Townsend who lives now in Durham and who, like his father before him, for many years went in first for Gloucestershire, and who was at the other end when that famous century was made:

C.L. TOWNSEND: This was the one and only time I ever saw W.G. Grace flustered – when the last runs were needed for his hundredth hundred. Poor Sammy Woods could hardly bowl the ball and the doctor was nearly as bad.

READER: May 20th, 21st and 22nd, 1895 for Gentlemen of England versus Cambridge University at Cambridge. W.G. Grace 52.

May 23rd, 24th and 25th for Gloucestershire against Kent. W.G. Grace 257 and 73 not out – in the field throughout the match.

May 27th, 28th and 29th, 1895 for England versus Surrey at the Oval – W.G. Grace 18.

May 30th, 1895. Grace wins the toss and Gloucester bat first in their game against Middlesex – W.G. Grace 169.

One thousand and sixteen runs in the month of May – made in only 7 matches and only 10 innings –

NARRATOR: This was the mighty swan song. A new generation, a generation which had bred fresh heroes for itself, saw the giant of an earlier age in all his greatness. There were still triumphs – another 24 centuries to come, and even Test matches. His last Test match, in 1899 when he went in first with another man who like himself became a legend, is a legend in his own lifetime. C.B. Fry, athlete and scholar, poet and conversationalist, probably the finest brain ever applied to cricket and whose recollection and critical opinion I am grateful to have here – Captain C.B. Fry:

C.B. FRY: Naturally, I remember the Test match of 1899: who wouldn't remember his first Test match and W.G.'s last Test match, especially if one had walked in with him first. I walked in with W.G. As we went down the pavilion steps, I must say he looked extremely cheerful, and brushing his beard aside as though he meant business; and as we passed through the gate, he said, 'Look here Charlie Fry, remember I am not a sprinter like you.' Anyhow we went in and we put up a very good stand – I think it was 75 before W.G. got out. (*Cut.*) The only thing was he could not run the second runs for the country and he could not run short runs in front of cover point. But it isn't known, I think, that he would not have played in that match unless he had been over-persuaded by Lord Hawke. (*Cut.*) W.G. didn't like the idea of not being able to bend down and catch a catch. That was the real reason why I think he retired. He was a very, very great man and we were all very fond of him and admired him as a very great Englishman.

ARLOTT: And how did W.G. look from the opposite crease, Captain Fry?

FRY: He stood his full height and he was a long way over six feet. He played every stroke with a real swing of the arms.

He came down extremely quickly from a great height and he very rarely missed a ball; and when he came down on it, the ball had to go – and it went. He was a very correct player, he stood by the old canons of style: he radiated on his front foot and he was a tremendous driver on both sides of the wicket. He used to hit with a full swing of his arms and a tremendous turn of his hands at the end of his swing and – well – I tell you he made bowling look very small when he was on the job. And I will tell you another thing – when he was in he made everyone else on the field look like a boy. (*End*)

NARRATOR: Thank you Captain Fry. 'Blocked shooters to the boundary' – yes, an old Gloucester critic saw that –

GLOUCESTER VOICE: He dab 'em but seldom and when he do dab 'em he dab 'em for four.

NARRATOR: And another Gloucester cricketer is W.S.A. Brown, one of the wonderful group of Gloucestershire off-side fieldsmen of the 90s – Grace, Brown, Sewell and Jessop and here is evidence again that Grace was a human being and not an automaton of a cricket field – W.S.A. Brown:

W. S. A. BROWN: Yes, the old man was much more than an automaton: he was almost the perfect captain to begin with, thinking about his players and never failing to give them kindness and encouragement.

Now I remember quite vividly our August Bank Holiday match with Sussex at Bristol in 1898. When we came to take our second innings, there was not much possibility of a finish on an easy wicket on the third day. When I went in to bat, W.G. was still in and had got about fifty and I was very keen to stay with him until he got a hundred.

Now, in those days the score-board did not show every run as it was scored, but only the total – and that only every ten – nothing to show how much each batsman had got. We went on playing for sometime when W.G. sent for the scorer ... He got his answer and we went on playing again. But two or three more times he sent for the scorer to ask his score. Then, having scored a single, and in the middle of an over, he turned to W.L. Murdoch, the Sussex captain, and said he was declaring the innings closed. I was astonished at this because W.G. had scored 93 – and there were only forty minutes left for play which was plenty of time for his hundred and no time for a result. As we were walking back to the pavilion I said, 'Doctor, do you know you made 93 – aren't you going to stay and get a hundred?' His reply amazed me even for W.G. – it was: 'I have got plenty of hundreds and they tell me I have got every score from a duck to a hundred in first-class cricket except 93 and now I have got 93 so I am declaring the innings closed.'

NARRATOR: Grace managed the London County side into the early years of this century – played until 1908 – but the loss of his son aged him –

DR GRACE: I never liked cricket more than I do now, and the only regret I entertain is that my career is ending instead of beginning –

Some who are veterans when I was a youngster are dead and perhaps are forgotten; some who were of my own age have dropped out of active cricket and I am painfully conscious that my eye cannot long remain undimmed, that my muscles must soon lose their elasticity and that in a year or two my name like those of the companions of my youth will drop out of the averages. At least I can say after all my years in the cricket field that the joys have far exceeded the pains and as I look back along the vista of years now growing dimmer I rejoice that I participated so long in the delights which cricket affords.

NARRATOR: On October the 23rd, 1915 at a time of the year when even the latest bats are put away for the winter and under the heavy pall of the ugliest war the world had known, at Eltham in Kent, died William Gilbert Grace, member of the Royal College of Surgeons, licentiate of the Royal College of Physicians of Edinburgh and a cricketer. And here let me turn again to Charles Townsend who said to me:

TOWNSEND: To do justice to W.G. in a few words is impossible. You see, I was one of the family and I

Grace carrying his girth with good humour.

dearly loved them all. W.G. loved his home – this much I can vouch for – that all cricketers who played with him from boyhood, as my father did, through to those who played with him to the end of his life, all loved him as a great and sincere man. Don't try to draw comparisons, but let him remain as that great sincere simple man who gave so much pleasure to countless thousands of people during his long career.

NARRATOR: But perhaps the last word was spoken by an earlier Bishop of Hereford when he said this of W.G.:

BISHOP OF HEREFORD: Had Grace been born in ancient Greece, the *Iliad* would have been a different book. Had he lived in the Middle Ages, he would have been a crusader and would now have been lying with his legs crossed in some ancient abbey, having founded a great family.

NARRATOR: As he was born when the world was older, he was the best known of all Englishmen and the king of that English game least spoilt by any form of vice.

ANNOUNCER: You have been listening to *The Old Man* a centenary programme in honour of W.G. Grace, written and introduced by John Arlott. Others taking part were Preston Lockwood as W.G., George Holloway, Phyllis Smale, Hedley Goodall, Lewis Gedge, Paul Rogers, Myles Rudge, Robert Bashford, Alan McGilvray, Edward Lee and S. Kumar; with W.S.A. Brown and the recorded voices of Jack Hobbs, C.J. Kortright, C.B. Fry, Arthur Paish and C.J. Barnett. The programme was produced by Desmond Hawkins.

BBC West of England Home Service, July 1948

8

Two Charlies

John's ability to assimilate and then disseminate thoughts which you had assumed were yours alone has always been an enviable part of his art. This is never more obvious than when he assesses a player's personality. Two contemporaries of the thirties and forties provide illustration, both opening batsmen, but of somewhat dissimilar temperament.

Farewell to Charlie Barnett

When Charlie Barnett plodded back to the pavilion from his last innings of the 1948 season, high-shouldered and swinging his bat like a walking stick, the first-class game in England lost a unique cricketer whose successor is not yet to be seen. Always a master of timing, he wisely left county cricket while men could still say 'Why is he retiring?' rather than wait until they asked 'Why doesn't he retire?' He had experimented with mere utility in batting in that last season and, characteristically, he had rejected it. When he found he could no longer consistently play great innings in the grand manner, he left the game rather than be less than himself.

An Attacking Batsman

The perfect wickets and defensive batting methods of the thirties conspired to reduce competent batsmen to a level of anonymity, but Charlie Barnett was not to be confused, even for a single stroke, with any other batsman. No other opening batsman in the game was so likely to hit the first

Charlie Barnett, Gloucestershire and England.

ball of a match for four. On his day – which came often – he would make a bowler believe that freshness, the new ball, morning life in the wicket were no more than the ingredients of another Barnett century.

It would be an error to suggest that, because he was an attacking batsman, Charlie Barnett was not shrewd both as a man and as a cricketer. He played the first match of his twenty-two year cricket career for Gloucester against Cambridge University, in 1927, before he was seventeen. He followed his father, C.S. Barnett, and an uncle, E.P. Barnett, in the Gloucester team as an amateur. With a wisdom not always shown by young cricketers, he played as an amateur in 1928, as well, making sure of his footing before he became professional in 1929. A natural hitter, who added considerable thought to his power of stroke, he was a bright, rather than a great, number five in his county's batting. But, with the retirement of Dipper in 1932, he replaced that master of subtle defence as Gloucestershire's opening batsman. He was an *attacking* opening batsman – almost a contradiction in terms in modern times – more, he was a successful attacking number one. In 1933 he scored over 2000 runs at more than 40 an innings with 6 centuries, and he played his first Test – against the West Indies at the Oval.

For six seasons until war, Barnett triumphantly rode his whirlwind of batting. He not only threw the boldest of bats at any bowling, but he played chiefly on the off side where the true graces of the game lie. To be sure he could hook viciously, but he liked best of all to stand up straight hunching his high and powerful shoulders, and thunder the ball anywhere between mid-off and third-man. He was no maker of the pedestrian hundred, neither did he take his runs greedily against weak attacks. There is an essential quality about Charlie Barnett's batting which is sometimes missed. In a day when caution among opening batsmen is the fashion, it is easy to dismiss a free-scoring number one as a 'risky selection'. But Charlie Barnett was as likely to make runs against the greatest as against the small fry – often more likely to do it against the strongest attack. He *believed* that he was the master of any bowler alive – and what was more, he often proved it.

No English batsman, not even Hammond, was so effective as Barnett against the great Australian O'Reilly. Where many others faced O'Reilly tensely and anxiously, Barnett swung at him, scientifically but powerfully. Perhaps he never had a greater moment than when, still not out, he was only one short of a hundred before lunch in the Trent Bridge Test of 1938. Only three batsmen in the history of England-Australia Tests have scored a century before lunch – and they are all Australians – Victor Trumper, Charlie Macartney and Don Bradman.

99 BEFORE LUNCH

No Englishman has ever achieved the feat. But, in that first Test of 1938, with McCormick, O'Reilly, McCabe, Fleetwood-Smith and Ward bowling against him, Barnett swept to 99 not out in an unfinished partnership of 169 with Len Hutton in the two hours before lunch. He drove and cut majestically – and almost 'murdered' Fleetwood-Smith. When Len Hutton played out the last over before lunch as a maiden, the Australians were, certainly, baulked in their attempt to trap Barnett as he pressed for his hundred. But I think he would have scored that other single which, in the event, he scored off the first ball bowled after lunch.

He has played a great innings in almost every county – perhaps most memorably his magnificent century in eighty minutes against Larwood and Voce at Trent Bridge in 1936. But to pick among Barnett's innings is almost impossible because he could not and would not be shackled, he could not bat other than handsomely. Once he was 'set', it was almost impossible to bowl a length to him. Even disaster to his fellow-batsmen had no effect upon him because he believed so firmly in himself as a batsman.

His greatest service was, perhaps to his native Gloucestershire, for whom he played more innings than all but

Billy Neale of the recognised batsmen of the county's entire history. Many of those innings won matches – as much by their psychological impact on the other side as by their size.

As a medium-pace bowler he was steady, with that life from the pitch which such a high easy action as his always produces. In post-war years, I think he was sometimes amused that his in-swingers and leg-cutters took cheap and regular wickets at reduced pace, but he was always a useful bowler. He could field, too, with brilliance in the deep-field to round off that something always more than mere usefulness which he had to contribute to the cricket of his time.

The measure of Charlie Barnett's greatness as a cricketer lies in the fact that his like is not to be seen in our cricket today.

Day and Mason Cricket Annual 1949

CHARLIE

The county cricket captains, at their annual meeting, included, as a 'new appointment' in their list of umpires to stand in first-class matches in 1954, the name of C.B. Harris (Nottinghamshire). In many autograph albums he is represented by the page-wide and unmistakable signature 'Charles Bowmar Harris' underlined with a fine old-fashioned flourish; but a full generation of county cricketers has identified him satisfactorily as 'Charlie.'

He will have his place in the sun, this summer, for the second time: and, for the second time, he will have it in defiance of probability.

Many great players have come to the summer-long green fields of first-class cricket from the pit-head pitches which dot the Nottinghamshire and Derbyshire coalfield, but they have been only a small proportion chosen from the thousands who have played there. Charles Harris, of Underwood, was seventeen when he left the pit, packed his new leather bag, and, prepared to stand on his own feet, went to join the Nottinghamshire ground staff. It was 1925 and the feudal order of things still ruled at Trent Bridge. G. Gunn, W. Whysall, W. Walker, A.W. Carr, W. Payton was the order of the side's main batting. Notts were in one of their periods of plenty. The young men could think themselves lucky to be alive and there in such a time.

The figures of Charles Harris's cricket career are those of a good, workmanlike county batsman. He first played county cricket in 1928; was given his county cap in 1931, and retired in 1951. He scored something over eighteen thousand runs for Nottinghamshire. Meanwhile, with greater pleasure, if less technical justification, he took 196 wickets with off-breaks which did not always break but had the backing of tactical conversation.

On those pitches near the pitheads, where the black coal shows through the grass blades, batsmen learn not to flinch when the ball rears at their ribs; neither do they rub their bruises, for that, they know, merely encourages the bowler. Charlie always batted the more determinedly for being hit.

In the long-enduring Nottinghamshire opening pair of Keeton and Harris, Keeton was the heavier scorer, a brilliant stroke maker who, in his time, went in first for England. Yet many bowlers found it harder to bowl to Harris.

The temptation of the high-thrown ball or the floated half-volley would evoke from him a defensive stroke of elaborately infuriating ease and certainty. To play back maiden overs to the irritation of both crowd and opposing fieldsmen would often divert him for hours. On other mornings, a small half-past-eleven crowd has seen him cut, hook and drive good-length, new-ball bowling with the certainty and range of stroke of that mercurial George Gunn whose temperamental successor he so often seemed in his county side.

He liked best to be the one rock of resistance in a crumbling innings. Then his lean shoulders jutted, his cropped hair seemed more bristly than ever, his bat was wary as a cat's paw. When his side's batting was going well, how-

Charlie Harris, Nottinghamshire.

ever, sheer lack of the challenge which made him his true, angular, batting self would often bore him to the point of the wild stroke of utter impatience. He was, they said, unpredictable. He was also, in an age of cricket which has been called characterless, an original.

(There was deep irony in some of the tactics he adopted, but there is none in his feeling for the game. He is an incurable cricket spectator. I was surprised on one occasion, at a relatively unimportant Derbyshire match to find Charlie sitting in the pavilion. An injury from the previous match had kept him out of his own county side which was playing in London, so he had come to watch the nearest first-class match, and for all of each of the three days he watched intently, with both perception and generosity.)

The craft of the game was deep in him, and so was knowledge of men. One spin bowler who played often for England lost much of his effectiveness in face of Harris's 'nomination.' 'That's the google,' he would say, as the ball left the hand: or, 'That's your leggy.' Then he would play a stroke of elaborate care to the covers, or hit the googly savagely, with the spin, through the less closely covered leg-field. It was more than the bowler could bear. At the crease, one minute before half-past eleven, he would survey the field with a solemn air and greet his opponents with, 'Good morning, fellow workers.' Charlie's formula for unsettling a famous fast bowler by stopping him in the middle of his run-up in order to wave an imaginary spectator from the sight-screen or to adjust an already well-fastened pad-buckle, was a shrewd piece of clowning.

By 1951, he had largely lost his place as Keeton's opening partner to R.T. Simpson. In June of that season, however, with Keeton injured and Simpson at a Test match, he went in first against Hampshire at Trent Bridge. He saw the first four Notts wickets fall for 22 runs on the 'green-topped' wicket which often occurs at Trent Bridge on the first morning of a match. Harris carried his bat for 239 out of the eventual first innings of 401.

At that time, only his closest friend, reluctantly admitted to the secret because of the need for his assistance in treatment, knew that Charlie was in constant and acute pain. He was already in an advanced stage of the illness which, last year, was treated by two operations of such proportions that his friends held little hope for his life. In hospital, he was forgiven much of his exuberance not merely out of respect for his courage but because exuberance was, clinically speaking, impossible from one so gravely ill.

He quoted the odds on his recovery with an objective accuracy, which startled some who did not know him well. Eventually he announced, 'I have beaten the book.'

As an umpire he will be the central figure of a saga composed in roughly equal proportions of his doings and apocryphal revivals of old stories. While he will miss little, he will certainly speak his personal and unusual mind. Some of his more sardonic remarks will attempt to conceal the simple gratitude and delight he feels at taking his place in the sun for the second time.

The Spectator, March 1954

9

The Mystery of Cricket

'The mystery of the Trinity is as nothing compared to the mystery of cricket.'

Whether this entirely facetious comment made by a BBC drama producer to a youthful broadcaster sowed a seed for that which follows is entirely debatable.

THE MYSTERY OF CRICKET

A programme which asks the question – but will certainly not find the answer – 'What is the peculiar fascination of this game to so many different types of people?' Written and produced by John Arlott and Edward Livesey, with contributions by S. F. Barnes, Len Hutton, C. J. Kortright and J. E. Walsh.

ARLOTT: The Mystery of Cricket – you may think at first that this is a programme explaining cricket. It's not. If a man has to have the fascination of cricket explained to him, he'll never really feel it. We're talking tonight of those of you who are already converted (if that's the right word?). We want to put before you all this extraordinary problem – why does this game have such a peculiar attraction for so many different people, and what in fact do they get out of it. Well, to attempt to elucidate the mystery, we've got here the written testimony of several cricket writers, and here in this studio are a couple of honest-to-goodness Saturday afternoon cricketers.

AUKLAND: Duffers!

ARLOTT: Well, that was autobiographical, not from the commentator. One of them's a Derbyshire man, the other is a Shropshire countryman, and we've got some recorded and completely unscripted interviews with several of the game's greatest players, but I warn you, before you start you may think now you can answer the question, but you won't be able to at the end of this programme. Righto. Let's begin with the evidence as laid before us by E.V. Lucas.

READER: How to explain the fascination that cricket exerts: that is not simple. That it should attract the proficient is understandable, though they are liable to continual mischances and mortifications such as no other game presents. But the curious thing is that it attracts the incompetents as well, those who never make a run and cannot bowl, and yet, doomed only to dreary waiting in the pavilion and to fatiguing fielding, they turn up punctually on every occasion, hoping for the best, and even, such is the human heart's buoyancy, expecting it. There is no other game at which the confirmed duffer is so persistent and so undepressed. It is for the experts – victims of misfortune – that depression awaits. It is they who chew the cud of bitterness. The phrase about the glorious uncertainty of cricket applies to the individual as much as to the fortunes of the struggle, for there is no second chance. The batsman who is out first ball must retire to the pavilion and brood on his ill-luck until it is time to field and forget it, when, as likely as not, he'll miss a catch and enter purgatory again. This constant risk of making no runs would, you'd think, deflect boys and men from the game. But no. The cricketing temperament, always slightly sardonic, accepts it. The uncertainty spells also glory.

AUKLAND: Ah, that's cricket.

STOCKTON: That sums it up absolutely. The gist of the thing is the uncertainty of it, especially in the lower classes of cricket.

AUKLAND: That's right, the duffers.

STOCKTON: I saw an instance last summer when the three crack batsmen on our side did nothing, but the fellow who wasn't used to playing and was really very nervous about it, lashed out and hit two sixes and a four.

ARLOTT: Add to that C.B. Fry's comment on the game:

READER: To some people cricket is a circus show, upon which they may or may not find it worthwhile to spend sixpence; to others, it is a pleasant means of livelihood; to others, a physical fine art, full of plots, interest and enlivened by difficulties. To others in some sort, it is a cult and a philosophy and these last will never be understood by the profanum vulgus, nor by the merchant-minded, nor by the unphysically intellectual.

ARLOTT: The profanum vulgus! There you see the 'mystery' begins to come in. Cricket, too, is a magic, never more a magic perhaps than for the very young, when the very names of cricketers are Olympian names and then there are the memories of the old cricketer looking back at himself as a young cricketer, as they are in this poem:

READER:

There's music in the names I used to know,
And magic when I heard them, long ago.
'Is Tyldesley batting?' Ah, the wonder still!
... The school clock crawled, but cricket-thoughts would fill
The last slow lesson-hour deliciously.
(Drone on, O teacher: you can't trouble me.)
'Kent will be out by now' ... (Well if you choose
To keep us here while cricket's in the air,
You must expect our minds to wander loose
Along the roads to Leyton, Lord's, and Leeds,
Old Trafford and the Oval, and the Taunton meads ...)

And then, at last, we'd raid the laneway where
A man might pass, perchance, with latest news.
Over his glasses he would smile to hear
Our thirsty questions as we crowded near.
Greedily from the quenching page we'd drink –
How its white sun-glare made our young eyes wink!

'Yes, Tyldesley's batting still. He's ninety-four.
Marlow and Mold play well. Notts win once more.
Gloster (with Grace) have lost to Somerset –
Easy: ten wickets: Woods and Palairet ...'

So worked the magic in that dusty lane.
The stranger beamed. Maybe he felt again
As I feel now to recall those lovely names
Jewelling the loveliest of our English games.
Abel and Albert Trott, Lilley, Lillywhite,
Hirst, Hearne, and Tunnicliffe – they catch the light –
Lord Hawke and Hornby, Jessop, A.O. Jones –
Surely the glow they held was the high sun's!
Or did a young boy's worship think it so,
And is it but his heart that's aching now?

ARLOTT: Now Thomas Moult, who wrote that poem ...

AUKLAND: A Derbyshire man that was – Thomas Moult. He lived in Dovedale.

ARLOTT: But on the bus route to Lord's now. Well, anyway, I think he ought to have mentioned Sydney Barnes, one of the greatest pace bowlers who ever lived, and who played in his time for many a League Club, for Staffordshire, Warwickshire, Lancashire and England, one of the legendary figures of cricket and whom I'm going to ask to recall one of his brightest legends. Well, Mr Barnes, I want you, if you will, to take me back to the days before I was born – that Test match against the Australians at the Oval in 1912.

BARNES: Certainly.

ARLOTT: It was there I believe, that you bowled both Warren Bardsley and Charlie Macartney without either of 'em knowing very much about it.

BARNES: Yes, I remember it quite well. Warren Bardsley came in and he hadn't been in long. I whipped one down to him, which was an outward swinger to a right-hander – an off-break.

ARLOTT: What, coming in to left-handed Warren Bardsley?

BARNES: Yes, that's so. Well, he watched it go by past

his toes and next he knew about it, it knocked his wickets down. Then MacCartney – to him I bowled an inward swinger – a kind of leg-break; it swung across his toes and suddenly he found his wickets were disturbed.

ARLOTT: More than disturbed, I should think.

BARNES: Well, knocked back.

ARLOTT: Floating one way in the air and coming the other way back off the pitch.

BARNES: Up against the swing.

ARLOTT: And sometimes it'd go on with the swing?

BARNES: Oh, certainly.

ARLOTT: And then other times it'd come back?

BARNES: The break bowler doesn't always make it turn, you know.

ARLOTT: And that at a fairly considerable pace.

BARNES: Yes, a pace.

ARLOTT: Well, fast enough for Archie MacLaren to call you a fast bowler?

BARNES: That's right.

ARLOTT: But we're not breeding that sort now. Have you got any idea why?

BARNES: Well I fancy they've got more sense.

ARLOTT: More sense, why?

BARNES: Well, it's hard work you know. I gave up bowling as a fast bowler pure and simple because I could never see the ball going fast enough.

ARLOTT: But I think I'm right in saying, aren't I, that even after you were sixty you could wrap a few batsmen round the knuckles?

BARNES: Well, I used to try to.

ARLOTT: And succeed?

BARNES: Sometimes. I got a few wickets. But the last game I played was when I was about sixty-eight.

ARLOTT: Did you get any wickets in that?

BARNES: Yes, that year I made over a hundred wickets.

ARLOTT: You see, to find out about the mystery of cricket, you've got to enquire into the mysteries of playing in it, even into the mysteries of the Chinaman.

STOCKTON: John, what's the difference between a Chinaman and a googly?

AUKLAND: I should like to know why it's called a Chinaman, too.

ARLOTT: Well, there's no difference at all off the pitch between a Chinaman and an *ordinary* googly, because the Chinaman is a ball bowled out of the side of the hand by a left-arm bowler which is an off-break to a right-hand batsman. A googly is bowled by a right-hand bowler, and that's also an off-break, but bowled with a leg-break action. The intent is to deceive.

ARLOTT: But anyway, Jack Walsh, of Leicester, I suppose is the man who knows more about the Chinaman than anyone else, but like any really wise man he doesn't broadcast *all* his wisdom.

Well, Jack, we know you as bowling the Chinaman, but didn't you once bowl the orthodox slow left-arm breakaway?

WALSH: That's correct. I started off by bowling slow left-hand with leg-spinners in Sydney in about 1932.

ARLOTT: And did you bowl them well enough?

WALSH: Well, on the opinion of one of my skippers, a very prominent New South Wales player, he thought that there was a possibility that I might be able to play for Australia, bowling the old leg-spinner.

ARLOTT: But you gave it up, Jack?

WALSH: I gave it up. I decided to concentrate on the Chinaman and the googly.

ARLOTT: Now when you decided that, there was nobody in first-class cricket bowling it, was there?

WALSH: I don't think so. I think Fleetwood-Smith appeared on the scene for Victoria about the same time.

ARLOTT: I see, but it was your own idea to bowl it?

WALSH: It was my own idea.

ARLOTT: Why, Jack?

WALSH: Well, I'd had the impression that if a right-hander could bowl leg-spinners and googlies, I thought the left-hander could do it and do it as well.

ARLOTT: And then, you took it up more or less as an experiment?

WALSH: As an experiment, yes.

ARLOTT: And on that experiment you chanced whether

you ever made a Test place as an orthodox left-hand bowler and let that go.

WALSH: That's the way I thought, yes.

ARLOTT: Because the problem appealed to you?

WALSH: That's why I liked it.

ARLOTT: And now you bowl the Chinaman and googly?

WALSH: And the googly, yes.

ARLOTT: Only one googly, Jack?

WALSH: Two, John.

ARLOTT: Only two, Jack?

WALSH: Two, I think.

ARLOTT: No one, least of all English first-class batsmen, can be quite sure that they're still only two. They're wiley birds, these left-arm bowlers. One of the first of them was Johnny Briggs of Lancashire, who always used to upset the Australians, and that's why I think it could have easily been for an Australian that this poem was written.

READER:

Let me whisper in your ear, Johnny Briggs,
I must pick with you a rather biggish bone.
Now you needn't sprint away like that, Johnny Briggs,
I shall catch you, Johnny, sometime all alone.

You bowled me with a nasty ball, Johnny Briggs,
Which twisted three or four times in the air;
Then it broke and shot like lightning from the pitch:
Now I think that is not altogether fair.

And then after this achievement, Johnny Briggs,
You smiled and you grinned, and then you chaffed,
Till a chuckle of delight went round the field,
And you winked that wicked eye of yours and laughed.

STOCKTON: Huh, that's all very well, but I've always said that the real cricket is played on the village green, not on the county grounds.

ARLOTT: Now then, Ernest Stockton, you're not going to give me the romantic line about village cricket, are you?

STOCKTON: Well, no, I'm not. You'll find the average village lad keen enough to win, but if he gets a lickin', well again it's always in the game. Many's the time I've come home with the lads from an away match and been asked, 'How did you get on?', and if told that we'd lost, heard the remark, 'Well, I'll be dashed, I thought you must have won by the bally noise you were making.' But people misunderstand village cricket. They think the thing's funny when it isn't. There's a true story that illustrates that. I know the fielder in question. This chap was wearing a pair of flannels much too big for him round the waist. He was fielding in the deep, and presently he got under a skyer. It slipped through his hands and as he wasn't wearing a belt, the ball dropped down his trousers. While he was trying to secure it, and thus make the catch, some silly chump called 'lost ball' and turned what should have been a good catch into a six hit. Oh yes, you can laugh all right, but the point is that that was a tragedy, not a comedy. The fool who called out 'lost ball' might have lost us the match. We play cricket seriously in the country.

ARLOTT: That's the point. Funny things may happen in cricket, they do happen in cricket of all classes, but cricket's played seriously. This is what Len Hutton has to say about big cricket:

HUTTON: When young I studied all the cricket books that I could possibly get hold of and studied various styles and various methods of obtaining success, and I must say that I still feel that I know very little about this game, which is such a wonderful game and a wonderful team game.

ARLOTT: Well then, it's become something more than a job, it's almost a craft?

HUTTON: Yes, I do think that there is a great deal of science in this game, particularly in Test cricket against Australia, where the opposing chaps think of all kinds of ways in which to get you out.

STOCKTON: Well, I've seen Hutton make one or two big scores.

AUKLAND: And it looked as if he couldn't possibly make a mistake – child's play to him.

ARLOTT: It may be child's play till you try to do it. But in that connection, have you ever heard this story about Bill Ponsford?

READER: After all that had been said about Ponsford's wonderful sight, the doctor who examined him when he volunteered for the Air Force was astonished to find he was colour blind. He couldn't distinguish between red and green. A dialogue like this followed:

Doctor: What colour did the new ball look to you?

Ponsford: Red.

Doctor: What colour did it look after it became worn?

Ponsford: I never noticed its colour then, only its size.

STOCKTON: It's the size of the ball that always worried me – always like a pink pill when you're batting against it.

AUKLAND: Well, we've said nothing yet about spectators, but really they're half the game. I love watching on a county ground where every little bit of strategy is noticed and commented upon. Mind you, it's a great education – to listen to the remarks of people who know nowt about cricket.

STOCKTON: There's no doubt about that.

ARLOTT: How right you are.

AUKLAND: You can hear people who are sitting right across – at right angles to the wicket – appeal for a man being out leg before. There's a lot of fun in being a spectator, especially in the peculiarities of the players. One thing about Hutton: he always touches his cap at the bowler.

ARLOTT: Yes, there's a lot to notice at a first-class cricket match, or at any cricket match, and I wonder if we do always really want the bright cricket and the big batting. E.V. Lucas said something extremely wise about that:

READER: Cricket is not a series of spectacular events, a display of sparkle, and it never can be. Cricket is a stealthy, protracted, and often very dogged and unexciting form of warfare. Big hitting bears the same relation to cricket as wit to a Parliamentary debate, or champagne to dinner. They are exhilarating when we find them, but just as legislation can go on without wit, and dinner can go on without champagne, so can the game of cricket go on without fireworks. The spectacle of a watchful and astute captain assisted by a bowler and nine fieldsmen trying to get a man out should be as entertaining as one dashing hitter. It is the whole concerted attack and the determination of the resister that make cricket. Splendid, no doubt, when the resister finds the boundary again and again, but not less admirable when, doing his best, he merely succeeds in keeping his end up and either winning or preventing defeat.

Cricket is not big hitting or consistently bright batting, although big hitting and bright batting are a part of cricket. Cricket is big hitting and bright batting plus no hitting and anxious batting, plus even dull batting, plus bowling, plus fielding, plus strategy, plus chance. That is the game: all those ingredients are essential.

STOCKTON: Not from a spectator's point of view.

ARLOTT: I think they are, but there again you're getting back to the old subject of big hitting, and I must say I'd dearly have loved to have been with Cyril Foley in 1911 – thirty-eight years ago, at Hove, when he watched Alletson batting for Notts against Sussex.

READER: Between twenty-five minutes past two until five minutes to three, Alletson gave an exhibition of hitting which has never been and never will be approached. He scored no fewer than 139 runs. That meant that he himself was, for half an hour, scoring at the rate of 278 runs per hour. Words fail me. In one over from Killick which included two no-balls, he hit 34 runs: 4-6-6; 4-4-4-6. Indeed, had it not been for some unavoidable delay he would have made even more runs than he did in that last half hour. Time was wasted to prise one ball out of the new stand, into whose soft wood Alletson had driven it, no chisel being available. Alletson is the only person who has ever driven into a stand. One ball was lost for good and all.

Sinking a pint with Charles Kortright outside his Brentwood home in 1949.

ARLOTT: One of the major mysteries within the mystery of cricket is the mystery of Alletson, that big hitter; what happened to him afterwards?

READER: Later in the season I went to see him again and happened to sit in the Notts dressing-room next to A.O. Jones, the Notts skipper. Jonah was in despair. He said to me, 'The man can't be normal. I told him that I'll play him in every match right through the season even if he makes a run of ducks, as long as he will hit, but he just won't do it. You'll see for yourself presently.' And I did. In came Alletson with a huge crowd on tip-toe with excitement and made the most scratchy 11 runs possible. Never once did he attempt to hit the ball. As he was not a bowler he had to be dropped from the side.

ARLOTT: On the strength of that one innings, Alletson becomes the legendary hitter. The legendary fastest bowler of all time is Charles Kortright, still alive, still enjoying life with immense gusto, down in Essex where I was able to talk to him.

Well, Charles Kortright, I believe you played cricket for many years, just because you wanted to and at your own expense and not for any profit at all?

KORTRIGHT: That is so.

ARLOTT: And why did you?

KORTRIGHT: Because, well for one thing there was mighty little else to do in the summertime and because I enjoyed it, every moment.

ARLOTT: Well now, you knew, didn't you, that the life of a fast bowler, the effective life of a fast bowler, is shorter than the life of, say, a slower bowler, or a batsman, or even a wicket-keeper?

KORTRIGHT: Oh sure, yes.

ARLOTT: Well then, why did you bowl fast?

KORTRIGHT: Well, there's a great satisfaction in helping a stump out of the ground with a fast one: a slow one doesn't often do.

ARLOTT: How long did you go on playing?

KORTRIGHT: Till I was forty-two.

ARLOTT: A good innings.

KORTRIGHT: Yes, yes.

ARLOTT: And if you had your time all over again would you do the same again?

KORTRIGHT: Certainly.

ARLOTT: And it's what, rising forty years ago since you played first-class cricket.

KORTRIGHT: Oh no, forty-six.

ARLOTT: Forty-six is it?

KORTRIGHT: I left off in 1903.

ARLOTT: And would you say those fast bowlers wickets are the best memories you've got?

KORTRIGHT: Well, on one or two wet wickets I did one or two quite decent performances; like I finished off an innings against time down at Southampton against Hampshire. I got the last 6 wickets in about half an hour for 10 runs. That was one example. Again I took – I finished off a match at Edgbaston once, on a very sticky wicket – a mud wicket – I won't say sticky. I took 5 wickets for 12 there – well, that finished that off.

ARLOTT: What did it mean to you, Charles, to play cricket?

KORTRIGHT: To play a clean game and that was always the understanding in my day – that you played clean. And if anyone didn't play clean, well he heard all about it. If a man played cricket, he was understood to be a good sportsman.

AUKLAND: Well, if I'm alive at his age and as good a man as him, by gow, I'll have a couple. That is a good life, that is.

ARLOTT: Yes, a good life at 79, and I think he'd have that couple with you, Sam.

Well, as Charles Kortright says, if you play cricket you're a sportsman. But I'm afraid you're apt also to be a human being. I wonder how many of these excuses you've heard, and remember these were first printed in *A Cricketer's Guyed*, first printed in 1886: the first few of them – 'On Being Bowled Out':

READERS: 'My dear fellow, can't think how I missed it. Easiest ball ever saw in my life.'

'Worst wicket I ever came across. Wouldn't play here again if you paid me.'

'Umpire slick behind his arm; couldn't see a bit.'

'Filthy thing shot and broke half a yard.'

'Never tried to play it; feel rather seedy; glad to get out.'

ARLOTT: And these – on being caught out:

READERS: 'I'll swear it was a bump-ball, if I never speak again.'

'I never went within a yard of it! You heard it! Why, that was a man chopping wood in the next field.'

'Devilish good hit; would have been out of any ordinary ground.'

'This infernal bat don't drive a little bit.'

ARLOTT: Or on being run out:

READERS: 'No use playing against an umpire.'

'I swear I was past the wicket. There's my heel marks to prove it.'

'It wasn't his call at all, fool!'

ARLOTT: And of course there is always doubt on being leg before wicket:

READERS: 'No one but a cad would have asked such a thing.'

'Umpire means to earn his money at any rate.'

'What? Our umpire is it? Well, all I can say, he's an old fool.'

'It hit me on the back of my head.'

'I hit it hard.'

ARLOTT: Or these, on missing a catch:

READERS: 'The sun was bang in my eyes.'

'Funny thing – never missed one before that I can remember.'

'Good God! there *was* a lot of spin on that ball.'

'Ooh, right on my old sore place.'

'Shouldn't call that a chance, should you?'

ARLOTT: Lastly, when being taken off bowling:

READERS: 'I'd just found the right length, too.'

'Well, they didn't get many runs off me.'

'Oh, what's the use if fellows can't hold catches.'

'Hate bowling with a sticky ball.'

'I'd have *asked* to be taken off at the proper time.'

'Well, I shan't play for the Bottlejugs again.'

ARLOTT: Well, and now in this mystery which we've elaborated even if we haven't solved, the last word must come, traditionally, from a woman – from Mary Russell

Mitford of *Our Village:*

READER: 'Who would think that a little bit of leather and two pieces of wood had such a delightful and delighting power?'

Midland Home Service, May 1949

10

LOUIS MACNEICE AND FEATURES DEPARTMENT

'Jim' Pennethorne Hughes, 'Headmaster' of the BBC Staff training section where John was an instructor in the early fifties, public school boxer, poet, writer, broadcaster, collector and 'rufous Hanoverian' of distant Royal lineage by George IV and Mrs John Nash, was a man of ambivalent personalities – amiable, amusing and urbane, also sensitive, reticent and shy. Betjeman wrote that, 'he was much loved by an intimate few, and much liked by very many. He seemed lonely.' John was one of the few.

Hughes had been instrumental in consolidating the fledgling commentator's success with Eastern listeners in the minds of the BBC hierarchy when he sent a wire from Delhi: 'Cricket broadcasts greatest success yet East Service. Must be continued all costs.' This, of course, referred to the first post-war Indian tour and at that time Hughes was working for the Corporation in the sub-continent. Incidentally, nearly a quarter of a century later John contributed to a published volume of poems by Hughes and also was bequeathed his collection of books on magic.

The administrators' quick realization of the impact that John was having with the cricketing fraternity in India, encouraged the young broadcaster, now wearing his production 'hat', to begin formulating ideas that would appeal particularly to his newly-won audience. One such was a discussion chaired by Learie Constantine that assessed the Indian tour with Professor D.B. Deodhar and Abdul Hamid Sheikh, the Hindi commentator, on one side of the table and Arthur Russell and J.A. on the other.

His most demanding undertaking as a BBC producer

had been to mount a memorial feature on Gandhi just after his assassination. He had an hour to prepare a one-hour programme. By narrating and acting himself and with the assistance of two readers, three books of Gandhi aphorisms and a record of the Gujarati prayer-hymn of the bells, he managed it: 'Every time I ran out of ideas, we put the disc on.' Gandhi was a man he would most liked to have met: 'To take on the whole British Empire and win – without raising a hand in anger – to change the course of history. Fantastic.'

A number of John's first broadcasts had been as an actor and reader, in features, documentaries and poetry programmes such as The Metaphysicals, Book of Verse *and* England to Gibraltar; *the latter was in the series* Britain's Own Doorstep, *recorded at the old Monseigneur Studio in Piccadilly, for which he was paid the princely sum of five guineas, complementing a third-class return railway voucher from Southampton to Waterloo and a subsistence allowance of £1. This was in 1944, when the difference between guineas and pounds could be the price of a three-course meal. And then there was an epic in which J. Arlott and one Deryck Guyler took the parts respectively of forward and rear-gunners in a 'bomber' that had been 'shot up' by the 'ghastly Hun'. 'Or was it the other way round?' queries John. 'Perhaps Deryck was at the front and me at the back.' Chuckle. 'I do remember that, as supposedly the plane went down in flames, we both had to sing, "We're gonna hang out the washing on the Siegfried Line" I think it was, accompanied by the whole BBC Symphony Orchestra. Deryck sang sharp, I sang flat – the orchestra got it about right!'*

Many of those broadcasts were the product of the old Features Department. Even today, at almost any gathering of programme makers, rumours fly: 'I hear they're going to bring back Features!' Everybody knows it is not true. Times have changed and people have gone. There is no harm in wish-fulfilment.

Between its birth in 1936 and dismemberment in 1963, the Features Department of the BBC, beyond reasonable argument, produced the most original, imaginative and deeply satisfying work ever contributed in that medium. Laurence Gilliam gave the department its character, chose its widely diverse members, and gave them an atmosphere of ease which was reflected in a high quality of creativity. Few who have examined the relevant output would dispute that, of all that extremely talented group, the outstanding artist was Louis MacNeice.

The name of Louis MacNeice still evokes a memory picture no less sharp for being almost forty years old. Its setting is 'The Stag' (properly 'The Stag's Head') across New Cavendish Street from Rothwell House where Features Department lived its casual but stimulating life.

If Rothwell House was its official headquarters, there is little doubt that 'The Stag' was the breeding ground where a myriad of good and bad ideas was spawned, exercised, embraced, or rejected. For a first-time visitor in 1943 it was a revelation. The picture stems from that experience. The group at the bar consisted of Francis ('Jack') Dillon; Leonard Cottrell, Robert Kemp, Michael Barsley, Robert Barr, Geoffrey Bridson; Cecil McGivern – a late arrival, as usual – Laurence Gilliam and Louis MacNeice. To an aspiring young writer, MacNeice was a figure for distant admiration. He sat inches, yet only inches – mentally rather than physically – detached from the main cheerful, welter of conversation. Jack Dillon was, as usual, setting up ideas for the pleasure of knocking them down; Bridson amusedly grave; McGivern tautly incisive; Gilliam expansive. MacNeice looked the romantic idea of a poet: long, sensitive face, quizzical nose, deep, dark eyes, forelock dropping across left forehead, languid air, his forearm lay along the bar counter, long slim fingers fidgeting gently with a cigarette. Two, three, four times he made as if to enter the conversation, only to retreat in face of louder competition until Jack Dillon said: 'Yes, sorry Louis, what?' 'I was only going to ask,' he said, in the pause, with the most leisurely and unemphasized voice, 'whether anyone would like a drink'. He relished the anticlimax, with a smile which went no further than his eyes.

This man was one of the leading poets of his generation;

Louis MacNeice, poet and Features producer, casting a quizzical glance.

but it might be claimed that he was the finest of all writers for radio. At first he hesitated about entering the servitude of an institution. BBC Features, though, was not an institution in the usual sense. Laurence Gilliam gave his staff the utmost – some other BBC departmental heads thought inordinate – liberty. He had an innate sense of the creative atmosphere; only such an attitude could have won from Louis MacNeice a trust so relaxed that he produced probably the finest of his work, more historically important even than his poetry, in the bondage which, towards the end, won his loyalty. It was sadly appropriate that he and Gilliam should die only a little before its final bureaucratic assassination, which had been foreshadowed ever since the end of the Second World War that had provided the reason and the setting for its eminence.

Gilliam's argument that 'Teamwork is a key that unlocks great reserves of creative power' is one with which many would disagree on the grounds that, at the highest level, creativity must be individual. Yet it often seemed that this officially loose, but convivially close, association of producers, writers and producer/writers drew the best out of all of them. Over the twenty-odd years of its existence people as diverse as Douglas Cleverdon, Geoffrey Bridson, both of whom have chronicled the department valuably, Stephen Potter, Joe Burroughs, Reggie Smith, Rayner Heppenstall, Edward Sackville-West, Felix Felton, Leonard Cottrell, Robert Kemp, Michael Barsley, Jennifer Wayne, Terence Tiller, John Bridges, Robert Gittings, Patric Dickinson, Igor Vinagradoff, David Thomson, Bertie Rodgers, and Ludwig Koch (recorder of 'sound pictures') had apparently no common characteristic except that they contributed to a quite unique radio output.

Long before, in *Autumn Journal*, MacNeice had written of a desired community 'where the individual works with the rest, where people are more than a crowd'. Now he found it. When the end of the War made it possible for him to leave and return to the freedom of the freelance writer, as so many did, he chose to stay in the BBC. His first reputation was as a poet; radio gave him the opportunity to demonstrate the truth of his own argument that the poet 'is only the extension of the common man'. He had two gifts specifically valuable in radio: firstly, he thought in speech-rhythms so that his verse could be not merely read, but spoken. That is not a common attribute; some poetry perfectly acceptable to the eye cannot even be declaimed (try 'Ode to the West Wind'). He had, too, a superb ability of writing conversation in the rhythms and timing appropriate to character. Indeed, he took to radio script writing as if by nature.

He quickly recognized, too, the importance of the technical aspect of features – which Cecil Lewis described as 'the kaleidoscopic use of multiple studios' – with all the advantages of effects, music, chorus, changed acoustics. He always had an immense respect for other craftsmen in the medium and a highly perceptive understanding of their problems. He seemed intuitively to understand – to feel – radio:

> As with many other media, its narrow limits are also its virtues, while within those limits it can give us something unobtainable from print (though print, of course, will always retain its autonomy). When I first heard a piece which I had written for broadcasting, broadcast, I was irritated by details of presentation, but excited and delighted by the total effect (there was more to my script, I felt, than I myself had realized).

Louis MacNeice learnt quickly; he needed no more than the year 1941 to come to full terms with the medium. He had a most sensitive ear and, although not technically a musician, he recognized all its possibilities and William Walton, Benjamin Britten, William Alwyn, Anthony Hopkins, were among the composers who worked contentedly and successfully for him.

He was a meticulous, but not fussy producer. Concerned as he was to avoid 'the cold fish voice of the Narrator', his devices were never tricksy. He saw his characters as three-dimensional and was at pains to define them – usually in advance of rehearsal in a letter with the script – to the actors who took the parts and then, largely, to allow them to work their way into them. He had a particular set of actors whom he regularly engaged and who worked in close accord with him. Most of the feature producers had their particular favourites who helped to form the character of their work. (Jack Dillon, who employed a very tight circle of performers, once remarked: 'Nepotism in the BBC means you can only use your brother if he's good'.) Among MacNeice's teams were Howard Marion-Crawford, Stephen Murray, Cyril Cusack, Robert Speight, Alan McClelland, Mary Wimbush, Peter Ustinov and Esme Percy (The March Hare). MacNeice was calmly authoritative at the control panel. Sometimes, but always with a by-your-leave, he would take over a pot meter to adjust a sound-perspective he particularly wanted; but otherwise he was a relaxed listener.

There are certain landmarks in radio features. Apart from the valuable experiments of Lance Sieveking and Archie Harding, Geoffrey Bridson's *The March of the Forty-five* was the first major attempt to present the factual and documentary in dramatic form.

Cecil McGivern's *Bombers Over Berlin* and *The Battle of Britain*, both stemming from *War Report*, Gilliam's *Scotland Yard* and Felix Felton's *Underground* were early wartime efforts; yet Jack Dillon's pre-war adaptations from Hans Andersen of *The Nightingale* and *The Snow Queen* (and he continued in that field as well as in *Country Magazine*) showed how wide an umbrella Gilliam could spread.

Major wartime works were *Shadow of the Swastika* by Igor Vinagradoff and A.L. Lloyd, produced by Laurence Gilliam; Leonard Cottrell's *Coastal Command* and (1943) *The Rescue* by Edward Sackville-West. Later, a wartime idea, seven years in incubation, Dylan Thomas's *Under Milk Wood* – produced by Douglas Cleverdon, with the poet himself as narrator. Only the last two reached the standard which MacNeice so consistently maintained. Now, though, British radio – still, to many, 'the wireless' – was providing a standard of creative communication the world had never known before.

That eminence was enjoyed and appreciated by only a narrow generation. Although it began in 1936, it did not come into its own until about 1940 or 1941. Television had been shelved for the duration of war; but listeners in this country – and subsequently the audience in the United States for *Britain to America*, perhaps the first sustained major achievement of the department – enjoyed a unique artistic experience; now largely forgotten.

War always heightens imaginative – especially poetic – awareness (as witness the high wartime sales of verse). Now, for the first time since the ballad singers, a pattern was established of an uninterrupted flow of poetic creation into the mind, demanding not even the ability to read; and, freed from pictorial dictation (as in television or film), leaving the imagination free to create its own images. No other organization approached this level: from the inauguration of the Italia Prize in 1949 until 1955, of fifteen entries chosen as outstanding works of those years, fourteen came from Features Department of the BBC. Running commentary offered, of course, an equally - even greater - fresh opportunity of communication; but, and not solely because it had to be spontaneous, it never reached a remotely comparable peak.

Sometimes Louis MacNeice had to write topical documentaries in a hurry to meet the demands of wartime programmes. Yet always there was the touch of his own fine talent. In this facility he never lacked felicity. He was incapable of cliché, except those he created for himself, and others did not recognize as such.

To spend a day with him at Lord's or an afternoon at rugby - Haydn Tanner's match for London Welsh on his return from Germany was an epic essay in conviviality - was to discover his immense zest and sense of fun. Meet him in 'The Stag' over a drink - at times, towards the end, he drank quite heavily, but, in the early days especially, he gave less sign of it than most - and he seemed quite dilettante in his attitude to work. Yet his output shows that his industry was immense for, in addition to his BBC duties - invariably of production as well as writing - he turned out a fair amount of high standard poetry, a number of interesting and conscientious studies and reviews, and the extent of his studies - for features on Rome, Greece, India, Russia, Norway, Ghana, Oxford, the Nile - was considerable, for he abominated the shallowness of knowledge to which he was at times almost compelled by the demands of programme schedules.

All this time he was turning out most highly original work for radio. The first unmistakable indication of his genius in this form was *Christopher Columbus* (1942) which, because Louis was so close to it, was produced by Dallas Bower. His lighter touch, humour, facility in unlaboured puns, wit and satire were woven into *Calling All Fools, The March Hare, Salute to All Fools*. After the great Faust series (produced by Archie Harding in 1949), *Pri-*

soner's Progress (which won the Italia Prize), *Dr Chekhov*, the utterly sensitive *He Had a Date* and *Alexander Nevsky*, came the high peak of his achievement, *The Dark Tower* (1947) which realizes the potential of sound radio with immense control, dignity, imagery and conviction. The title appealed; of his period in a prep school at Sherborne he wrote: 'The boys seemed suddenly terribly young; I had learned their language, but they could not learn mine, could never breathe my darkness'; and in *Persons from Porlock*, his moving and much cherished last feature, 'all dark – leading to dark passages'. It is hard to believe that anything finer has been done in the medium, or will be done in a world where the standards of television are economically all powerful. Still to come, illustrative of his range and invention were *One Eye Wild*, *The Careerist*, *Enemy of Cant*, *The Burning of Njal*, *Portrait of Rome*, *The Queen of Air and Darkness*. A period of attachment to television did not attract him: he came happily back to his old office at Rothwell.

At the heart of his achievement lay the splendid quality of his poetry; and, which is not the same thing, his unfailingly poetic thought. Sometimes its depths were profound and tragic. From childhood, he was much engaged by the concept of death; at fifty he was depressed at the thought of his greying hair. It may be fanciful, but still is possible to feel, as some of his friends did, that he did not resist the illness – caused when he was drenched by a rainstorm while surveying a cave site in Ingleton for a broadcast – which killed him.

BBC Features with Louis MacNeice could never have achieved what they did without Laurence Gilliam. He shielded them from the tyranny of the bureaucrats who, temporarily repulsed by the urgency of wartime demands, returned in peace to bring the artists to heel. A classic example of the confrontation is captured in Louis MacNeice's reaction when the time-and-motion study man asked him what he had been doing in the period shown blank on his work-sheet. 'Thinking,' he replied.

Vole, 1980

11

Any Questions? and Politics

Any Questions? is now well into its fourth decade. With a mixture of civilized contention and adroit humour, it has become one of the long-distance runners of radio, a cheerful and not insignificant national ritual like Sunday lunch.

Any Questions?

To the generations now in their teens, twenties and thirties, *Any Questions?* is part of the broadcasting Establishment: old, if not old-fashioned, sometimes diverting, often revealing of its participants, frequently amusing, but in a predictable fashion. Yet in the early post-war years it was a crusading programme, beginning another regional try-out, with a life-expectation of a few weeks. It re-shaped broadcast discussion – and even the regulations governing current affairs broadcasts. It became the one enduring personality broadcast which was never distorted by its personality, Freddy Grisewood, who, last month, on his eightieth birthday, retired as its question-master.

All that, however, anticipates the growth of a programme which, as first envisaged in 1948, had as its 'gimmick' – a word not then invented – members of the audience asking questions, actually being allowed to speak into a live microphone. (This seemed to some officials to invite the disaster of some crank uttering an obscenity or, worse still, some biased political remark, to the listening public.) Meanwhile, the remainder of the audience, mustered by distribution of tickets through the various religious and social groups of the community, were encouraged to show approval or disapproval of answers by clapping or even booing.

Soon, however, it was apparent that the true appeal, and even importance, of the programme lay elsewhere. It was the least cautious programme the BBC had broadcast until then. It is odd, now, to recall the trepidation before the first performance in the Guildhall at Winchester on 12 October 1948. Freddy Grisewood, a sixty-year-old professional broadcaster, was the question-master (a title taken from the *Brains Trust*) and the members of the panel, thereafter called 'the team', were Naomi Royde-Smith, Honor Croome, Jack Longland and myself. We were genuinely concerned lest we should infringe one of the many written or unwritten rules of the Corporation in some gaffe which would ruin the programme and ourselves. The producer, Nicholas Crocker, and the West Region officials, on hand to pull out the leads at the first sign of an indiscretion, were even more anxious.

Within a fortnight the programme was a regional success; in two years it was a national one with a considerable press coverage. Its performance in any town on its West Country beat was a major local event and it played to packed town-halls. The listening public sensed that this was a genuine programme, that the questions *were* those of the members of the audience who asked them, that they *were* unseen, that they *were* discussed freely and *ad lib* and that there *was* genuine argument between the members of the panel.

After a winter overseas I became a regular weekly member of the team in 1949; in effect, the anchor-man, so that I watched the programme grow up. From week to week the political party headquarters became more convinced of the importance of this new platform, and it was at times amusingly obvious that some speakers came briefed to deliver some set-piece, which they often fired off in reply to a quite inappropriate question only for their true cue to come up immediately afterwards.

There was, too, a growing tendency among some speakers to take increasing risks, to fly more daringly in face of all the known and imagined aspects of the Corporation's political caution. A permitted looseness of form, abandoning the strict, single answer in favour of something near debate, often produced lively broadcasting, notably the Boothby–Michael Foot cross-talk act, at least one towering rebuke by Lady Violet Bonham Carter and some blisteringly funny repartee by Jeremy Thorpe. It was, and still is, an engaging mixture of sincerity and acting, spontaneity and dutiful set-piece, wisdom and propaganda, gravity and humour. Despite the producer's care to choose a panel with contrasting voices, *Any Questions?* in its formative days could have become a muddled programme. It was given order by its question-master. Freddy Grisewood was almost certainly chosen for the post on the grounds that, having recently retired on pension from the Corporation, he knew the BBC and its cautionary standards well, he was 'safe', and had an established and pleasing voice. No one, certainly not the man himself, can have imagined that in 1948 he was about to make a completely fresh reputation.

His first asset lay in being non-partisan: he is nostalgically conservative but not a party-political creature. His background was, superficially, wrong for the question-master of a topical programme which – because it was a true product of its time rather than by design – reflected the post-war rebellion. He is the product of an earlier period: the son of a Worcestershire country parson; Radley and Magdalen; good enough batsman to play a match or two for Worcestershire; international trialist at hockey; county tennis-player; a right back for the Corinthians; a keen fly-fisherman; studied singing in London, Paris and Munich; bass singer of high professional standard; all that before he was commissioned in the Infantry in 1914–18. He inherited some port but not a lot more and, after eleven years of estate-management in his native Worcestershire Cotswolds, he came to the BBC by the semi-accidental course of so many early broadcasters. Purely consciously and nostalgically an Edwardian gentleman, he imposed those standards on *Any Questions?*, like a host rather than a compère.

Before the programme there was dinner for the team. In the early post-war years many hotels in country towns of the West had, unknowingly, some extremely good pre-war wines. Often he was invited to inspect the cellars, where his knowledge of claret produced some memorable and cheap bottles for the team-dinner. He took the head of the table: his manners were infallibly good, his jokes gentle; he seemed genuinely interested in his guests and reinforced the confidence of the nervous with almost naive admiration. He continued the situation into the programme, never showing distress at anyone's political views but surprised and somewhat indignant at bad behaviour. The only rebukes he administered were for interrupting, ignoring his request to stop talking or, simply, being a bore.

So far as I know he was only once defeated along those lines, when a panel-member with a reputation as a raconteur embarked on a story which developed into a filibuster but clearly could not be stopped until it reached its pay-off. The expression of disgust on Grisewood's face was an accurate indication of the fact that the speaker would not appear again. Selection of the panel has always been the province of the producer – until 1952 Nicholas Crocker, subsequently Michael Bowen – but the question-master's rare personal expression of disapproval was, I believe, always accepted. Some militant and some intellectual speakers came to the programme wary of a question-master they thought less profound than themselves; but, like the rest, they invariably were charmed by him. It was that charm which gave Freddy Grisewood his control and the programme its after-dinner quality.

Its effect on broadcast discussion, however, can be measured by two incidents. In March 1951, at Itchen, Southampton, a questioner referred to a constituent's letter to his MP being sent on, by the MP, to the writer's superior – did the team think this opened the way to victimisation? Anthony Wedgewood-Benn and Sir Edward Boyle, both MPs making their first appearance in the programme, refused to comment, on the grounds that parliamentary privilege was involved. The producer ruled that the team might answer the question and Jack Longland did so. The matter was raised in Parliament and BBC staff who might be held responsible rehearsed their appearances at the Bar of the House for several weeks until a White Paper exonerated the Corporation from breach of privilege, and ruled that such comment was not likely to influence the Speaker or the House of Commons.

In November 1956, on the Friday evening before a special sitting of the Commons to debate the Suez war, the team were warned in advance that the '14-day rule' precluded any discussion of Suez. In reply to a question asking whether, in the present state of world culture, law was possible without the backing of force, Henry Fairlie posed the hypothetical problems of a nation he called 'Ruritania'. The BBC administrator in attendance decided that this was a barely veiled reference to Suez, pulled out the microphone-lead and stopped the broadcast. There were protests and ironic comments in the press, correspondence columns and the complementary *Any Answers?* programme, and it is generally assumed that the abolition of the 14-day rule soon afterwards came as a direct consequence of the incident. No doubt these two decisions, without which broadcast discussion of important themes would be intolerably shackled, would in any case have been forced by some argument or programme; but, in fact, they were both achieved by *Any Questions?*

The Listener, May 1968

In 1984, Any Questions? *went to Alderney. Taking part were Katherine Whitehorn, Edward du Cann, Ian Mikardo and John Arlott, who described himself as a 'former broadcaster'. David Jacobs, who had chaired the programme with his customary charm and poise since Freddy Grisewood had retired, spoke first:*

> *Now, just before we go to the first question, may I say personally what a joy it is for me to have John Arlott in the team, because he was on the very first* Any

> Questions? *programme all those years ago in the late forties and was also the man who took the trouble to teach me how to be a broadcaster –*

The first question centred on issues raised by a dock strike at Dover. John was exercised by wider implications:

> *I've been a trade unionist all my life – my father and grandfather under threat of the sack founded the Nalgo branch in Basingstoke – I'm no anti-trade unionist. But the fact is, you see, the trades union movement has become sloppy. People like Ernest Bevin and Aneurin Bevan would have been picked up by the modern educational system, they'd have gone to University, they would have become University Dons, they'd never have been in the trades union movement at all. Now the modern educational system scoops up all those with good brains and takes them away and it leaves those who can't pass their O levels to be trades union leaders. (Laughter and applause.) If your intellect is thus limited and for this reason you have a chip on your shoulder you're not an ideal leader of working people.*

John has been no stranger to controversy. In fact, he landed in a considerable amount of scalding water after an early Any Questions?, *in which he stated explicitly his views on the South African régime and apartheid. His radical political convictions are inherited; both grandfathers were passionate Gladstonians and he believes his mother was the first Liberal agent in Basingstoke to get a member into Parliament.*

John himself twice stood as a Parliamentary candidate in the fifties, after being elected President of the National League of Young Liberals. On the first occasion, he polled over 7,500 votes which was the largest percentage increase of votes anywhere in the United Kingdom; the second occasion again found him in third place in a three-cornered contest, though this time he attracted nearly 12,000 votes. His election agent, Norman Hoddell, estimated that the same percentage increase next time round would see Mr Arlott as an M.P. 'I fled incontinent,' laughs John.

His platform theme during both campaigns was that, 'A Parliament divided into two groups, the haves and the have-nots, is contrary to the principle of democracy.' The truth of that principle applied nationally and internationally could be interpreted as the 'between the lines' basis of a televised debate from the Cambridge Union in 1970, when the Minister of Sport, Denis Howell, and John opposed the motion supported by Ted Dexter and Wilfred Wooller, 'that political commitment should not intrude upon sporting contacts':

WILFRED WOOLLER: ... I think ... we ought to establish what British sport has done and what it is. It has unquestionably given a great deal to the world. Apart from the game it has given us spirit and throughout its history and particularly the two games I am very closely connected with, rugby and cricket, there have been a mixture of all races and creeds and religions and a very happy association. One should establish this because at the moment both rugby and cricket are very sharply under fire from many walks of life and in many forums, but its record is a great one and it was a great one when there was racial segregation in this country. When a great and lovable sportsman like Lord Learie Constantine, or 'Learie' as he was when I played with and against him, was refused admission into a certain hotel, his colour was a bar and yet on the sporting arena he was very much loved ...

We're now approaching a point when politics is intruding into British sport. This was never done before and basically it's come in because of the South African question. I think sport's record stands on its own. It is opposed to racialism, it is opposed to the apartheid system in South Africa, but it doesn't believe that it alone can change it. It believes by mixing it might, it *can* show by example, and this it has always done in the past. We've reached a stage now where Labour Ministers and Labour followers in the house were suggesting and stating in fact that both rugby and cricket should cease to play South Africa. We have the Minister stating that he would not watch the cricketers play South Africa next summer, but I just can't measure up the double standards of a minister of a government which suggests that cricket should not be watched as far as he's concerned and by his ministers and Members of Parliament who suggest that we should not play against South Africa when they're busy trading with South Africa ... (*Applause.*)

If we bring politics into our sport in any shape or form – we've not done so yet – then at no stage in the future can you protect yourself from other people using it against you ... If you bring politics into our sport you're going to destroy the last bastion of sanity we have ... (*Applause.*)

JOHN ARLOTT: ... I should perhaps at an early stage state that I have known the Honourable third speaker [*Mr Wooller*] with great admiration for some thirty-seven years, in close personal contact for twenty-three years, during which we have dined, wined and argued together and in that entire period I have been completely amazed at the political naivity (*applause*) of one so shrewd in other matters and I must admit, Mr President, with due humility, that if the honourable third speaker had continued for the time that has been allotted to me he might have done the cause of the opposition more good than I could ... (*Applause.*)

There is a time in the growth of some political beliefs when they so offend against common morals that they are recognisable as evil and obnoxious to right thinking people ...

I cannot believe that any gentlemen on the other side of the house would happily have played a round of golf with Hitler or Goering, nor I trust do any of them want to make up a football match with the people who directed or carried out the suppression of the Hungarian Revolution or who battered down the rise of thought in Dubcek's Czechoslovakia ... This sir, is not a question of nationality nor of race but of political commitment, which is a personal matter. The ultimate clash of political commitment, Mr President, is war, which breaks down all contacts between nations except those between the bankers gathered in Switzerland ... (*Applause*.)

NEW VOICE: Surely if political commitment is a personal matter then it is indefensible for people to interfere with other people's personal inclination to play sport with whomsoever they wish?

JOHN ARLOTT: Yes sir, it would merely anticipate me ... The clash of political commitment is war, but even this, in present years, is not national nor racial. The major wars of recent years, those in Korea and Vietnam have been civil war in which a race has divided against itself on the issue of political commitment ... But this, I believe, argues that political commitment is a matter so deep and so profound that when the split is at its deepest then the breaking of sporting contacts is only a trifling casualty. So, Mr President, it would be my wish not only to show that this motion is fallacious but that the reverse, the converse, is a major truth ...

Mr President, I would go so far I think as to argue that political commitment is the only valid reason for breaking the sporting contacts. To see what other reasons we can find: national differences won't do, the World Cup proves that: nothing in football is more exciting than to see, for instance, West Germany playing against Brazil and a clash of method of character, of approach and of physique. And so, in the Glamorgan cricket team which won the championship this year race was unimportant. It had West Indians and a Pakistani, whom it's most happy to see here tonight, Majid Jahangir, who played distinguished parts in the winning of the Championship and were very happy members of the team in the dressing-room and in its hotels. Not nationality, not race, I would say not, Mr President, difference of sex, for as you may have heard, men play many games with women ... (*Laughter*.)

It is political commitment and political belief that

can make a man think that his opponent's views are so obnoxious that he will abstain from playing any game against him as a protest against what the other man believes and also, lest it should be assumed that by taking part in any activity with the supporters of that view, he gives it his tacit approval.

Any man's political commitment, if it's deep enough, is his personal philosophy and it governs his way of life, it governs his belief and it governs the people with whom he is prepared to mix. Mr President, sir, anyone who cares to support this motion will not exclude politics from sport but will in fact be attempting to exclude sport from life. (*Applause.*)

A reporter at the debate concluded that:

> *in some respects this was a most disappointing evening and the proceedings at times did not do justice either to their theme or their surroundings ... [however] ... the 'pièce de résistance' of the evening and the only lasting impression one has of it was undoubtedly the deep conviction which permeated John Arlott's stirring speech. The only man to eschew notes, he thrust his hands deep in his pockets and treated the audience to fifteen minutes not only of his inimitable and dulcet tones but also of thoughts and beliefs which came from the heart and made a deep impression on all present.*
>
> *He, surely, swayed the voting to his side of the house and thus the motion, that political commitment should not intrude upon sporting contacts, was defeated by 334 votes to 160.*

Ian Wooldridge came to the same conclusion in the Daily Mail*:*

> *He won the day not only with sane persuasion, but a faultless flow of English so beautiful in its construction that you could almost hear the commas and semi-colons fall into place. He sat down to a standing ovation.*

John found the debate 'a very moving occasion'. His admiration for Wilf Wooller remained undiminished.

12

VALETE WILFRED WOOLLER

There have been four major formative personalities in Glamorgan cricket history. The first was Norman Riches, whose highly talented batting carried them into the first class game (1921). The gracious, wise and loyal John Clay cemented the Club, playing from their entry into the Championship until they won it in 1948. Maurice Turnbull, as captain, secretary and fund-raiser sustained them through the difficult days of the 1930s. The fourth is Wilfred Wooller, all-rounder, captain, secretary and driving force of the post-war period.

His retirement from the post of secretary after thirty-one years deprives cricket of one of its most forthright and influential administrators. It is hard to believe, though, that he will not soon find himself deeply involved in some fresh aspect of it.

It was in 1937 that Jack Mercer said, in his softly confidential manner, 'Do you know the best swing bowler in England is playing club cricket in North Wales?' Pressed, he named him as 'That young Wooller, the rugby player; a big lad, he gets a lot of pace off the pitch and moves it about'. Born at Rhos-on-Sea, Wilfred Wooller went to Rydal School, played for Denbighshire, and in winning Cambridge sides in the University matches of 1935 and 1936. In 1937, however, he was too busy making a living in the coal trade to find much time for cricket. Maurice Turnbull, an old rugby team-mate, persuaded him to turn out for the county, but he could contrive only seven matches in 1938 and nine in 1939; nevertheless, he matured and developed steadily as an all rounder.

Rugby, though, was his main pre-war sport and he was three years a Cambridge blue. At twenty, playing in the first Welsh team to beat England at Twickenham, he dropped a goal from inside his own half. He won eighteen caps as a determined, high-kneed, extremely fast runner, at centre-three-quarter, and a spectacularly long and accurate kicker.

In 1942 he was captured, with his Royal Artillery unit, at Singapore. During three years as a prisoner of war of the Japanese, his immense determination, not only to live himself, but to carry his fellows through with him, won him the lifelong devotion of many of them.

By the same inflexible purpose and his immense natural physical resilience, he pushed himself back into action for the 1946 cricket season when, under John Clay, Glamorgan finished sixth, the highest Championship position they had ever achieved. In the next year he took over the captaincy; and, ninth then, they went on, in 1948, to win the title for the first time. If many knowledgeable judges were surprised by their success – for there were certainly several stronger batting and bowling counties in the country – they needed to look to the new captain. For more than a decade Wilfred Wooller lifted his side, again and again, to heights greater than the sum of the players' individual ability.

Memory will always recall him in those years, his wide, heavy shoulders slightly stooped, shambling down the pitch to his place, little more than a stride from the batsman, at forward short leg. There, eyes intent under his high forehead, jaw jutting, fists jammed truculently down on hips between deliveries, he dominated the outcricket. More than one batsman cracked under this psychological pressure; some were undoubtedly talked out by the exchanges between the captain and his wicket-keeper, Haydn Davies. Others, attempting to drive him away with aggressive strokes, were surprised by the speed of reaction of the large, fearless man who caught them. He was not alone in the practice of gamesmanship; but, unlike some, he accepted it in the same unyielding spirit as he indulged it. He was possessed of divine impatience; perhaps, indeed, he was temperamentally better suited to rugby than to cricket. Sometimes when he was frustrated by a cricket match that was going nowhere, it seemed likely that, in a sudden fury, he would buckle down with his fieldsmen and sweep the umpires, opposing batsmen and stumps over the boundary line to resolve the issue once and for all. He cursed opponents roundly and fiercely, but without malice. Many were amazed that one so belligerent on the field was so convivially generous off it. Again it was the rugby player showing through. He followed Maurice Turnbull in seeing catching as the means which lifted a team to competitive heights; he drilled his sides in fielding as a rugby captain might exhort a scrum: and he held 409 catches himself.

It is fair to say that, although the specialists of the pre-war Gloucestershire under Beverley Lyon had approached it, no other county side had ever before caught so well as his of 1948; they set a fresh standard. The evidence of one who watched every ball bowled, with the confirmation of several who took part in it, argues that Wilfred Wooller virtually lifted Glamorgan to win the decisive game against Hampshire – in that Championship season. They had only one more match to play – against Leicestershire – which they expected to lose – and did – because Jack Walsh was so deadly against their numerous left-hand batsmen. After losing most of the Saturday at Bournemouth to rain, Glamorgan reached 315 on the mild Monday pitch. In terms of cricketing probability, they simply had not time to win. Then, with no alteration in the conditions, after a few overs of the new ball, Wooller ostentatiously rubbed it in the dust, waved six fieldsmen closely about the bat. With no apparent technical justification, he called up his spinners – and in an hour, six Hampshire wickets went down for 24 runs. The rest was psychologically inevitable.

After the war his bowling was never more than medium in pace, but he consistently took good wickets (958 altogether) by his accuracy, variation of pace, movement

Wilf Wooller bowling for Glamorgan against Essex at Valentines Park, Ilford, in 1949. Non-striker is Alf Avery who was shortly to be dismissed by Wooller for 8.

either way and sheer hostile persistence. His batting looked heavy-handed, but he five times scored over a thousand runs in a season; 13,593 altogether. He could play either way as he judged the game demanded; defend doggedly and safely – as he did to save the match against the Australians in 1953 – or hit powerfully, especially to leg (108 in two hours against Lancashire in 1947). He played twice in strong Gentlemen's teams against the Players, but most of his cricket was for Glamorgan. He was invited to tour South Africa in 1948–9 but had to refuse because of the demands of his business; and, immeasurably the finest captain in the country at the time, he should have taken the 1950–1 England team to Australia. An extremely durable cricketer, he performed the double in 1954 when he was forty-one, was forty-seven when he gave up the captaincy after fourteen seasons; rising fifty when he returned to the side for a single match in 1962.

In 1946 he became County Secretary; and for the next thirty-one years he exerted more influence over Glamorgan cricket than some committees would permit. He stood in a strong tactical position. He came from North Wales; and, in consequence, while he could not be rejected as a non-Welshman, West Wales could not question him as being Cardiff; nor Cardiff for being West Wales. He rode out some turbulent times; made some wrong decisions, but more that were correct, and rarely one which did not stem from conviction and enthusiasm.

One story often told about him dates from 1948. Glamorgan had never beaten Middlesex when they met them at Cardiff in that triumphant year; thanks to the bowling of Hever and Wooller, they took a first innings lead of 138, and eventually set Middlesex 275 to win. Wilfred, opening the bowling, had a series of 'shouts' against Syd Brown the Middlesex opening batsman, each of which was refused by that idiosyncratic but wise umpire, Alec Skelding. At length, after his fourth or fifth appeal, Wooller turned on him with 'What was wrong with that, you blind old bastard?' 'He was not out, Mr Wooller,' said Skelding, 'and it is true that my eyesight is not good; that is why I wear these strong glasses; but I can assure you that my mother and father were married; and, I'll tell you something else, Mr Wooller, I don't think you're going to win this cricket match.' He never gave a decision against Syd Brown, who made 150 not out in a score of 275 for eight (no one else got as many as 30) and Middlesex won by two wickets. Some years later, when the county secretaries discussed the position of Alec Skelding – who was already over age – on the umpires list, Wilfred Wooller was the most vehement supporter of his reappointment, which was duly approved.

He has made many friends; and some enemies – mainly little men – but all who knew him would agree that, while he was sometimes lacking in tact, he infused immense drive and devotion into Glamorgan cricket. His ideal was a successful, all-Welsh team; and several times he came close to it. He used, too, to see Glamorgan's fixture with

Wooller smiting 30 in the second innings of a drawn match spoilt by the weather.

a touring side as a Welsh international match and the crowds responded to the feeling. He was chaired off the field after the splendid win over South Africa in 1951; and, in 1953, he and Len Muncer saved the game against Australia with a fine defensive partnership. Less obviously, he worked devotedly and shrewdly to set the club in a sound financial position.

A dogmatic extrovert, he brooked little argument; and his political views were not everyone's; but many who disagreed with him hold him in respect and affection for his honest and absolute loyalty. He was lucky after the war to marry Enid, a woman most splendidly his match, not least because her superb sense of humour has always set even his wildest extravagances in proportion. They have been happy with their five children and their odd – sometimes extremely odd – dogs.

An informed and successful Test selector from 1955 to

1961, he is now a press, radio and television reporter of cricket and rugby, marvellously, almost naively, biased in favour of Glamorgan and Wales and, of course, characteristically forthright in his opinions. Although he is no longer employed by the county, his boundless energy is not likely to be satisfied with inactivity. Without doubt we shall see him, pipe spurting smoke, bearing down, frowning, on some place or activity which, in his term, needs 'tackling'; and he was always a hard tackler.

Glamorgan Cricket Yearbook, 1978

13

Honest Harding

When, in 1951, Gilbert Harding was 'rested' from radio's Twenty Questions, *John was one of several personalities asked to do a stint as quiz-master. Just before recording he received a telegram: 'All good luck. Enjoy the programme. I'm sure you will. They're so easy to handle. It's so simple. Gilbert.'*

This so-called Century of the Common Man has created its aristocracy from below, through public acclaim and 'audience research'. Thence, there is no stranger phenomenon than the stardom of Gilbert Harding, who has always held – and shown – a very poor opinion of 'popular' taste.

Indeed, that taste, while acclaiming him, has misunderstood him. It has singled out as his salient characteristic his rudeness – which is as superficial as saying that a man who just won a marathon race is out of breath. To be sure he can be rude – infuriatingly rude – but never for rudeness' sake, always out of his fundamental independence.

That independence – of action and thought – makes him completely content to be an outspoken minority of one on any subject about which he feels strongly. He does not suffer fools gladly; even when they profess to be his 'fans'; and he will not suffer cruelty, injustice or meanness at all.

His taste is half-instinctive, half the product of study. He joined the Roman Catholic Church out of sheer conviction. The man in the street may have the power to pull him down from his precarious pinnacle, but that will not bring him the half of one kow-tow from Mr Harding.

Gilbert Harding in typical pose.

I have often strongly suspected that he considers the human mind to have been made for higher matters than *Twenty Questions* or *What's My Line?*. Since he is too fundamentally honest to bottle up his opinions, that irritation often reveals itself. Then his moustache bristles, his eyebrows lift and jut, his eyes pop, and he is capable of some of the most superbly barbed and spontaneous invective we have known.

I believe that more than one listener or viewer finds in Gilbert the expression of that rebellion against mass ideas which he himself has smothered in order to conform to the general pattern.

Rudeness is something more when it has point and wit. Mere rudeness is mean; Gilbert Harding has always been generous, not only of money to those in difficulties but generous of his advocacy for those ill-served.

There was genuine humility, too, we may feel when told that he referred to a company as 'third-rate', he answered with: 'If I said that, then I am fourth-rate.' A fourth-rate man could not say that.

During John's first electioneering campaign, Gilbert Harding agreed to chair an Any Questions? *public meeting at Waltham Abbey in Essex. As a prelude to setting off on the tiresome journey from Broadcasting House in the West End, Gilbert, who was by then a very sick man, sank a couple of stiff gin and tonics to wash down his remedial pills. Once into John's car, he lit a cigarette, then promptly fell asleep. Fortunately John, who was concentrating on manoeuvring his vehicle through the rush-hour traffic, noticed in time, took the cigarette from Gilbert's lips and stubbed it out. A little later the sleeper awoke with a Bashan-like roar when his 'chauffeur' had to brake sharply in order to avoid colliding with another car that had 'cut in'.*

John described the incident in his News Chronicle *column shortly afterwards:*

I cocked my ears for a characteristic judgement on the driver, but Gilbert wearily closed his eyes. Five minutes later came the remark: 'The nation has two things to thank me for – I do not drive a car and I have no children.'

Matters for regret, rather than thanks, I should have thought. What a comforting feeling to know that somewhere on the roads, Gilbert Harding was spontaneously telling 'the other driver' just what we thought of him. Neither would any generation suffer for a few more Hardings to express independent ideas with the whip of wit.

Evening News, April 1954

14

The Hungry Traveller

A few years before that journey with Gilbert Harding, in pre-motorway days, John had driven a hundred miles along a major route in England without being able to buy a meal between 8.30 p.m. and midnight. He was not amused.

Today, happily, that cannot happen. For an article written in 1954, though, it is noticeable that his savoured gastronomic memories concentrate mostly on Continental cuisine:

The Hungry Traveller

It is a pleasant idleness, the recollection of meals relished in the past. The elevation of that rumination to delight is, perhaps, the foible of one normally, at meal times, hungry, thirsty and inclined to extravagance and, at all times, emotionally vulnerable to places and people.

The professional gastronome – chef, restaurateur or wine-taster – may completely separate his palate from his emotions, cooking from the company, his taste-buds from the *genius loci*. He may even, for all I know, be capable of minute criticism unmitigated by hunger. His province, however, is cooking, not the blend of food and mood which is the amalgam of imagination.

The tourist may expect to eat a local dish in perfection, and drink the local wine knowing that very few wines travel perfectly. Much of unhappiness at the dinner-tables of Soho derives from the failure of 'the jolly little wine I discovered in San Remo last summer' to live up to the recollection of its discovery.

I recall a dinner of leisurely – yet almost heart-rending – relish under the moon in Venice: two days later, that meal was duplicated – in strictly culinary terms – at Treviso in driving rain, when it seemed a commonplace experience.

With the memory of that first meal reviving a mild nostalgia, my first dish here will be *scampi* – and they *shall* be *scampi*, not Dublin Bay prawns. I enjoy Dublin Bay prawns – under their own name – but when they push their antennae into the menus of almost every expensive restaurant in London under the pretence – and even the waiter's ready guarantee – of being *scampi*, I resent them too much to eat them. These shall be true *scampi*, fresh this very morning from the Adriatic, fried, and served with a dandelion salad; and I will even take with them, for memory's sake, the nondescript but sympathetic white wine which was that night described as 'of Verona'. The two together will call back that jumble of warm, volatile Venetian conversation whose true background is the motorless rush of the canals.

Little more traffic-noise comes from the narrow streets about the restaurant terrace which is also the roof of the monolithic chapel of St Emilion. There, one day, the second course of a lunch was lampreys prepared Bordelaise fashion – cooked in the local claret, with onions and mushrooms, and served on croutons. To two of us, at this first taste, Henry I's 'surfeit of lampreys' became the most understandable – indeed, the most desirably regal – cause of death to be imagined. It was the rare sympathy of a fatherly and observant host which arranged that, for us, the next three courses consisted also of lampreys. The wine was a Frenchman's choice, *Cheval Blanc* 1928, grown and pressed within hailing distance of the sands where the uncloying lampreys had fed.

On another occasion when a single course lengthened into a meal, the wine was also remarkable. I do not know its name in catalogue terms – if it has ever reached a catalogue, which I doubt – but, in the little trattoria at Monrupino, toppling on the edge of Yugoslavia, it is simply *'il vino'* drawn from the barrel and brought to the table in unlabelled bottles. It is wine to underline the accuracy of Homer's image of 'the wine-dark sea' or Fletcher's 'purple bubbles winking at the mazer's brim' – so dark that it clouds the teeth grey-black. It is lusty and round in the mouth, warm in the stomach. We drank it contentedly with *prosciutto crudo*, the salted uncooked ham, sliced casually and eaten on crusts of bread from a bare wooden table, with another glass of the wine in place of a savoury, and another instead of coffee.

Despite the interval of *prosciutto*, the remembered richness of succulent lampreys makes the boyish excitement of kidneys prepared Carvalho fashion – that is, fried in butter and served on toast with truffles, mushrooms and Madeira sauce – too rich even for recollection. The *paella*, however, was meant to be a meal in a single dish. We ate it near the sea, at a Spanish dinner-time so that it was midnight before we finished. Cooked shellfish – largely mussels – rice, and chicken in a rich gravy: that night, the three were separate heaps on the dish: the next day, a mile away, they were mixed together and fried for the last few minutes of their preparation. Yet, through all its varying details of cooking, *paella*, with only its flavour of saffron constant, is a juggler with mouthfuls of great variety and shifting emphasis. The wine, a red *Rioja*, the year – the year available; safe, however, to specify the Paternina bottling. That was indeed a meal of artful surprises, which would have been ruined if a sweet had followed it; even coffee was too harsh for the echoes it left on the palate.

So, no sweet; but a mild regret for figs and pomegranates eaten in Sicily, with the *Muscato* of Syracuse, gentlest of sweet white wines. A wine of Mediterranean history, at home beside the stones of the Greek theatre – and, under its own sun, a match for most Sauternes – the *Muscato* is a poor traveller, tired by a journey of twenty miles from its vines, a vinegary mockery when brought as a prize to England.

The cheese must be British – not, as a rule, a well-received demand even in a London restaurant, where Roquefort, Danish Blue, Camembert – of a gluey messiness never seen when it is served in France – and Brie, are presented as if they were the only cheeses fit to eat. So far down the menu, the French, the Spanish, even the Italians, have moistened the mouth in anticipation until the English are too humble to claim – and the rest of the world too loth to discover – that British cheeses are the finest in the world. Clean, rich, subtle, strong, of fine variety, they are a half-forgotten, but still great, catalogue – Cheshire, Blue Cheshire, Lancashire, Caerphilly – not only from Wales, but Wiltshire, Dorset, even Ireland – Wensleydale, Blue Vinny, Gloucester, Double Gloucester, Cotherstone, Dunlop, and, too, the decent Cheddar, eaten at its due time and after half the cosetting given to an indifferent Port-Salut. Shall I ever, now, be able to taste Cottenham, Slipcote, Leicester or Truckles? The return of Stilton evoked, perhaps, a little too much enthusiasm. Did it, in fact, unduly press the factors, or is it ill-luck that has faced me with more than one Stilton which seemed to have been hurried to the table? Much tempted by both Cheshire and Wensleydale, nevertheless, out of a single, distant tasting, I shall ask for Gloucester. With it, I will take, if I may, a 1934 *Chambertin*, a wine as big as a house, a drink to put the imagination of five Shakespeares into one jobbing journalist. Every Briton who ever bought a handbook on wine in order to impress a lady by arguing with the wine-waiter has learnt that a burgundy should be allowed gradually to come to the temperature of the room and be drunk, in the language of winesmanship, *chambré*. The French, for whom wine is less unusual and less expensive, are not always so pedantic. It is not out of vandalism that I would ask for this burgundy at cellar temperature, to drink the first glass cool and refreshing as a foil to the subtlety of the cheese. Thereafter, with its cork drawn, the wine will breathe, its temperature grow more mellow, and we shall expand together, drowsily.

I have drunk bad coffee in sixteen countries and expect to do so in as many more. So, I will be satisfied with the coffee that any English housewife – the gaucheries of glue-drinking Americans notwithstanding – can prepare if

A slightly pained expression.

she is not too lazy to use freshly ground coffee beans; for the sake of certainty in this case, I will ask my wife to make it.

Increasing weight, short wind and bulging suits do not seem too high a price to pay for these felicities and, happily, if heavily, I will move again into that deep chair in the slightly faded but unhurried restaurant in Vienna where the waiter's smiling hope that you have eaten well seems to derive as much from goodwill as from expectation of a tip. Somewhere far enough away for the sound to seem to come from history, a man with a glass of cool beer beside him is playing a zither. The cellar here was laid down in days of imperial splendour, and the music reinforces the gentle sadness that there is no replacing the half-litre bottle the waiter has so gaily brought up. It is the Tokay *Essenz*, nearly ninety years old, gentle as silk, yet fresh as grass, liquor of immortality. As we drink it, we are all immortals, and it is Sydney Smith who murmurs – 'Fate cannot harm me. I have dined today.'

The Spectator, January 1954

15

BASINGSTOKE

As a youngster, John often stood outside Kingdon's iron-monger's in the town market-place and looked at others doing the same.

BASINGSTOKE

Of Basingstoke in Hampshire
The claims to fame are small:-
A derelict canal
And a cream and green Town Hall.

At each weekend the 'locals'
Line the Market Square,
And as the traffic passes,
They stand and stand and stare.

16

Wiltshire Line

Inspiration for poetry can arrive along an unexpected track:

'I did go to the stations – they reminded me of the drawings of Osbert Lancaster. At one, as I passed the level-crossing, a porter called out, "You've missed the train." "No, I haven't," I replied. He was adamant, "You have, it's gone." I said, "I didn't come to catch the train." "What d'you come for then?" he demanded. I gave in. "I've come to look at the station." He thought I was round the bend.'

Wiltshire Line

The stations, like toy-castles, make
A children's wooden-soldier game,
Along the winding Wiltshire line
And hide the villages they name.

From hazel copses down the line
The sulky, green-black engine calls:
The porter shuts the crossing gate,
The lonely signal creaks and falls.

The dusty station drinks the smoke,
The porter loads a box-cooped hen;
The train jerks on towards the fields,
The village is alone again.

Nostalgia haunts the village cross.
The silence floods the disused forge
And frames in empty guestlessness
The sunlit, stucco-fronted 'George'.

The weathered shop-fronts seem to yawn
Beneath their red-and-white striped blinds:
The church-clock's golden fingers mark
The path of age-untroubled minds.

The distant engine strikes a flag
Of sharp white steam that lazes clear
Against the rim of cupping hills;
Its cry comes faintly to the ear.

Across the vacant station-yard
The air is rippling down in heat:
A mongrel dog, stretched out asleep,
Is squire of all the white main street.

17

A Little Guide to Winchester

Nearly all of John's poetry is the concentrated essence of impressions during the first fourteen years of his life. 'A Little Guide to Winchester' is consciously satirical.

A Little Guide to Winchester

At Winchester the smell of guide-books lies
Across the streets with rich mediaeval names,
And snap-views of the long Cathedral rise
Through alley-ways and leaded window-frames.

The buzzing traffic down the High Street pours
To where the Butter Cross juts out, then stops
By old St Maurice's half-hidden doors,
And cakes and shirts in mild, unbrazen shops.

See, cycling blithely through the grumbling cars,
A Wykehamist, with brightly banded tie,
And, in the basket on his handlebars,
The biscuits, cakes and books he came to buy.

Now, like a matron, over-jewelled and laced,
The Gothic Guildhall by Sir Gilbert Scott,
And, phoney-Tudor, beam-and-plaster faced,
The jeweller's shop Hostel of God-Begot.

Silk stockings and fur coats and dove-grey gowns
Take tea, crook-fingered, in a Norman keep;
While, as the sun moves round behind the downs,
The quiet clergy court cathedral sleep
In houses calm, where time is but a guest:
These men, who soothe a death or bless a birth,
Should know themselves as truly soothed and blessed
By houses that are stone-spelt peace on earth.

18

BRIGHTON

'With the exception of Bath, Brighton is the most exciting English town I've been to. I couldn't aspire to write anything about Bath but tried this half-mocking thing about Brighton. The town's a splendid mixture of majestic architecture and seedy life.'

BRIGHTON

All-electric, down from London,
Every hour the green trains run,
Bearing tribes of worshippers
To the doubtful Brighton sun.

Postcards of the Sussex Downs,
Ice-rinks, music-halls and beer,
Dance-halls, snack-bars and the rain
On the domed and garnished pier.

There's an elegant Adam fireplace
In a third-rate dancing-club,
Forgotten print of the Regent
In a dusty, smoke-fumed pub.

Regency houses, row on row,
In crescent, square and street,
With pediment, pillar and portico,
'BED AND BREAKFAST' all complete.

Strange-wrought Gothic street-lamps,
Churches a-gleam with tile
Jostle the chrome and marble
Of super-cinema style.

From the tomb-like cold Pavilion,
Drawing-Rooms and Dome
Regency ghosts are sweeping
Through the town that was their home.

Do they see the plaster peeling?
The fly-blown fluted ceiling?
Regency houses tumbled down?
Hove another, *nicer* town?
The Phaeton gone for the family car?
Electric light in the Oyster Bar?
And buses bluing the salt sea air
Under the trees in Castle Square?

And would they return to Hell by way
Of Brighton beach on a summer day,
Would they trip with trippers up-to-date,
And, Regency ghosts immaculate,
Arm-in-arm and devil-may-care,
Past the whelk-stalls and through the profanity,
Step
        down
                the
                        steep
                                stone
                                        stair
Into this huddle of hot humanity?

19

Marine Parade Hotel

'Which hotel did you have in mind?' was the question. A slow smile accompanied the reply. 'Ah – probably it was an amalgam of several.' The questioner persisted. 'But any one more than others?' A long pause, then a quick smile. 'Possibly the old Metropole, Brighton, mixed with the Grand, Eastbourne.'

Marine Parade Hotel

Fantastic as Fonthill, yet crudely staid,
It bulks like a cloud on the Esplanade:
Gothic-mad architect's crazy trick
Worked in public-convenience brick.
Against the pavement, so greyly prosaic,
It flaunts its name in pink and white mosaic:
The steps are bath-bricked far too white,
The hand-rails burnished far too bright:
The tall walls echo the lightest tread,
The noise-shamed walker averts his head.

The manager, pigeon-holed and sly,
Watches his narrow world go by,
Knows each numbered impersonal door
On each monotonous self-same floor
Hides the betrayal, the secret dirt,
Innocent-seeming, yet selfish hurt:
How under conventional cheap veneer
Of pomp, or hearty tweeds-and-beer
Are false-teeth, wigs and too-bright dyes,
The corsets, the pads, the drops-for-eyes –

Shams to make the shams respectable.
Never suspecting their tricks detectable,
Daily they move in ghoulish charade
Across the pseudo-Baroque facade.

From 'Tudor' bar and beer swill-tainted,
Walls and women bogus and painted,
At half-past ten I must stagger away
As they count the cash of a well-spent day.
Into the sea-front's wind-crammed night,
Where, from squat windows, curtained tight,
The narrow jets of light escape
To fall across the road like tape.

There are quiet women in the shadows, waiting,
A smell of cabbage rising from the grating;
No, the people scuffling at the refuse-bin
Do not consider they are 'living in'.

20

Come Unto These Yellow Sands

'The whole thing is a joke – not to be taken seriously.' Even so, it is the best kind of joke, one that few can fail to recognize.

Come Unto These Yellow Sands

Sing the sands of Bournemouth,
Sing the Bournemouth Belle,
Pokesdown, Boscombe, Bournemouth West –
You can sing for an hotel.

Come down for a week in the sun,
And sit on the pier-end and booze,
Go back with a sun-blistered nose,
And tintacks and sand in your shoes.

Here you may revel your savings away,
You may rollick or ramble or ride;
But whatever you do or do not do,
Don't cross the GREAT DIVIDE.

For a gulf splits the people of Bournemouth,
A gulf that is wide and sheer,
Between barmen, whores, pimps, and waiters –
And those with three thousand a year.

West from the Bournemouth West Station,
In still roads with limes at the side,
The unburied mummies of Bournemouth
Do not *live* but consent to *reside*.

They only come out when the sun does,
To sniff up the ozone and pines:
They take dinner at eight - sacramental -
But served with *appropriate* wines.

No children shout out in their houses,
Nobody utters a word -
Only the ignorant sparrows
And pens scratching cheque-books are heard.

The Daimlers pass by like a whisper,
The servant-girls pray they may please,
Even taxi-men bow from the waist
And the tradesmen go down on their knees.

For God has made friends with these people,
Reserving for them from their birth
A separate bathroom in Heaven,
The freedom of Bournemouth on earth.

21

Churches of Bournemouth

As the 1960s approached the 1970s, John spent three weeks or so looking at churches in Bournemouth in preparation for a Guide to Hampshire, which, in the end, did not materialise. His research was used in an article that appeared in Hampshire – *the county magazine – with the headline: 'There has been no comparable concentration of church-building in Britain'.*

Churches of Bournemouth

There is no other town in Britain like Bournemouth. At the beginning of the last century it was a stretch of cliff and scrub around the mouth of the Bourne, ideal smuggling country, crossed by a few tracks and with four or five isolated farms over on the Christchurch side. Partly within the parish of Christchurch and partly in the chapelry of Holdenhurst it was hardly more than a map-location. In a little over a hundred years it has grown into one of the wealthiest towns in the country with a population of 150,000 people – one in every four of them of pensionable age – spread out at the generous average rate of a dozen to the acre over some 12,000 acres and with the staggering rateable value of £10,635,175. In the season it has, too, a vast hotel and boarding house population and a constant influx of day-trippers.

Such a brief life means that it has sparse historic interest apart from archaeological diggings and that, built in a period by no means outstanding for its taste, it contains little of architectural distinction.

The beauty of Bournemouth lies in its natural features –

the roll of the land, the mild drama of the chines, the long curve of the coast, the fall of the cliffs; all that lies to man's credit is that, given space in good measure, he found it most profitable to use it generously in wide roads and uncrowded houses. Indeed, a writer in *The Architect* in January 1874 commented 'it would be almost impossible to find anywhere such a vast array of houses of all sorts and sizes in which there is less architectural merit; Cockneyfied Gothic, or vulgar, pretentious would-be Italian monstrosities obtain everywhere' and added 'one is thankful for the mask which Nature, as a rule, places before them in the shape of pine trees and shrubs which flourish luxuriantly in the light, sandy soil.' When William Morris visited the town in 1883 he described its villa architecture as 'simply blackguardly, fit only for ignorant, purse-proud digesting machines.' To quote from *The Builder* of the same year 'it is to be hoped Bournemouth may rise a little presently to a notion of the desirability of employing a higher class of architecture when any of the streets have to be rebuilt but for the present the mischief seems to be pretty well done.'

Since that day there has been similar ostentation, and often a split-minded attempt to reconcile commercial needs with residential enterprise. So, although there has been a certain amount of unexceptionable – but unexceptional – domestic building, there has been much that lacks taste or character.

In most towns, even those apparently least favoured, the Victorian age created industrial or civic buildings of functional dignity; but Bournemouth has none such. The station is too late (1885) to catch the best of the railway age and even the Town Hall was formerly an hotel. So, apart from a bricky, mock-Tudor club formerly called The Knole, the engagingly simple, 19th century, Talbot Village, and Talbot Heath Girls' School, those who search for interesting architecture can confine themselves to the churches. More than fifty ecclesiastical buildings must have gone up there between 1850 and 1950 and virtually every one of the major late Victorian church architects –

J.D. Sedding, J.L. Pearson, G.E. Street, Norman Shaw, William Butterfield, J.A. Chatwin (best known for his work in Birmingham), A.J. Pilkington, John Oldrid Scott – is represented.

There has been no comparable concentration – in time and place – of church-building in Britain. This is explained not simply by the need to provide for a quickly growing population from scratch, but because Bournemouth in the latter half of the nineteenth century contained a quite amazing number of people with considerable enthusiasm, time and money to lavish on churches. Victorian England has been described as 'one of the most religious' civilized countries the world has known. It is for others to argue whether they were truly religious or deeply concerned with the trappings of religion.

Certainly they endowed Bournemouth for some odd reasons. The parish of Holy Trinity, for instance, was created – and two churches built when St Peter's, the mother church of the town and parish, was more than large enough for all the parishioners – because some of its congregation were Evangelicals (St Peter's was Tractarian) and wanted a 'preaching church' rather than the 'praying church' of the Pusey-Keble faction. Moreover, when Holy Trinity was built it had to be even as architecturally different from St Peter's as was reasonably possible. Yet again, St Paul represented a breakaway – from Holy Trinity – at the expense of building a new church because, while most of the congregation of Holy Trinity supported the Church Missionary Society, others favoured the Bible Churchmen's Missionary Society and that minority decided to have a church of its own. As another instance of the town's prodigality, A.M. Bennett the founder and first vicar of St Peter's and the original driving force of the – Tractarian – Church in Bournemouth had a son who, in due course trained and was ordained as a priest; he became first vicar of the Church and Parish of St Stephen, created as a memorial to his father and to serve the Anglo-Catholics of Bournemouth.

Even after the cost of building these churches, there

Holy Trinity, Old Christchurch Road.

was much money available for church furnishing – by modern standards over-furnishing – commissioned from the finest artists and craftsmen of the time. So there is a profusion of church plate as fine as any of the period: St Peter's is prodigally full of painting, decoration, carving, sculpture and stained glass: the reredos in Holy Trinity was painted by Byam Shaw; at St Clement Sedding was engaged to design tombstones for a vicar and his wife and a curate of the church. These stones, incidentally, seem to be in danger; several nearby have already been dug out: and this is the church where, quite alarmingly, the charming oratory and vicarage were demolished only four years ago. Otherwise, wherever one looks in these Bournemouth churches – font, pulpit, lectern, altar, screen – the workmanship is the finest of its time. In fact it represents the Church of England's last phase of opulence.

The non-conformist buildings are too recent to have the character of the late eighteenth, or early nineteenth, century chapels; and they are generally less adventurous than the Anglican. Richmond Hill Congregational Church – where the famous preacher, John Daniel Jones, was once the pastor – the centre of Congregationalism in Bournemouth and its first church after the little mud and thatch chapel at Pokesdown; Westbourne Congregational – which is scheduled for demolition to make way for shops – and St Andrew's Presbyterian Church are all roughly in the Anglican-Gothic tradition. There is, though, some 1900-ish influence in Charminster Road Congregational and Holdenhurst Road Methodist. The most original of the nonconformist buildings are the Wesleyan Punshon Memorial Church, consciously 1950s, angular in its search for lightness, but making some interesting external use of colour; the unsophisticated Kinson Methodist and Immanuel Congregational, Southborne.

The Church of the Sacred Heart (1874) was not adequate for the Roman Catholic congregation of the central area and was enlarged in a skilful, though not entirely sympathetic, marriage of yellow brick with grey stone by A.J. Pilkington in 1898. The Church of the Annunciation in Charminster Road is a more impressive unity. Designed by Sir Giles Gilbert Scott in his middle twenties, it is built of red brick and the exterior has a thickset air; but the inside is white and gives an impression of simple austerity, firm but not heavy. Corpus Christi, Boscombe, also in red brick, was built in 1889 but the west tower was added in 1932. In the south Chapel there is a painting of some English martyrs – several of them from Hampshire – which experts have thought may be the work of Frederick Rolfe, better known as 'Baron Corvo' of *The Quest for Corvo:* he lived in Christchurch during the 1890s.

The Anglican churches – 26 of them – make, however, the more coherent story. The exception to it, by far the senior among them, is in the originally Dorset village of Kinson – once a centre of smuggling activity – which was brought into Bournemouth and Hampshire in 1931. The church – still in the diocese of Salisbury – has a sturdy, late Norman, ironstone tower and retains the original chancel within extensive Victorian rebuilding. Still standing relatively alone beside an arm of the Stour – though refuse tips are creeping up on it, heralding the mass building to come – St Andrew's is essentially a village church.

Holdenhurst – another 1931 addition to the County Borough (although it is, strictly speaking, the Mother Church of Bournemouth) – also retains a separate quality, shut off by the fencing of the Bournemouth-Ringwood clearway and approached along a half-mile *cul de sac* from the direction of Throop. It is only three miles from the centre of Bournemouth yet there is not a pine tree to be seen. The churchyard of St John the Evangelist beside the village green and which once served the entire Bournemouth area, stands in a churchyard in which the cypress and yew are well established. The original building was put up in 1834 but, forty years afterwards, Benjamin Ferrey of Christchurch, topographer, architect and artist, added a chancel. It has some rare plate much earlier than the building.

There was already a St Peter's of 1843, with a south aisle of 1845 before, in 1853, Bennett ambitiously – for his congregation was still small – commissioned G.E. Street, whose reputation as an architect was now growing, to build him a church large enough for 1200 people. The result is not warm, but it is impressive and, although it lies at the bottom of the town and has to compete for attention with some recent high buildings, its 200 feet spire still arrests the eye from many angles. There are statues by Frank Redfern, paintings, carvings, glass and ironwork by Bodley's, Comper, Earp, Sir Thomas Jackson, Morris and Burne-Jones (who also did some mosaics for the altar but they faded and were replaced). Shelley's heart is believed to be buried at St Peter's: so is his wife, Mary Shelley, author of *Frankenstein*; and her parents, William Godwin who wrote *Political Justice* and her mother, Mary Wollstonecraft, author of *A Vindication of the Rights of Women*, lie in the same family tomb. Both

St Peter's, Hinton Road.

Keble – to whom there is a chapel in the South Transept – and W.E. Gladstone made their last communions at St Peter's.

St Peter's is basically Pugin-Gothic, but Holy Trinity, which *had* to be different, was designed by Charles Ferguson, who had studied in northern Italy, in a Lombardo-Gothic fashion with a separate, Italian-style campanile. While Byam Shaw was painting the reredos, Holman Hunt, one of the great pre-Raphaelite painters, died, and Shaw incorporated him in the painting as St Luke. Holy Trinity is essentially an auditorium, with fine acoustics and seating for 1,000 people; in recent years it has developed a reputation for music. A plaque near the baptistry recalls that Rupert Brooke worshipped there.

St Stephen, the third – Ritual Anglo-Catholic – of the central churches is usually considered architecturally the best of them. A memorial to A.M. Bennett, whose son was its first incumbent, it is a unity in harmonious stone by J.L. Pearson, a highly religious Tractarian who worked on it with infinite care for the last seven years of his life. The building of the tower, ten years later, was supervised by his son but the spire of Pearson's original intention has still not been built. An unusual amount of rib-vaulting, some reverent surprises and, as at St Peter, a general complexity of construction apparent when one looks towards the altar, are all assimilated in the lofty, cool building. It, too, is handsomely furnished.

St Clement, Boscombe, is in many ways equally remarkable. It was built in yellow stone by J.D. Sedding in 1873, but twenty years afterwards a grey stone west tower, with an unusually wide arch and window, was added. The former wealth of the parish is obvious; the furnishings and decorations are superbly, even extravagantly, made. The high altar and reredos – of Caen stone and alabaster – are based on those which Sedding restored at Winchester. The west window is probably the best in a town where much of the stained glass is more ambitious than happy. Originally the pleasing brick and wood covered-way on the south side, which now ends batheti-

St Stephen's, Stephen's Way.

cally in nothing, let to a harmonizing oratory and vicarage which have disappeared: church buildings, it seems, are not 'protected'. Observation suggests more alterations, involving the formerly attractive, but now somewhat neglected, churchyard are afoot.

St James, Pokesdown, which stands high above the entrance road to King's Park, was G.E. Street's last church. Originally part of an ironstone-banded composition including the neighbouring schools, its balance and character were ruined by a clumsy lengthening to the West end in 1931, additions to the school and, especially, a recent enlargement of the vestry.

An avenue of cupressus macracarpa leads to the door of St John Baptist, a busy church which has the local clock in its stubby tower. The original work was by Street – 1874 – but the chancel is by Bloomfield and a decade later. It is lit by a generous wheel window at the west end.

St Mark, Wallisdown, the parish church of Talbot Village, set among pines leaning from the prevailing south west wind, faces on to bleak heathland. It has a good tower; transepts but no aisles; it is antiquarian but not so impressive as its churchyard.

St Michael, Poole Road, is the second St Michael – the first was a memorial chapel. The lofty nave is the only part of Norman Shaw's original design to be executed in its entirety.

St Swithun in Gervis Road, also by Norman Shaw, less orthodox, of towering greying white stone, darkly screened by pines, is in one of the central wealth-pockets. The architect was parsimonious with window space apart from the huge, plain, west window which, even on a dull day, spreads the impression of high light through the vast, line-washed nave.

St Andrew, Malmesbury Park, by J.A. Chatwin, is an unobtrusive, rock-faced building with an interior of lime-brick banded with red.

St Luke, Wimborne Road, Winton, is large, red-brick, Edwardian ecclesiastical in medium-sized, red-brick, Edwardian residential.

St Alban, Charminster Road, by Fellowes Prynne, is built on a slope so that the east end, facing on the main road, sheers up abruptly like the prow of a ship. The east window is admirably restrained, the west bolder and effective.

St Ambrose, West Cliff Road, is in the heart of the chine country, built in yellow stone and good taste, well appointed, expensively furnished and with ample parking space.

Christ Church, Westbourne is an unpretentious, grey stone building of 1913, with no spire or tower, and set in guest-house territory.

St Andrew, Boscombe, is in white stone on the edge of the hotel country; three separate roofs, consciously antiquarian.

St John, Boscombe, by J. Oldrid Scott, on the main road, flint-faced and spacious, serves a multitude of guest-houses.

St John Evangelist, by T. Stevens, in Surrey Road, Branksome, hoists a Gothic revival steeple, tall and clear, above the surrounding cedars, pines and bungalows.

St Francis, Charminster Road, has the partly Romanesque air fashionable in the 1920s: high and light, it has a good, plain wheel window.

Holy Epiphany, of Ronald Phillips, at Moortown, is in red brick and white stone to harmonise with the rapid, high-density, low-storey building of the area. It has a separate campanile that might be an after-thought and a sympathetic, non-lofty, pulpit.

St Mary the Virgin, Holdenhurst Road, has a severe red brick exterior; but the interior is wide, white and light with gaily painted tie-beams and pulpit.

St Paul is a grey unity based on the school which was the first building on the site, followed by church and vicarage, but not enhanced by the Church Hall. It is in several ways the least important of the churches of the central area.

St Saviour, Iford is modern, red-brick, Italianate with a wide, simple, three-arched interior.

Close to the sea, at Southbourne, St Katharine – 1882 – is earlier than most of the brick and stucco villas about it. It is Gothic Revival and has a striking, stained-glass portrait of Queen Victoria. All Saints, by John Oldrid Scott, is later, set among later and smaller houses: it has a memorial east window. St Christopher's – 1933 – is trim red-brick with a wide, white, brick interior.

St Augustine, Charminster Road, was Butterfield's last church; it has an oddly-shaped bell-turret and, when it is not locked, it is possible to see its lately limewashed interior and to appreciate the east window.

The most recent, and probably the most exciting, church in the Bournemouth deaconry, however, is St Barnabas at Queen's Park, built in the centre of the new estate on a steep slope. The architect has made an even greater virtue of the fall of the land than Prynne did at St Alban. A square, light-red brick and glass building with a pointed roof, it has the church on the upper floor with an entrance on the top ground level and the altar in the east corner; the lower storey is a hall to be used for parish events of all kinds. It is light, informal, yet with a simple dignity and lack of affectation. If there was something of a falling away in the standard of church architecture in this area during the earlier decades of this century, St Barnabas marks a bright and sensitive revival.

Hampshire, the County Magazine, February 1970

22

Morning Prayers

'"Morning Prayers" was the result of reading Victorian novels.'

Morning Prayers

Sullen, separate, down the stairs
To the cold, dark, waiting chairs
Set in rows for morning prayers
The family came.

Papered wall, a floral stream
Dimmed by tea-urn's wreathing steam,
Lit by struggling yellow gleam
Of gas-jet's flame.

Tired and silent in hindmost row,
Meek domestics kneeling low,
Tight-tied hair and starch-stiff bow,
Each one the same.

High on the wall, in honoured place,
Devoid of heart, or light, or grace,
Heavily scowls grandfather's face
From gilded frame.

Papa with patriarchal air,
Accosts his God in strident prayer;
For vengeance – 'Strike and do not spare'
Makes urgent claim.

Vengeance on an erring child,
A son defiant, callow, wild,

The son he thrashed, renounced, reviled,
But could not tame.

Who now, the reckless, outcast boy,
Crime his living, vice his toy,
Finds in sin unholy joy,
And knows no shame.

Mother and sister love him well
But dare not break pap's stern spell
Consigning the black-sheep to Hell
Who smirched his name.

. . . .

Best-seller of eighteen-fifty-three,
In three-decked uniformity,
It contemplates the brevity
Of literary fame.

23

THREE HYMNS

The Rev. R.R. (Bert) Philip, one time minister of Paisley St James' and Scottish county cricketer, recollected how on the Sunday of the Trent Bridge Match between England and Pakistan in 1954, John gave a talk to a local Boys Brigade bible class. The class was run by H.A. Brown, secretary of Notts CCC and John's subject that Sunday morning was 'A Sense of Values'. His own reaction afterwards was, 'What a good Sunday morning – I knew all the hymns, but not all the tunes, which is the perfect service; and the boys were lively (facially) and quiet – the perfect audience.'

John broadcast several times on religious programmes such as Christian Forum *and in 1969 was asked by the BBC to put new words to three English traditional melodies for their new Hymnal. 'There's an essential simplicity to lyric writing,' says John, 'which very often a poet doesn't have. Arguably, it's a difference between Thomas More and W.B. Yeats – More wrote better lyrics and Yeats better poetry.'*

When asked by the BBC how soon they could have the lyrics, came the reply: 'Tomorrow.' 'Now, don't be silly, Mr Arlott,' said the rather staid lady commissioning the work. 'I'm not being silly – I don't take long to write a lyric,' countered John. Sure enough, the hymns were finished by the next day.

Since, John realises that: 'The twelve lines of the one about Harvest Festival have been about a hundred times more remunerative than almost anything else I've written in my entire life. It's in virtually every modern hymn book in the English language. Quite amazing.'

Recently, representatives of Britain's two million Methodists decided to expunge 'God Save the Queen' from their new hymn book. At the same time, they voted to include, 'God whose Farm is all Creation'. Hallelujah!

I

By the rutted roads we follow,
   Fallow fields are rested now;
All along the waking country
   Soil is waiting for the plough.

In the yard the plough is ready,
   Ready to the ploughman's hand,
Ready for the crow-straight furrow,
   Farmer's sign across God's land.

God, in this good land you lend us,
   Bless the service of the share;
Light our thinking with your wisdom,
   Plant your patience in our care.

This is first of all man's labours,
   Man must always plough the earth;
God, be with us at the ploughing,
   Touch our harvest at its birth.

2

We watched the winter turn its back,
   Its grip is loosened now,
And shoot and leaf have signed their green
   On brown of field and bough.

From ambushed frost that kills by night,
   And storm with bludgeoned hand,
From soft and secret-moving blight,
   Dear God, protect our land.

And send soft rain to feed the crops,
   Sun-warm them gold and red;
So great the prayer we learned from Christ,
   Give us our daily bread.

3

God, whose farm is all creation,
   Take the gratitude we give;
Take the finest of our harvest,
   Crops we grow that men may live.

Take our ploughing, seeding, reaping,
   Hopes and fears of sun and rain,
All our thinking, planning, waiting,
   Ripened in this fruit and grain.

All our labour, all our watching,
   All our calendar of care,
In these crops of your creation,
   Take, O God: they are our prayer.

24

ROUND ENGLAND WITH AN EAR-TRUMPET

Some readers with long memories and soft hearts may recall with nostalgia The Saturday Book. *Others with shorter memories but equally soft hearts may like to be told that* The Saturday Book *was a most literate, amusing and enterprising magazine. In 1950, its editor Leonard Russell decided on a little light diversion:*

ROUND ENGLAND WITH AN EAR-TRUMPET

Yes, yes, we must all do what we can to help the Festival of Britain. Here is our own contribution, a small gazetteer of English place-names pleasant and unpleasant, compiled by JOHN ARLOTT for the mystification of tourists from abroad. Nothing, of course, is invented.

PLEASANT

Beaudesert
Beaumaris
Beaurepaire
Berry Pomeroy
Brown Candover
Cherry Hinton
Cross-in-Hand
Dieulacresse
Dolor Hugo
Hannah Cum Hagnaby
Henley-in-Arden
Hinton Admiral
Holme-next-the-Sea
Ivelet
Margaretting
Merry Maidens
Midsomer Norton
Providence Place
Red Roses
Ryme Intrinsica

Shepherd's Forstal
Silk Willoughby
St Just in Roseland
Talk o' th' Hill

UNPLEASANT

Albright Hussey
Balsall Common
Bawdeswell
Bloody Oaks
Blubberhouses
Bullslaughter Bay
Caldron Snout
Crows-an-Wra
Dripping Well
Dunnose
Gummers How
Helion Bumpstead
Hellifield
Horridge
Hucknall Torkard
Lothing
Little Sodbury End
Lustleigh
Muker
Old Wives Lees
Peover Superior
Piddletrenthide
Port Soderick
Ramsbottom
Sinwell
Snailwell
Sour Milk Force
Spital-in-the-Street
Swineshead
Ugglebarnby
Ugley
Unthank
Wrangle

The Saturday Book, 1950

25

Euphonics *v.* Crakes

The cricketing equivalent of that topographical tour was culled for The Spectator *from the obituary notices in Wisden's Almanack.*

Euphonics *v.* Crakes

Wisden, contemporary chronicle of our cricket, is constantly revised as a work of reference. Since 1933 the 'Births and Deaths of Cricketers' section has been often pruned, so that now, apart from the greatest earlier names, it includes only players who have taken a defined part in first-class cricket in England and who died – or will die – after 1925.

So compactness is achieved at the sacrifice of contemplation. Only in the vast and kindly ramblings of the older volumes can the idle eye now come upon the Rev. T. Duodecimo Platt, who played for Harrow, and died in 1902. The Welsh schoolboy cannot find, in the up-to-date editions, echoes of his princely houses in the Cambridge fast bowler of the seventies – W.N. Powys – or that Dr Cadwalader who played for Philadelphia. Dr Damian is gone, along with Lawless and Lovering, Trudgett and Tryon; and the poet's eye misses the four Coleridges who played for Eton (and two of them for Oxford University as well).

Recalling a lesser literary eminence, 'Craig, A. ("The Surrey Poet"), d. July, 1909, aged 59' was there, with his poignantly incomplete data; now he, with many others, has lost his last line of immortality.

That Mr T.S. Pix played for Harrow in 1824 has remained in my mind for over twenty years, but I had to turn to an old *Wisden* to find that he lived for seventy-six years after that great day.

It was intriguing to obey the instruction of the entry 'Blayds, Mr E. (see Calverley, Mr E.)' and find – '(formerly Blayds)'. Why? – Was some great fortune left him conditionally upon a change of name? – or, for I see he was at Cambridge, was his reason reverence for the light verse of C.S. Calverley?

The long series of 1914–18 tragedies has come under the sub-editorial pencil. 'Bailes, Gunner R. (Yorkshire Club Cricket) d. Oct. 1918' has followed 'Childe-Pemberton, Major C.B. (Harrow) b. Sept. 27, 1853, d. at Potgeiter's Drift, Jan. 21, 1900' into the limbo of unnecessary reference; but their story is told afresh in – 'Turnbull, Major M.J. (Camb. Univ. and Glamorgan) b. March 16, 1906, d. Aug. 5, 1944'.

I remember, too, a Dumas-musketeer cricketer – d'Albertanson, Mr R. – and my disappointment at finding that his only quoted team was Sutton Valence School. More prosaically, there was Puddephatt, F. (Islington), born on January 11, 1831, and, seemingly – and, I hope, happily – still alive in 1923.

Few names – and no initials – are held in such reverence as those of cricketers. Which of us, as a lad, would have dreamt of referring to Stevens without the essential 'G.T.S.', Chapman without 'A.P.F.' or even that Mr Case of Somerset – whose team-mates called him 'Box' – without the initials C.C.C.?

Sounds mean what association makes them mean, especially in the mind of the hero-worshipper. A Rhodes by any other name would bowl as well. It is hard to fall back on the ear alone, to realise that Trumper, for all its connotation of dashing batsmanship, is an ugly name; that Woolley, synonymous with lordly strokes, sounds the same as 'woolly': and that Hobbs and Bradman would be dull, unlovely sounds but for the memory of the two cricketers who bore them.

The oldest of after-dinner cricket games is that of

picking imaginary teams and handsome names against ugly ones would be as good a match as any to while away the time in Hades.

The form of the very early cricketers is uncertain, so we may allow Nyren and Beldham – how much more handsome, somehow than Beldam and, remember, he was 'Silver Billy' – to cancel out Hogsflesh and Stevens, of Surrey, who was so often recorded in the score-sheets of the eighteenth century as 'Lumpy'.

We must agree, too, I fancy, to omit the obvious puns of such crickety names as Fielder, Batson, Scorer, Driver, Holder and, prudently, Rashleigh. Meanwhile, to pick on such as Pigg (Mr Herbert, of Cambridge University and Hertfordshire) is to labour a joke which must have wearied him all his life.

Grace, of course, is clearly first choice for the Euphonics and his own choice of partner – 'Give me Arthur' – brings with him to the wicket Shrewsbury, a name of mediaeval richness.

R.L. Stevenson's theory about the beauty of 'v' and 'i' sounds is not valid for Vialls, nor for Vidler: Vyse will not do, and some lurid Victorian work of fiction has left me with the feeling that the name Vibart is villainous. Vane, Vizard and Valentine are tempting, however, and Verity, doubly handsome, in both sound and meaning, must be included. From Verity, clearly, must follow Trueman. Perhaps, too, it is the 'v' in the word Graveney that gives it a quality as mellow as his batting.

The names from Debrett will not, alas, strengthen the side very much. Lord Burghley (1825–95) did not get a 'blue' at Cambridge. The Earl of Redesdale is described only as a 'Patron' of Gloucestershire cricket, and Venables (R.G.) never progressed beyond the rugby eleven. M.A. Noble will do for an opening bowler, though, and Lyon, with its heraldic ring, provides us with a wicket-keeper.

I am tempted by d'Ornellas but it is followed by 'Private F.A. (Ottawa)' – not quite a good enough player, I fear. So, for the Gallic word-taste, we might have C.A. Ollivierre of Derbyshire and the West Indies, or Lionel

Palairet, de Courcy or de Lisle but that the Victorian Hampshire elevens included 'Champion de Crespigny, Mr P.A.' whose claim must be unquestionable. Mead – as pleasantly pastoral as the Middlesex opening pair of Lee and Dales – the simple dignity of Lord, and the rounded history of Rhodes, and the first eleven is complete.

If there is to be a twelfth man, let it be J.W. Juniper, of Sussex, who was a bare twenty-three when he died in 1885.

Even then, we have omitted Rylott – in full, even more impressively, Arnold Rylott – who played for Leicestershire; the country richness of Haygarth and Appleyard, the courtesy of Knightley-Smith, the picturesque Ravenhill and the gentle sound of Aird.

The rougher-sounding batting we have already started with Trumper and I think perhaps Fuller Pilch makes him a harsher partner even than Ubsdell (G., of Hants.). Sprot, of the same county, however, makes an explosive number three. Perhaps Nicholas Wanostrocht's assumption for cricket purposes, of the name 'Felix' excludes him; but Curgenven we must have, and Gaukrodger, J. Smurthwaite, and J.W. Zulch, in place even of Goatly (E.G., Surrey) or one of the three Baggallays. Sugg, I feel is slightly to be preferred to Sprinks, who has a merry sound, and Jiggins, who, I am sure, was amiable enough.

A relatively unknown – Stileman-Gibbard (Bedfordshire) – would force his way into the side but that we need a fast bowler – Kortright – perhaps the fastest of all. Snary, of Leicestershire, is 'preferred' to Stuckey (Victoria) and Slinn (Yorkshire) and Pougher – pronounced 'Puffer' – rounds off the eleven. As twelfth man, Runting must probably give way to the surprising uncertainty of Unstead (J., of Kent).

So, the two elevens might be:

Euphonics	*Crakes*
Dr W.G. Grace	Fuller Pilch
Arthur Shrewsbury	V. Trumper
T. Graveney	E.M. Sprot
Philip Mead	J.W. Zulch

M.D. Lyon
Thomas Lord
M.A. Noble
P.A. Champion de Crespigny
Wilfred Rhodes
Hedley Verity
Freddie Trueman
Twelfth Man: J.W. Juniper

F. Sugg
H.G. Curgenven
J. Smurthwaite
G. Gaukrodger
C.J. Kortright
H.C. Snary
A.D. Pougher
Twelfth Man: J. Unstead

The Spectator, August 1954

26

The Night Train to Berlin

John's career as a broadcaster and journalist took him far afield – Fiji, Singapore and Korea are but three less likely locales.

At the end of 1953, he made a journey into Europe for Forces lectures and also the Evening News. *Every day for a fortnight the paper highlighted his travels and 'trailed' the series on the front page:*

> *He went there to see for himself the places where history is being created day by day. He did not go to collect the official utterances of politicians, but to see for himself what these places look like, what the people do and talk about, to create a picture of the background to the history that is happening about us.*

Once in the Eastern Zone of Germany, a British officer drove him to Potsdam. On the way they were 'flagged down' by a military policeman. As the car slowed, the officer remarked with heavy humour, 'What are you? Police, Special Branch, Liberal and the BBC? Huh! Don't fancy your chances. I don't think you'll ever get out.'

The Night Train to Berlin

A foretaste of tension lies in the journey to Berlin in a train which travels all night through the Russian Zone with its blinds drawn, not to prevent passengers looking out but as a precaution against some trigger-happy Russian taking a pot-shot at a passing light.

Then, with the morning, you are passing through allotments, dotted with little box-houses of timber, or, sometimes, of brick, bare this year, stuccoed next, as the money comes slowly in. These are impermanent houses for, as every Berliner feels beyond doubt, Berlin, as it now is, has none of the characteristics of permanence.

This is the capital of Germany – or a desperately small Western bridgehead in the Russian Zone, according to one's viewpoint. Russia occupies almost half the city and controls all the routes into it, a power she wields peremptorily and hostilely.

Berlin is not Germany; and, while Berliners are Germans, they are unlike the people of any other part of Germany. They have a metropolitan quickness about them, in which you notice resemblances to the Cockney and, even more, to the Parisian. They are far less stolidly unquestioning than the provincial German, their women are far more smartly dressed and their sense of humour is keener.

It is a strange city, this, with Russian outposts even in the Western sectors – at the radio station and in the quarter-share of the guards on the stark Spandau Prison with its German war criminal prisoners.

Nowhere is the situation more tense than along the boundary between the British sector of Berlin and the Russian Zone of Germany. The road runs outside, beside the Gatow Airport and on, with only an occasional house breaking comfortably wooded country. It is a lonely road; no one from the city has any wish even to approach it, and you may drive its length and back without passing another vehicle.

At first the entire road is in the British sector and there you notice that, on the Russian side of the fence, the trees and bushes have been cut down to ground level for a depth of some thirty yards back. This is the 'death strip'.

See, there – look hard, for it is well camouflaged – that wooden look-out post up among the branches of the trees? From there the escapees, breaking from cover, are shot before they can cross the narrow belt of open land into the British sector.

Soon the *centre* of the road becomes the frontier. Road, indeed, only in name, for no one but the few boundary-dwellers and its guards use it as a route, and all lesser roads leading off it on the Russian side are blocked by barbed wire.

On the inner side it is worn and clear as far as a white line – drawn by the British Military Police – about six inches on our side of the centre. On the other, it is grown over with grass, for we patrol the road openly, the Russians do not. A few weeks ago one of our patrol Jeeps took a corner wide, its off-side wheels crossed the white line and the driver, faced with levelled tommy-guns, was taken prisoner, to qualify for a day of irritation 'in the box'.

Every guard-post – manned by the Berlin police but visited regularly by our patrolling Military Police Jeeps – faces a Russian point – like chessmen moved up against one another.

Let us stop at one of these points, if only because this is one of the few places in Berlin where you will see a Russian soldier. He saunters out of his hut, smoking; a fair-haired, sturdy, amiable-looking man but with a tommy-gun swinging familiarly from his shoulder. He gives us a glance which is half a smile and returns to his fireside, leaving us to the effective guards of this once quiet country road.

They are members of the Volkspolitzei or East German People's Police – 'Vo-pos' as the Berliners call them. Recruited by the Russians they fall into two groups. Some are ex-Wehrmacht men whose roots and families were in East Germany and who, offered a high post-war wage (for the Eastern Zone) of from three to five hundred marks a month *plus* special ration-cards for all their family, accepted it and stayed.

A practical joke by my guide faced me with one of these V.P.s when by Russian standards I was where I ought not to have been. I was uneasily silent. 'Well,' said my guide, to the People's Policeman, 'where would you sooner be, here or in Nottingham?' 'Nottingham, my oath I would,' was the answer in the English of a man who had been a prisoner-of-war in the north Midlands.

These men, after all, have known total war and defeat, and have been matured by those experiences. There is no doubt that some of these older men turn a blind eye to refugees seeking escape to the West.

The younger members are different. Born in or on the edge of war, they grew up knowing only wartime Germany, Hitler and then the Russians. Small wonder that they are the firebrands of Europe, youths with an enthusiasm for war possible – as a German professor once said of the Hitler Youth – only in those who have never heard a machine-gun fired in hate.

We stood well back from the white line, on the grass verge, and, talking, looked up and down the half-and-half white and green road. The young People's Policeman swaggered up until his toes all but touched the white line, rifle slung, hands in pockets, chewing gum. His hat was tilted, his loose Russian-style tunic covered the heavy shoulders of a well-built lout of nineteen or twenty.

He scowled at us. We ignored him. He looked straight at us and calmly – and childishly – spat heavily and deliberately across the white line and looked at us again.

He stood there, unmoving until we climbed into our car and moved off, and, as we did so, shouted an offensive remark in German and spat again.

The young People's Policemen are the scum of Europe, the types who, falling under the influence of a dictator, become enthusiastic bullies and even murderers, in or out of war. Small wonder that, with such men as these along the boundary-lines, incidents occur: in fact, it is remarkable that they are so few, for these thug-fingers are trigger-hungry.

It was a relief to return to the city and not, one felt, surprising that the people of Western Berlin hug the centres of their sectors. It is surprising, however, that in this inflammable atmosphere they should yet preserve some gaiety, produce such a fine, friendly, reasonably priced café as the Quartier Boheme, with its newspapers, dishes and wines of all nations, its smoothly cosmopolitan conversation.

Nowhere so much as in the quiet countryside on its outskirts is Berlin truly and deeply and ominously unquiet.

Evening News, November, 1953

27

The Austrians Still Sing

John's memory of Austria has little to do with its environs and reveals more of his state of mind following the stay in Germany. One evening in an hotel room in Graz he was reading Thomas Hardy's Jude the Obscure, *which he regards as the greatest of English novels:*

> *'Nothing has ever moved me so much as that novel. I was on the sixth floor and had just got to the point where they open the closet door and find the bodies hanging there – I dropped the book and dashed down six flights of stairs to find anybody who could speak English – I was so frightened.'*

The Austrians Still Sing

After the uneasy cross-currents of Germany it was mental fresh air to wake and look through the train windows at Austria.

The castles on the Rhine were grim with the suggestion of dark secrets, but here gay castles of 'happy ever after' look down from the peaks of contours as extravagant as those a child makes in modelling clay – more of the Alps are in Austria than in Switzerland.

The slopes are dark with pines – the air is full of their scent – down to grass green with an Irish greenness. The shallow, blue-white streams carry the snow water down through meadows dotted with red and white cows and silky white goats.

Scattered over these lower slopes, haphazard as toys strewn across a nursery floor, are the fresh doll's-house, wooden chalets. Their roofs are flatter than those farther north, for this is sun-country, where, under wide eaves, the maize-cobs hang ripening to the colour of the pumpkins which lie like golden blobs in the pastures.

Austria is a southern country with its own unique features: the onion-shaped church spires; the hay-poles standing up like ranks of scarecrows on the farms; the wayside shrines – carefully roofed crucifixes or sentry-box-shaped brick pillars, alcoved to house the picture or image of a saint, surrounded by gay offerings of wild flowers.

The men of Austria are not content to follow the humdrum clothing-pattern now accepted by the rest of the world. The Carinthian or Styrian dress – grey with green piping or brown with green piping – or the hunting costume of bottle green, topped by the Tyrolean hats, with their huge shaving-brush decorations or badges fixed to the hatband make the Austrian male sartorially unique.

Yet all is not so well in Austria as the look of this fat-as-butter countryside suggests. It is said, with characteristic middle-European wryness, that 'The position in Germany is disturbing but not impossible; the position in Austria is impossible – but not disturbing.'

Even in 1939 it was all but impossible. Austria, as it stands today, is the core and all that remains of the great Austro-Hungarian Empire: less than one-sixth the size and population of its domain in 1914, when it included Yugoslavia, Czechoslovakia, Hungary, Bulgaria and large parts of Italy and Poland. Now what is left bereft of its major sources of modern wealth – the oil wells and the industry of Wiener Neustadt, which are in Russian hands – struggles to maintain Vienna. The capital matched the size of the old empire, but now, representing over a quarter of Austria's 1953 population of about 7,000,000, it is an impossible burden.

Like the British and the Americans, the Germans and the Austrians are often considered to have much more in common than they actually have because they speak the same language. In fact, they are two very different peoples, though the Englishman notices that while Austrian motor traffic is much thinner than German – for few Austrians own cars – their driving is just as bad as the Germans', over roads whose condition is that of 'make-do-and-mend'.

In the towns the shops are gay and well stocked with every kind of food and clothing; but prices, by comparison with wages, are high. You may see whole shop-windows full of those fantastic Austrian pastries, bursting with cream; but a dozen of them cost a day's wages of the average workman.

I was standing in the back of a tobacco shop in Klagenfurt – tobacco is a government monopoly – when I saw a man come in who was obviously a regular customer. Nothing was said but the assistant at once handed him two loose cigarettes – his day's supply – and he paid and went out.

Burdened with a vast number of pensioners from two wars and a huge, clumsy Civil Service based on that of the old empire and which no one seems to have had the heart to reduce, the Austrians are renowned as bad tax-payers. Their main hope of wealth is their tourist trade, which has grown steadily since the war. Indeed, every other building through the southern roads seems to be a guesthouse and along the lovely lakes by Meria Worth and Welden there is not a house but will provide you with bed and food.

Let them cook you a meal of Wiener Schnitzel – a slice of veal fried in breadcrumbs – or of the Tyrolean pork and dumplings, to be eaten with their beer or the light white wine of the country, for they are good cooks and they love food.

They love laughter, too, and uniforms; the gallant station-master, throwing back his long cloak and raising his hand imperiously to indicate the precise spot at which the train should halt is as gloriously attired as a field-marshal in some Ruritanian musical comedy.

The policeman is even more splendid. On a green cap with a red band he has one cap-badge in the usual place, another above it and yet another over his left ear. His high, turned-down collar carries a red strip bearing gold insignia of stars, and so do his epaulettes. His green tunic is piped with red and sparkles with silver buttons, while a huge silver badge decorates his left chest. He carries a revolver in a black leather holster on a shining belt and his black trousers are piped with red – above the dirtiest pair of boots you ever saw.

Walk into the streets of any Austrian town at night and, still as it all looks in the clear air, hush for a moment, and you will hear music, the zither certainly, probably the guitar, and singing. Track it down and in some *keller* you will find the Austrians sitting drinking their beer with its traditional concomitant, the long, narrow Bierstangerl, the salt caraway-flavoured biscuit-breads. On the walls you may read *'Politischiers wird hier nicht'* – 'Do not talk politics in here' – or *'Nicht laut singen'* – 'Do not sing too loud' – but no one takes much notice, not even the landlord.

These easy people of a top-heavy, bankrupt State precariously placed within Russian pincers have little to laugh or sing about – but they do.

Evening News, November 1953

28

. . . And So To Trieste

'I met two friendly Yugoslavs. The only language we had in common was French which we all spoke very badly. They introduced me to slivovic, which we drank from authentic old glasses – right in the mouth. I remember not liking it very much so I bought them some whisky. It was a hillside tavern on the border – the front door went into Italy and the back door into Yugoslavia.'

. . . And So To Trieste

I travelled to Trieste by the Vienna–Rome express. At least, after years of film-going, I was to travel in a trans-Continental. There would be beautiful spies, of course; perhaps not more than a dozen, but enough to give everyone a chance. I wished I had a couple of nice military secrets to make the girl's time worthwhile. I put on a clean shirt in preparation for the luxurious dining-car, with shaded lights and the pop of champagne corks.

If there was a beautiful spy on the train she was well camouflaged, and there was no dining-car. For refreshment, a heavy-footed man padded up and down the train with alternative loads in his tray – iced beer when the train was cold, and hot coffee and frankfurters when it was stuffy.

I could, however, have a sleeper – a clean and comfortable cabin – at a price which made me wonder if I was hiring a special train. Here I realised that this was an international express: the conductor in charge of the wagon-lit said 'Yes' to show that he was a cosmopolitan; the steward said '*Oui*' to show that Wagons-Lits are a

French undertaking; meanwhile the ticket collector said '*Ja*' because it was an Austrian train.

The sleeper was wonderful. The only snag was leaving it, at four in the morning, for a Polish second-class carriage from Gdynia, its green plush worn down to an oily black gleam and smelling of sweat and sauerkraut.

To enter Trieste by train was too simple. So out on to the road that runs between the slope of stony hillside and a sea impossibly blue as only the Mediterranean or a picture-postcard ocean can be under a hot, late-autumn sun.

Then over there – that dark line among the bushes – a field-gun surrounded by Italian soldiers in camouflaged waterproof jackets. And the pack-mules and the Jeeps, the quick-stepping troops of the Alpini – sturdy, cheerful and in conversation easy with the English they learnt in prisoner-of-war camps.

Then into Trieste itself. A smart, flashy city, with little in its atmosphere to label it Italian, Yugoslav or anything else. The city, so they say – and with fair reason – of the prettiest and best-dressed girls in the world.

Trieste has been Austrian, French, Austrian again, and Italian; and, at regular intervals, what is now called Yugoslav. The four strains have combined to produce the unique strain of the true Triestini.

Standing in a friend's window on the slopes above the city I commented on a superbly dressed woman passing by – she would have been striking even in the West End.

'That,' he said, 'is our maid. You must have seen the price of clothes here; yet, on a few pounds a week, she dresses better than my wife. They all do.' Shopgirls in Trieste are better dressed, more impressive in features and in carriage than any in Paris.

Then an older woman walks past them, carrying a huge bundle of shopping or laundry balanced on her head – and you realise that those straight backs, poised necks, and the rippling walk have developed from generations of women who carried their loads on their heads.

Outwardly Trieste is calm. The political Parties within

the city are surprisingly pro-Trieste. No one in the city will admit to being 'Italian' or 'Yugoslav'; he says, 'I am a Triestini.' The 'tourists' are the danger. Meanwhile the real people of the city are more on edge than they seem. The local Parties seem to have realised that fact, and it may well explain why there have been so few demonstrations – except on the Italian 'armistice day'.

When the film of *Desert Rats* came to the British Army cinema in Trieste the enterprising cinema manager constructed a little machine-gun position with sandbags in front of the box-office as a publicity stunt – and scared a number of the population into panic demands for facilities to get out of Trieste before the shooting began.

Walk a few yards out of the trattoria inland towards Tito country and there is a rattle of rifles. Who are you and where are you going? The Venezia Glulia police, for all their appearance – the blue helmets and uniforms of an English 'bobby' – are still potential frontier guards, and watchful ones. Across the hills are Tito's men, in their loose Russian-style uniforms; armed, ironically, with Sherman tanks identical with those of the Italians.

There has rarely been such an international problem as Trieste. The Italians and the Yugoslavs are on the spot, in a position to put up something of a fight for their claims. In fact, however, Trieste was made as a port by the Austrians, given some civic dignity by Napoleon, and then developed as a key-port by Austria.

Italy finds possession of the city vital on prestige grounds yet, between the two wars, she seemed deliberately to starve it, to develop the ship-building of Monfalcone and the maritime importance of Fiume.

The Yugoslavs could use a modern port, but their communications with Trieste are poor, and would take years to create. The country which needs this port – and needs is, indeed, the word – is Austria, land-locked, desperate for an outlet to the sea for her goods and now finding it almost as cheap to ship them out of Hamburg as from Trieste – and one look at the map shows what nonsense that ought to be in a sane continent.

This is a wealthy city, clean, with imposing and well-filled shops. Prices are high, but there seem many able to pay them in the better hotels and cafes.

Across the water you can see the skyline of Venice, resting quietly back on a history of forgotten wars and a long-lost empire. Trieste is still busy making its history. Aesthetically, socially, architecturally, even historically, it is of no nation, a place by itself, independent enough in outlook to be governmentally independent.

A flashy city, without real or continuous traditions, coveted by three nations and loaded, for all its matter-of-fact pretence, with the ingredients of explosion.

Evening News, November 1953

29

MANCHESTER UNITED AND MUNICH

It is sometimes forgotten that John had a lengthy career as a Football Correspondent, having covered the game for the Evening News, News Chronicle, Sunday Observer *and the* Guardian. *Many an article was penned under the nom-de-plume 'Silchester', the name of the village from which his family emanated.*

In 1983, he had good cause to remember with mixed emotions the catastrophic Munich air crash twenty-five years earlier, when the cohorts of Manchester United and the football press were decimated in a fatal moment.

The present day football follower may find it difficult to appreciate the depth of horror felt all through Britain twenty-five years ago at the murderous Manchester United-Munich air crash. Eight young footballers of splendidly varied and exciting gifts, three members of the club staff, and eight journalists were killed.

Only rarely does an event in the world of sport make any profound impact outside that field. That disaster was the second of two shocks to the body of post-Second World War English football. The first belonged properly and solely within the sphere of sport. At Wembley, in 1954, Hungary punctured one of the last of English unjustified self-satisfactions by beating England as convincingly as the 6-3 score indicated. That destroyed the fiction of English football supremacy. The national disillusionment extended beyond its football grounds.

The Manchester United party leaving for that fateful trip.

The second shock, the loss of the main body of the Manchester United team, was far more profound; a whole multiple of human levels more significant; yet, in a way, the more important for the previous event. To understand its impact it must be understood that standards then were different. The image of football had not been tarnished by hooliganism, vandalism, and stabbings as has happened since. The players involved were paid a weekly wage which would barely pay the present day English top-rated footballer's tip to his hair-draper.

The richness of those young men's capabilities was understood and sympathetically deployed by the Manchester

United club manager, Matt Busby. Of those eight footballers who did not survive Munich, Roger Byrne was a left-back who marshalled and controlled the defence, embraced the responsibilities of captaincy without reservation. Eddie Colman, nimble of wit and movement, was a thinking, combative right-half. Mark Jones, a monumentally reliable centre-half alternated with Jackie Blanchflower in that position through the Busby youngsters' rise.

Duncan Edwards, the glorious young giant of English football and a mighty man, could play anywhere, but had his greatest moments at left-half. Once, in a Wembley international, he hit a square pass from the left touchline which thudded against Stanley Matthews' instep on the extreme right; and no opponent had the chance to touch it. Matt Busby described him as the most complete footballer he had known.

Bill Whelan, a magician of ball control, wove uncheckable paths through often impossibly muddy conditions to turn games. In Tommy Taylor, Busby went out to buy the man; in 1958 England's centre forward, he combined many merits; strong, competitive, industrious, fast, graceful; and a match-winner. David Pegg, lively orthodox outside-left of the 1956–7 Cup Final team, was in competition for a place with Albert Scanlon, preferred in Belgrade. Pegg travelled as a reserve. So did the local – Salford-born, full-back, Geoff Bent. Six of the team were internationals: Byrne, Edwards, Colman, Taylor and Pegg for England; Whelan for Eire. They were not only good footballers; Matt Busby, a devout and good-living Catholic, wanted them, he said, to be as proud of their club as public schoolboys of their school. Happily accepting that situation, they were gentlemen both on and off the field; and they dressed and groomed themselves with such self-respect that Matt Busby was proud to sit down to dinner with them.

In a very real fashion, English football's second shock stemmed from the first. Manchester United had done much to justify English football, even to promise its revival, in face of the European competition which, personified by Hungary, had brought about the disappointment and disillusionment of 1954. That achievement brought them support and admiration far beyond their local area.

In the immediate post-war seasons, Manchester United under Matt Busby, Jimmy Murphy and captained by Johnnie Carey were three times runners-up in the League Championship. They won the Cup in 1948; then, at last, as many had expected them to do before, they won the Football League in 1952. The players, though, were ageing; and the manager, the astute, honest and compassionate Matt Busby, set about building a fresh team largely from the talented youngsters the club had discovered and trained.

The cynics who doubted that his idealistic approach could succeed were proved wrong when, in 1956, his new team - with an average age of less than twenty-one - won the League Championship. As a result they were asked to join the - almost - new European Cup for national champions. That competition had been first staged in the previous season. The then English Champions - Chelsea, which shows how long ago it was - were persuaded to refuse the invitation to enter because it was thick-headedly feared that it would, somehow, impair the standing of English football.

Manchester United - certainly Matt Busby - had no such hesitation. They went in and, most memorably, in the second leg of their tie against the Belgian champions, Anderlecht, they made their win overwhelming by scoring ten goals. They were beaten in the semi-final by Real Madrid who were on their way to one of their six European Cup wins.

Already, though, Manchester had won a respect which extended far beyond mere local support. So, when they became League Champions again in 1957, a vast proportion of sporting - and even some of non-sporting - England was at their shoulders as they went into yet another European Cup.

To introduce a personal and parochial note, this paper, still then the *Manchester Guardian*, based there, and with its strong local affiliations, had been much involved with the progress of Busby's team. The sports editor was the charming and literate idealist Larry Montague of the great *Guardian* family; and his soccer correspondent, H.D. – 'Donny' – Davies, former player for Bolton Wanderers and Lancashire cricketer, who signed his reports – invariably thickly and relevantly larded with quotations from Dickens – 'Old International'. The paper had, for some years, run a Friday 'football essay' written by a series of correspondents, no one of whom had ever sustained it for as long as two seasons. That was not surprising on so unpromising a press day, with virtually no hope of a topical peg.

Writing it was, simultaneously, stimulating yet frustrating; the problem to discover a satisfactory theme at that end of every week. Nevertheless, ploughing on into a second season, it was apparent that the problem could be largely solved by experience of Manchester United's European competition which was so deeply absorbing soccer followers – and many non-footballers – throughout England. Number two to Donny Davies, though, was, most definitely, number two. The sports editor's reply to a request for a sight of that rarified world was met, simply, but quite unequivocally, with 'The football correspondent has first choice of matches; if and when he decides to miss a European Cup match, you can have it.' For more than a year that was highly improbable.

Despite an anti-climactic second leg, United won their first tie of the 1957–8 European Cup against Shamrock Rovers of Dublin by 9-2; went on to beat Dukla of Prague 3-1; and were drawn against Red Star of Belgrade in the third round.

Then, during the last week of January 1958 came a friendly call from the sports editor: 'Danny can't get away from work to go to Belgrade, do you want it?' Protestations of gratitude were met with 'Then you had better go and watch them against Arsenal at Highbury on Saturday; and write your report looking forward to the Red Star tie.' It was bound to be a hard match; Red Star had lost by only 2-1 at Old Trafford in the first leg.

That report, under the eyes now, is bitterly nostalgic –

> By the unqualified attacking approach which so many present-day managements fear, Manchester beat Arsenal by 5-4 at Highbury ... More than 63,000 spectators, Highbury's biggest crowd of the season came to see them, and all but the most partisan among them must have gone contentedly away. They saw some of the striplings carrying a few more valuable pounds of weight than on their last visit, and a forward line as effective as ever, though with a changed balance and method.
>
> United had one or both wing halves always poised on the frontal limit of defence ready to move forward and make a sixth or seventh forward. Thus deployed they could not help but leave gaps behind them and three times in the first five minutes only Jones, by superb tackling, prevented Bloomfield or Herd breaking through an almost contemptuously thin defence....
>
> Taylor with a second shot gave Manchester United a lead of 3-0 at half time.... Another run by Nutt and Bloomfield headed his centre just inside a post. Instead of the anticipated exhibition of Manchester goal-scoring the sides were level and the match a match indeed.... Such a situation would have made most teams hesitate over an attacking policy. There, though, were Edwards, massively, and Colman, jauntily, moving up, cross-passing until the situation was to their liking, then sending the ball forward and following up behind it as if they were half a dozen goals ahead.

The report was lengthy but, in short, Viollet and Taylor scored; then Tapscott for Arsenal and – 'That, though more might have come, was a fine game's last goal.'

In the normal sports-page fashion, the telephone account on Sunday afternoon was followed an hour later by a clearance call to the sports editor. 'Yes, good; but I must tell you, Donny has found the time off and is going to Belgrade tomorrow.' (Expletives deleted.) 'No use cursing; it is the correspondent's choice.' Again on the Wednesday United took a 3-0 lead; and again their opponents – this time Red Star – caught up at 3-3; that, though, was enough for Manchester to pass into the semi-final 5-4 on aggregate: the press duly celebrated.

On the Thursday return journey, they refuelled at Munich where, after a hitch on the runway, the aeroplane, making a second attempt to take off, overran and crashed into a house beyond the airfield. That afternoon, still irritated:

'Going out.'

'Still riled about Belgrade?'

'Yes, never mind, going out to buy a book.'

At the fourth bookshop: 'A call for you.'

'There can't be; no one knows I'm here.'

'It is still a call for you.'

'Ah, was tracking you south through the shops; you're to ring Larry Montague before the *Guardian* PBX chokes: the Manchester United 'plane has crashed; be ready to write a lot of obituaries – starting with Donny's.'

A shudder of horror mixed with guilty relief; nausea; then the phone call: 'Get to a phone, sit by it; piece the story together; you knew them; good luck.'

Sitting in the Press Club with John Camkin, picking up the cables from his *News Chronicle* office, reporting the deaths as they came in, writing obituaries beyond midnight, was a morbid experience.

Eight journalists, members of that club, had been killed; H.D. Davies (*Manchester Guardian*), Frank Swift (*News of the World*; former Manchester City and England goalkeeper), Tom Jackson (*Manchester Evening News*), Henry Rose (*Daily Express*), Archie Ledbrooke (*Daily Mirror*), George Follows (*Daily Herald*), Eric Thompson (*Daily Mail*), Alf Clarke (*Evening Chronicle*, Manchester) who almost missed the plane; he was embarrassed that it was held back for him. The only one to escape was Frank Taylor of the *News Chronicle* who survived savage injuries to write *The Day a Team Died*, a moving account of the disaster. Tom Walley, the Manchester United club secretary, Tom Curry the trainer, Bert Whalley the coach, too, were ticked off the passenger list. Jimmy Murphy who had stayed behind to prepare Wales for an international escaped, but went out hurriedly to Munich, desperate to be involved.

The instructions came through: 'Duncan Edwards not expected to live; Matt Busby only a 50-50 chance; build both into the story without indicating death.' The beef sandwiches were thick in the mouth; almost impossible to swallow even with a glass of burgundy.

When the body of the story was written; to the intro –

> Yesterday, on Munich airfield, Association Football shrank to a small matter. Twenty-four hours before, Manchester United had drawn with Red Star in Belgrade to pass into the semi-final of the European Cup on aggregate. It was yet another triumph for the finest club team ever produced in Britain. For the moment that victory seems slight; at best, a memorial to young athletes now dead.

Duncan Edwards died of his injuries; Matt Busby recovered and, with Jimmy Murphy, built a new and highly successful team. That, though, is another story. This one ended with:

> No club in the history of football had ever shouldered such a burden of strain as the Manchester United team of the past two seasons, which strove so mightily for the triple honour no British team has ever attained. Yet, even under that weight, they invested the playing of a game with something near, indeed, to glory in the imaginations of hundreds of thousands who had never come within miles of Manchester. This was to have been another triumphant homecoming to Old Trafford. If their triumph has become a wreath, it is one which, in many memories, will not fade.

The Guardian, 1983

30

THE LOCAL DERBY

Football flourishes away from international stadia. Two local sides in John's home town of Basingstoke and the reports of 'the greatest trafficker in clichés I ever knew', fuelled the following:

THE LOCAL DERBY

Although my boyhood affection for the United was strong, I cannot pretend that they were an exceptional football team. Indeed, I cannot say truthfully that the results of the league in which they played ever appeared in the results column of even the most soccer-conscious Sunday paper. On the other hand, they had, in that vintage period which coincided with my support, three professional players. Two had had trials – in one case protracted – in the reserve team of the nearby Third Division club: the other was a local player who had played 'hard to get' at the annual end-of-season smoking concert. Each received his train fare, where applicable, the cost of a taxi from the station to the ground (sheer profit), but not from ground to station (sore point), and a weekly payment of ten shillings.

The ground sloped steeply and was grazed by cattle all the week; but it had a corrugated-iron grandstand, two dressing rooms, and a bath which was filled from the rain-water tank, warmed, a few minutes before the end of the match, with a second boiling of the kettle which was used for tea at half-time. From this ablution – commenced on muddy days with boots on – the players came out shining, if sometimes streaked with mud at the hair-line, to walk through the winter evening gloom into the shop-lights of Saturday night and public admiration.

Their chief portion of fame, however, came on Friday afternoon, with the appearance of the local paper, in which an entire column was devoted to their doings of the previous Saturday. The report was signed 'Detinu' which, as his readers soon divined, is 'United' backwards. This critic's weekday life as a bookkeeper at the brickworks was obscure enough. On alternate winter Saturdays, however, he was an important figure. Swinging a cherry-wood stick, wearing tweed cap, brown overcoat and discreetly unstriped muffler, he would enter Hacking's Field precisely fifteen minutes before the match was due to start.

He did not mix with the players: that would have weakened his impartial authority. Usually he sat alone in the 'Press box' – the two seats in the stand with a shallow shelf in front of them. But once a year – twice if the draw for the local Cup worked out so – he shared that position with his imitator, who reported the matches of United's rivals, the local railway locomotive works, and who signed his reports 'Chemin de Fer' which, as Detinu knew, was French for railway.

They would nod only briefly on meeting. Each would scribble throughout the match. Perhaps they both had the good football reporter's knack of seeing the important play and writing during the unimportant: certainly I never caught either of them watching.

Detinu had plenty of time to prepare his critique, as he called it, for the following Friday, and always after the match with the locomotive works, he would rise to the heights of that period football prose which has so sadly gone down before paper rationing and 'hot' news.

From years of weekly reading, I can reproduce one of Detinu's reports as faithfully as if I had succeeded in my early ambition to become his successor:

UNITED'S GREAT WIN

For the local Derby with the Locos, United brought in the veteran Shelley in place of Donovan, recently recruited from Upsham, between the sticks. Otherwise they relied upon the stalwarts who held the Trojans to a draw in last Saturday's encounter. Their rivals were unchanged from last week. Thus, the two elevens lined up as follows: *Bradley United* (white shirts, blue shorts): Shelley; Holland and Delaney; Rees, Tipper and Balchin; James, Andrew, Elder, Mibord and Timothy. *Railway Athletic* (red and white shirts, blue shorts): Scriven; Watson and Robertson; Johnson, Clunes and Hartcup; Pryce, Jones, Percival, Brown and Grimston.

Delaney was fortunate in the spin of the coin and elected to defend the Town goal in the opening period, despite a stiff breeze. The turnstiles were still clicking merrily as referee Daniel's whistle set the game in motion and Percival touched the ball to Jones who set Pryce away on the right. Delaney, however, came across to stop the advance in sterling manner and clear his lines. United at once launched an assault on their rivals' citadel. Andrew was only fractionally wide from James's centre and shortly afterwards Elder missed a golden opportunity when Mibord served up a pass to him 'on a plate.'

The Lily-whites, however, returned to the fray but Dame Fortune frowned on them when Elder shook the cross-bar of Scriven's charge with a thunderbolt. After a spell of sparring in midfield, the railway boys took play to the other end where fate took a hand when Delaney was adjudged to have fouled Percival as the visiting spearhead stumbled in front of the goal. Shelley had no chance with JOHNSON'S shot from the whitewash.

Stung by this reverse, the homesters swarmed to the attack and from Timothy's flag-kick, Andrew fully extended the visiting custodian with a skilful header. United were not to be denied and, after MIBORD had fired over from close range, United's French star burst through to leave Scriven helpless with a daisy-cutter. Although the home forwards now battered unceasingly at the Loco's redoubt, no further goals materialized and the teams went in at lemon-time with the honours easy.

Half-time: United 1. Athletic 1.

Immediately upon the resumption, United, playing like

giants refreshed and gallantly refusing to accept a checkmate, threw all their resources into the fray and the 'Latics were fortunate to see Elder's first-time effort rattle the framework with Scriven beaten. In one of the invaders' isolated sorties, disaster almost befell the natives, but Holland retrieved the situation in the nick of time with an heroic goal-line clearance. United at once swung into action and after Scriven had thwarted James, they went ahead, when from Timothy's centre ELDER shook the enemy's rigging with a crashing drive. The home team were now definitely in the ascendant and launched attack after attack. Their efforts were rewarded when a model pass from Andrew left ELDER with the visiting goal at his mercy and the home leader made no mistake with a pile-driver.

The cherry-and-whites fought back in no uncertain manner but the experienced Holland was a tower of strength in the United rearguard. Balchin also proved a bulwark of defence and his purveying was well nigh perfect as was evident when he fed the fleet-footed Timothy to send the diminutive winger flying down the wing with the leather seemingly glued to his toes. The youngster's pass was so accurate that ELDER had only to nod it past the helpless Scriven to increase United's advantage with their fourth goal and the leader's third, to complete his second hat-trick of the current season. There was now no holding the white-shirted United: the leather passed from foot to foot in a manner which would have done credit to a side from a far more exalted sphere. When Elder was grassed inside the area, Nemesis, in the shape of Mr Referee Daniel (a second Daniel come to judgement) exacted retribution and Locomotive were rightly penalised. The ice-cool DELANEY calmly placed the leather on the fatal spot and crashed it home to increase his side's tally to a nap-hand. In the closing moments United's vanguard rained shots on the Loco's 'chicken-run' from all angles and in the penultimate minute Mibord fired narrowly wide from Andrew's feeding. But any further score was averted by the heroic Scriven, who fully deserved the ovation he was accorded by an appreciative gallery at the end when United trotted off worthy victors by five to one in a memorably contested local Derby. At last the home eleven have justified the high hopes held for them by their supporters since the opening of hostilities in the current campaign. All concerned are to be congratulated on a contest fought out in the best traditions of both sides under the admirable control of Mr Daniel.

RESULT: Bradley United 5, Locomotive Athletic 1.

'DETINU'

The Spectator, November 1954

31

THE PROFESSIONALS

As a football correspondent, John identified with the ordinary Third Division 'pro' as much as the star player. In the two pieces reprinted below, 'George Manymans' can be seen up and down the land on any seasonal Saturday, performing with honest endeavour in front of a hardy few hundred; of Sir Stanley Matthews, nothing more yet not enough can be said.

A HARD-WORKING FOOTBALLER

Call him George Manyman. One name will fit him as well as another, for, in our time, his name is legion.

I met him last Tuesday at Euston Station: his face was familiar: we smiled in mutual recognition and, as we walked towards one another, I racked my brains to place him. Surely he was a footballer? Tentatively I said:

'Surely you're not playing in London this week?'

'No,' he said and, confidentially, after a pause, 'I'm down here trying to get fixed up for next year: old Jim tipped me off that he wouldn't be re-signing me – he's pretty decent, he's giving me a "free".'

I remembered him now: a reserve wing half with a Second Division club: a pleasant man: a useful, but not great, footballer. I was not surprised that his club was releasing him. A professional footballer in his late twenties who cannot command a first team place is fortunate if he is kept on the books when there are promising youngsters clamouring for the chance to come on to the pay-roll. We went for a drink together. The talk was of the season's play, of some great players, and, eventually, of George himself.

What was said and what passed through my mind are fused together in my memory, for conversation served only to supply almost unnecessary confirmation of the details of a familiar story. Five years ago, George, in his early twenties, was a useful half-back with a works' team. The local professional club signed him as a good, strong, willing lad with football in him. There are many such, and one in twenty of them will become a really sound League player. Half-way through George's first season, the regular right-half was injured and George took his place for a few games. In the second of them, he hit a ball on the volley from long range and scored a goal which won the match. This put him on Christian-name terms with the crowd – 'Good old George,' they said. 'Come on, George.'

Under this encouragement, he played to the top of his honest, straightforward game: the side continued to win matches and, although the regular half-back was fit again, the manager did not disturb a winning team, but left George in. The local paper once made him headline news: he has the cuttings still. Everyone in the town read it: locally he was famous, and it was then that he finally arranged his marriage.

The team's winning run ended in a home match, and the deciding factor in the game was George's sheer helplessness against the international inside-forward whom he was deputed to mark. Again and again his dribbling left George standing: twice his body-swerve so baffled the outclassed half-back as to make him fall over and feel very foolish indeed. The crowd laughed at first, but not for long. 'Come on, Manyman: pull yourself together,' they said, reverting strictly to his surname and with a note of anger in their voices. It was almost a season later before George played for the first team again, turning up an average job in a losing side. In the reserves, he was tried out at full-back, at inside-forward, and once, with the club's goal-scoring its weak point, at centre-forward. He never played a bad game because he always tried so hard:

but he never played a great game, for the simple reason that great football was not in him.

Last season, the club bought a good right-half from a First Division club: this season a twenty-year-old local lad took George's place in the reserve side. Did it, I wonder, surprise George when his manager told him that he would not re-sign him this year? His former trainer now manages a Third League side. I fancy he will take George – for a couple of seasons at least: after that the going may be a little hard for a man in his thirties. Then – ? Back to a works' team, probably, directing their training, playing like two men every Saturday afternoon and, eventually, if he is luckier than most of his kind, a job in the factory while he acts as trainer and groundsman to the football club.

I know a George in an older generation. Mention his name to any football follower except some loyal supporter of the club he played for, and it will mean nothing. Visit that older version of George, however; look at his scrap-book, where provincial papers tell the detailed story of matches homeric in their day but now forgotten: single-paragraph accounts, pasted in at the side, show how the same appeared in the national press: three of these papers mentioned George by name. A cartoon from the local paper has a whole page to itself: it shows George in action: the original hangs over his sitting-room mantelpiece. If George has outlived his fame, he is not bitter about it. There is no such thing as undying fame: fame is long or short; those of short fame may retain its warmth for the fact that it did not last with them long enough for them to perceive its emptiness.

A million people watch football in England every week: without the Georges of our day there would be no football; let us bow him out of the game gracefully and gratefully.

Concerning Soccer, 1952

Stanley Matthews

He has been photographed in every possible pose and setting, he has been interviewed, presentations have been made to him, public meetings have been held about him, posters have been plastered through the Potteries – and we have seen him play at outside-right, a footballing experience we shall never forget. But, when a future generation which never saw him asks itself, or us, just how good he was – and why – we may find that we have committed little to print which tells the essential facts. Thus it may be that our grandchildren will look at the photograph of this quiet, short slight man and say: 'Ah, yes, Matthews; he was probably quite good, but not so good as you say, not so good as our modern players.' Let us then, briefly, consider this footballer under three headings – his character in so far as it affects his approach to football, his purpose as a player, and his method. We shall then find that his football is not a mystery but a series of facets each of which has been painstakingly perfected.

First of all, in his approach to the game, he is the answer to the manager's prayer. Conscious that he is a great player, he will do almost anything to maintain or improve his standard, and he is always thinking to that end. It is doubtful if any footballer of our time is fitter than Matthews, for he realises that the relative degree of fitness of two players in opposition may, in a single moment, decide a match by inches. This fitness means that, ply Matthews with ball after ball, and each will find him cool, balanced, breathing easily, capable of his best. The man marking him may become flustered, panting, but not Matthews. He does not drink or smoke – partly because neither interests him, but even more because it might detract by a fraction from his performance. He nurses his fitness, too; notice his completely relaxed stillness in the field, only his alert eyes moving when he is not directly concerned with the play.

His father, Jack Matthews, the Fighting Barber from Hanley, was a boxer with a reputation as a battler. He

Stanley Matthews playing for the RAF during the war and about to make a pin-point cross.

brought his sons from their beds at six in the morning to do deep-breathing exercises, to lift barbells and to use a chest-expander. If these exercises did not give Stanley Matthews a huge physique – for he is narrow-chested and has a slight stoop – it taught him to train, and to value the general physical well-being which fitness generates. So, too, did the two miles each way – in the morning, before and after lunch and again in the evening – which his father made him walk between their house and the Stoke City ground, when, in 1930, fifteen-year-old Stanley Matthews, ex-schoolboy international winger, began to work on the ground staff of the local club. To this day, Matthews trains, of his own volition, far harder than a trainer *asks* any player to do. He is quite single-minded in his determination to be a great footballer. Once, when he recovered from an injury, the Stoke City management were reluctant to change a winning team and asked Matthews to play in the reserves. He asked for a transfer. He recognized the wisdom of not changing a successful eleven. But, as he saw it, that winning combination might go on winning while he lost some of the 'edge' on his play and, above all, some of his confidence in the 'stiffs'. Granted an interview with the director, he was firm but reasonable. He regained his place and withdrew his transfer request. The second time it happened, he stood out for his transfer and, on 10 May 1947, Blackpool bought the finest footballer of our age for £11,500, as a fit, loyal, gifted player, his main ambition still to be a success in his career: twenty years of big football have not changed his original aim.

Both in the broad sense and in detail, Stanley Matthews has *worked out* his football. Since football is a team game, he realises – as some narrower-minded players have failed to do – that the greatest individual success is gained by effective work in the team's interest. He consciously works towards his team's success by two methods – by psychological attack on the confidence of the opposing side and, simultaneously, by actually playing the ball to the end of making goals. Thus, if he breaks the confidence of the left-back opposing him, or if he immobilises two players deputed to mark him, he has done his share towards defeating his opponents completely apart from what he does with the ball.

His actual playing method has been described as 'wizardry' – and left at that too often for the demand of the future: 'What manner of footballer was Matthews?' Much of this lack of description, of course, derives from the fact that the spectacle of a Matthews dribble is so stirring as to demand a positive effort of will to concentrate on technical detail. Let us, however, examine his playing method – noticing, as we go, to what an extent his clear and eminently practical thinking enables him to make use of facts so simple that many people ignore them. He is, by nature, and training, fast on his feet: he was a successful sprinter as a schoolboy. He has made himself faster still, merely by observing that a man in plimsolls runs faster than a man in boots and, hence, that a man in football boots lighter than those his opponent is wearing might gain a vital foot in twenty yards. Therefore, Matthews designed for himself – and also marketed, for he is not in football or business for charity – a pair of football boots half a pound lighter than the normal type. Already they have become a commercial success. These boots, size 6½ for his neat, well-kept size-8 feet, he wears unpadded for perfect 'feel' of the ball.

Given this background of pace and fitness, and with detailed care even to such details of his equipment as constantly renewed bootlaces, let us watch Matthews at work. In his early days he was a frequent shooter at goal, but he soon recognized that the angle from which a winger is usually forced to shoot gives him every opportunity of putting in a shot which, as he says, may look good to the crowd but is no trouble to the goalkeeper. Thus, he now concentrates on disorganizing the opposing defence and then making a precise pass to the better-suited inside-forwards who can head or shoot at goal from square-on. It is here that the significant difference is to be observed between Matthews and Finney of Preston, for so long his rival for his place in the England side and public esteem. Often as spectacular and effective as Matthews in beating opponents, Finney demonstrably lacks Matthews's keen appreciation of the moment at which to 'loose' the ball to a better-placed colleague. On this vital count Matthews shows himself the greater.

Like all real footballers, he is a fine player *without* the ball. Few wingers of our time, and certainly none so habitually closely marked as Matthews, have managed to give themselves so much room in which to receive and initially control the ball. In order to get the ball, he will often go back well into his own half or even, when his side is on the defensive, move across to the inside-left position. Then, the opposing full-back has either to leave Matthews unmarked or, by following him, throw the entire defence out of position. This is deliberately conceived strategy on Matthews's part. Often, too, even before he receives the ball, a body swerve, little more than a shrug, will send a defender the wrong way, away from him, as if to check a move at which Matthews, with intent to deceive, has only hinted. The same difficulty arises when he is in possession of the ball. The defender marking him *must* play the ball: to watch Matthews's body, with its feints and swerves, is to be sent in every direction but the one Matthews proposes to take. In the same way, it is almost useless to try to shoulder-charge him for he has so many different running paces and such close and controlled variation of them that it is virtually impossible to keep step with him or even level with him from stride to stride.

Much of Matthews's so-called dribbling is not dribbling at all. Particularly this is so when he backs away from a man, seeming to take the ball with him; in fact, he has merely allowed the ball, as it comes to him, to continue its course while he backs with it, not actually touching it, but passing his feet over or across the ball and drawing the defender with him. When he does dribble, he possesses the rare gift of compelling decisive action. He will take the ball up to the defender and, either force him to tackle and then beat the tackling foot, or take the ball quickly on. Here, too, he exhibits a rare gift which tennis players, in particular, will recognize. When one is in constant practice at tennis, one becomes so adjusted to the flight of the ball that it is possible to take the eye off the ball for a second in order to notice the opponent's position. Matthews, I suspect, is in such sympathetic touch with the football at his feet that he does not need to concentrate on it to the degree that most dribblers do, but can take his eye off it to observe the reaction of his opponent. Once the opponent commits himself to a tackle with a particular foot, which he does as soon as he takes balance on the other, Matthews is away, past the anchored, non-tackling foot.

In dribbling, he much prefers to use his right foot because, as the natural foot, it grants him that last degree of accuracy to which he always aspires. On the other hand, if you tackled him twenty times consecutively to the right, he would go twenty times to the left. With his continual tap-tapping on the ball, he keeps it closer than any other dribbler of such speed; his body over the ball, his control utterly perfect. It is this minute precision, absent from the spectacular loose dribbling of so many famous players, which characterizes Matthews's ball play. Thus he will control the ball, comfortably, bare inches from an opponent on the touchline. He has been described as over-elaborate; in fact, he will always go directly for goal when he can, going backwards or on the inside of a full-back only often enough to leave doubt in the defender's mind. One of his favourite dribbles is to start to go away to the right of the full-back, and then check as if to suggest the usual dribbling gambit of going the other way, only to move off again to the right with that immense burst of speed which derives from his intensive short-sprint training methods and with which, even now, in his thirties, he can pull away from almost any defender in the game. He is still fast enough, too, to push the ball to one side of a defender and go the other way round him. 'When I have got the ball,' he says, 'I have the advantage; I know what I am going to do, the full-back does not.'

When a fellow-forward is in a good position, Matthews will pass to him at once, but when he goes on, he will often work his way in along the goal-line, not for the sake of elaboration but because it disorganizes the opposing defence, because it allows of the shorter pass – always more accurate and less likely to be intercepted – and, above all, because it guarantees against the offside decision so often caused by the winger's forward pass. Very rarely indeed does he merely 'cross' the ball, hitting it into the goalmouth in general, as most wingers do; a centre from Matthews is a *pass* to a specific position. Again, with a balanced sense of the worth of the simple argument, his corners are never the fashionable inswinger kicked with the left foot, but the straightforward right-foot cross which carries the ball away from the reaching hands of the goalkeeper to where his fellow-forwards have an even chance in the 'climb' with the defenders.

At Blackpool there is a cheer on the rare occasion – about once in two or three matches – when Matthews heads the ball. He is simply not interested in heading; he prefers to play football with his feet, where complete control may be achieved. There would be still more surprise if he were to show anger or if he indulged even the mildest foul: he recognizes, with his usual good sense, that control of temper is as vital as control of ball or body.

It was in 1932 that Stanley Matthews first played for Stoke City's first team. Over the twenty years since then, he has been increasingly closely marked, his play has become better known, more widely examined and discussed by those whose business it is to stop him. Now, perhaps, he is growing old, as footballers go. Every great player has his 'off' days – only the mediocre can be completely consistent. Yet, Matthews out of form for one match is news – 'Is he finished?' Under the increasing burden of marking, defensive strategy, age and criticism, to be – as Matthews is – still the greatest of them all, is to be great indeed.

Concerning Soccer, 1952

32

A Southampton Football Epic

Although it was Reading, residing in the lower reaches of the Third Division South, that captured the terrace support of boy John, it is Southampton that now catches his eye when looking at the results in the papers.

A Southampton Football Epic

On those exalted levels of football where continental competition – the European Cup, or Cup-winners Cup – is regarded as economic necessity, to be eliminated in the semi-final of the FA Cup would be regarded as failure. That event for Southampton this year, however, marked the end of a brief but glorious period, in which both the team and its followers were lifted to unforgettable heights.

It is a long time – six years – since Southampton last reached the Cup Final; and thirty-six years since they were in a semi-final. In between fell the tragic season of 1948–9, when it seemed that promotion to the First Division was within their grasp, only for Wayman's injury to leave the forward line starved and unable to clinch the issue. There was, too, the Championship-winning year of 1960 in the Third Division; but in local eyes that merely put the club back in the setting which was its least entitlement – the Second Division – compensating for relegation seven years earlier.

So this season's Cup progress was Southampton's first experience of the high elation of success since most of their supporters could remember. The fine fever lasted, to be precise, from 8.41 p.m. on Wednesday, April 3, until 4.43 on Saturday, April 27: only twenty-four days, but for those who knew it a truly memorable experience.

A few months ago, no one near Southampton would have given them any chance of glory at all: indeed relegation seemed a considerable probability. The side was weak at right back, right half, inside forward and in the killing-area before the opposing goal. Then came the buying of Williams, Burnside and Kirby; and, as if that were his cue, Wimshurst suddenly began to play in the manner of the great ball-masters at right half, bringing the ball confidently forward, working almost impossibly close and linking with Burnside to give the other forwards a subtle and constant service. York City and Watford were not dangerous opponents in the third and fourth rounds of the Cup; but Sheffield United, hard First Division team, were by no means easy: form would have given them a draw at the Dell and a win at home; but they were beaten. Nottingham Forest away looked like the end; but a 1-1 draw brought them to Southampton for a replay. A few minutes after half-time they were 3-0 in the lead and were packing their defence so tightly there seemed barely room for a ferret to have wriggled through it. Then, at 19 minutes to 8 by my watch, Paine ran in on a long free kick by Traynor and flick-headed it past Grummitt. The whole ground flared up – but, offside. (There are people in Southampton who still believe that Paine's inward run was from an onside position, but that he moved too fast for the linesman's judgement.) That decision would have knocked the spirit out of most teams, and out of most crowds, too. Yet, instead of the silence of disappointment, that single incident seemed to convince the spectators that Southampton *could* win. The roar mounted, took on a strange – to visitors utterly inexplicable – quality of exultation. Here were a Second Division team, three goals down to a well-ordered side from the First Division, with a bare half-hour left for play, yet there was an illogical but half-convincing air of triumph about the losing side.

Wimshurst now was moving with suave confidence,

finding O'Brien and Paine, switching on the right: from time to time Sydenham went galloping down the left: Kirby was needling away in the middle. Now it was 16 minutes to go; Forest still led 3-0, when Kirby went up to a cross and headed a goal. Now belief was absolute. As Southampton rose, so Forest fell back, rattled by the incessant stream of crosses as Paine, again and again, twisted clear and inwards on the right to search out the hungry heads of his inside forwards, sweeping in against a defence which was losing its earlier discipline. Another cross and Kirby was in, butting his head into the ruck, and young Grummitt, only half an eye on the ball, pushed it into his own goal.

Only time was now the enemy. The packed crowd inside the closed gates and the less comfortable watchers, perched precariously in the trees across Archers Road, were merged in a complete unity and in a mass voice that lifted the team to an equal belief. Only one minute was left when Burnside, in a cold split second, measured his right-foot shot and hit it low and accurately wide of Grummitt's right hand into his goal.

Jimmy Gallagher, the Southampton trainer suddenly popped out of his dug-out, ran on to the pitch and kicked a ball sky high: the impossible had been done. Pressmen tore up the copy they had half finished and began to write fresh stories. One Southampton businessman, who had trailed sadly off when the score was 3-0, had heard the first great shout from afar and spent the last quarter-hour phoning the Dell every few minutes to hear the news he could no longer watch for himself.

The crowd-voice went on and on, in an atmosphere at once warm and electric: one of those emotional moments which sport, unpredictably, and rarely, produces; which cannot be controlled nor, once shared, forgotten.

Even extra time was something of an anti-climax: a decision had been reached: nothing definable, yet utterly certain – Southampton had bested Nottingham Forest. Their subsequent 5-0 win at White Hart Lane – a prodigious feat for a team junior by a League to its opponents –

was, in a sense, a lesser achievement. It was important because it showed that the blend which has been made in the Southampton team can, on its day, produce some of the most exciting attacking football in the country; but Forest had, in spirit, been beaten five days earlier, when their certain victory was swept aside. The impetus of that night remained with the side, and with its supporters. Southampton's 'gate' is 18,000 people; but it is estimated that 25,000 followed them to White Hart Lane, by special trains and in coaches and cars that crawled, bumper-to-bumper, to a match which some of them never saw, so heavy and unanticipated was the congestion at the turnstiles. A whole area had become deeply involved in Southampton's football, in a manner not paralleled even when the semi-final was reached the previous time, in 1926–7.

The semi-final itself was a dusty answer. The Cup Final is worth, at a rough guess, £1,000 a player to the two teams: and that was how the game was played. Manchester United packed their defence, took a scrambled goal and held on to it. Of course, those supporters who had worn the 'lucky' Southampton gold favours to Villa Park were downcast: the defeat had not even shown the side playing the sweeping attacking football that is its essential character. If they had done that and lost, the blow would not have been so hard.

Yet still there is the feeling that defeat was not, in the hearts of the Southampton supporters, failure. They had shared with their team a half-hour of rare *rapport* under the floodlights of the Dell on an April night, a time which was, and remains, a triumph which nothing can ever take from them.

Hampshire, the County Magazine, June 1963

33

Southampton Water

'"Southampton Water" has a kind of loving acidity. It is not meant to be caustic.'

Southampton Water

The fog is lying, grey
As sorrow, on the tide
That clears the half-sunk buoy
In sulky, humping stride,
And sucks at shingle-banks
With fierce, eternal greed.
Beyond this grey-walled world
Of water, pier and weed,
With saddened foghorn cry,
An unseen ocean-tramp
Is trudging back to sea:
Her pistons' dogged stamp
And water-churning rush
Are filtered echo-thin.
Now, through the wall of fog,
The steamer's wash sweeps in,
A huge and crested wave
With writhing undertow
Of dimpled strength, to strike
With sudden, cunning blow,
The dinghy at the pier,
And then, in tumbling ride,
To climb the drying beach,
Reverse the ebbing tide.

Behind its grim retreat
In shingle-grinding boil,
It leaves the groaning stones
A rainbow coat of oil.
The fog-banks gently hold
The foghorn's dying wail
And, in their shapes, recall
A whispered ghost-ship tale.

34

The Navy's Other Mission

During 1954, HMS Bermuda, *Devonport Port Division, ran a monthly magazine* Venture. *The magazine managed to prise contributions from stokers and stewards as well as the odd captain and Commander of the Fleet and maintained an entertaining mix of personality parade, signalese humour and ultra-respectable pin-up. Alongside an inventive article shedding new light on 'My Matrimonial Problems' by an anonymous Henry VIII was a more circumspect offering:*

The Navy's Other Mission

While humbly admitting to being a landlubber, I may at least claim that I realise more clearly than some of my kind that it is by no means far-fetched to treat the cricket of the Royal Navy as an important factor in the history of the game.

While I do not by any means forget Services cricket at Chatham and on the United Services Ground at Portsmouth, the greatest contribution made to the game by the Navy has been in spreading it across the world.

Naval sides have been playing at Gibraltar – 'on the Garrison ground outside the North Front' – and Malta for over a hundred years, and in Corfu they planted the sport so deeply that the islanders continue to play among themselves with enduring enthusiasm. In Fiji, too, they have created a healthy tradition of the game and they have given the Canary Islands and Mauritius almost all the cricket they have seen.

Indeed, the first known instance of cricket being played

Cricket on the ice cap at Igloolik. The famous engraving from Parry's second expedition 1821–3.

outside Britain was recorded by Henry Teonge, a naval chaplain (of HMS *Assistance*), when in 1676, some of the officers of his ship, riding up from Antioch to Aleppo, 'did in a fine valley ... divert themselves with various sports including krickett'.

On a more important historical level, many a reader of that valuable chronicle of Arctic exploration, Parry's *Journal of a Second Voyage for the Discovery of a North-West Passage* will have been surprised to find that its frontispiece depicts a cricket match. It is titled 'Situation of HM Ships *Fury* & *Hecla* at Igloolik 1822–3' and the figures are heavily hooded and coated but, surely enough, while their ships lie ice-bound in the background, they have set up the stumps and are playing cricket in latitude 69 degrees North.

It was well over a hundred years ago that Frederic Tennyson – brother of the poet-laureate and great-uncle of England's Test captain – wrote to Edward Fitzgerald from Italy to tell him that, in the previous week, he had 'fought a match at cricket against the crew of the *Bellerophon* on the Parthenopaean Hills'.

From the same time dates the first report of a match from China – in Hong Kong – and also in Chusan, where the Navy met the Army. Prince Henry of Prussia, touring the area, reported that, at Kiao Chow he saw thousands of coolies building fortifications: at Port Arthur, tens of thousands of coolies were building fortifications: at Wei-hai-wei – under British occupation – the activity was confined to two British officers laying a cricket pitch.

The Rio Club in Brazil cherishes the minute to the effect that, in 1842, the local side beat the eleven of HMS *Southampton* on a day when the noon temperature was 132 degrees Fahrenheit. About the same time, the new Cape Town cricket club was beginning a long series of matches against 'The Navy and Army' (note the order in which the two Services were named).

HMS *Amphitrite* seems to have covered much ground – or rather ocean – to play cricket for, in May of 1852, its team beat the Honolulu club by eleven runs and, later in the same year, played two games against HMS *Portland* in Chile. While the score of the second Chile match has been preserved, that of the first 'mysteriously disappeared during the bottle-emptying process that followed the fight'.

That may well have been a 'friendly' fight, but the first cricket match to be played in Japan – Yokohama *v.* The Fleet – took place in 1863 when the country was so unsettled that the players had to go on to the field armed.

In Russia, even in 1875, there was strict surveillance over foreigners. Cricket's senior book of reference – *Scores and Biographies* – records that, when the English Residents played the team from the Royal Yacht *Osborne* at the Cadet School in St Petersburg that year, the Chief of Police was asked to account for the presence of this 'force of warriors' in so important a military centre.

Four years later, in 1879, the Mediterranean Squadron played a series of seven matches – of which they won only one – against the British Residents in Constantinople. The game took a hold there and a league grew up, but the players were mostly British. Indeed, a Turkish naval officer who joined in with them was arrested as a spy during one of the games. He refused to give himself up until he had finished his innings but, when he was bowled, a troop of cavalry took him into custody and the cricketers of Constantinople never saw or heard of him again.

A match between A. and B. Companies of HMS *Agincourt* and the Rest of the Naval Camp at Port Said in 1882 was played in similarly dangerous conditions, for the only possible pitch was within a hundred yards of Fort Gim-el, held by Arabi's forces. The game seems to have generated its own excitement, too, for it ended in a tie.

Never, however, can cricket have been planted more deeply by its naval missionaries than in Samoa, where it was first played by HMS *Diamond* in 1884. The natives were so delighted with this new diversion that soon they were playing village against village, with two hundred players a side, five umpires and three batsmen at each end, in matches that lasted a week. To such an extent did cricket break down the island's economy that, after the threat to excommunicate the players had failed to curb them, a Royal Proclamation, signed by King Malietoa on the 20 June 1890, made inter-village cricket illegal on pain of a fine of forty-five dollars or three months hard labour. In the neighbouring Tonga much the same position arose – and even threatened the area with starvation – but, as the King himself (Tubow II was at school in New Zealand) introduced the game to his subjects, the credit – or discredit – cannot in this case be given to the Navy.

My favourite naval-cricket story has waited until last. Sir William Draper, who took Manila in the eighteenth century, was an enthusiastic cricketer. Perhaps his influence lingered there: certainly there is an eighteenth-century flavour about later cricket as one player recalled it, with 'enormous tumblers of iced beer set down a foot or so behind the wicket and constantly refilled'. I wonder if that custom applied in 1898 when, during the Spanish-American War, HMS *Immortalité* anchored there? The *Penang Gazette* report runs 'under a blazing tropical sun, with the American fleet in the bay, a bombardment imminent, and the natives on the point of rising to massacre the whole crowd, a little game of cricket was arranged between Manila and the *Immortalité* team, and came off, too.'

Perhaps it is too obvious to recall Drake and the game of bowls on Plymouth Hoe. Is it, however, extravagant to wonder if the particularly British form of insanity called cricket, indulged at times of stress, may sometimes reveal much of the wider world and its greater activities as equally insane?

Venture, July 1954

35

A Hampshire Handkerchief

Cricketing ephemera, avidly pursued by a platoon of non-altruistic collectors, turns up in diverse forms, but perhaps none so human as a simple square piece of cloth with which to blow your nose.

A Hampshire Handkerchief

To speak of a handkerchief as historic sounds like a contradiction in terms: useful certainly: sometimes decorative: but not to be thought of as something to warm history into life. Yet luck and coincidence recently brought me a souvenir handkerchief which is at once sporting history and, in its unsophisticated rightness, a piece of folk art.

That it should have come intact down to today is a minor miracle. As a rule such ephemera hardly outlive their original owners. If they are not thrown away or lost, they rarely survive the removals, changes of interest and taste, or the multifarious minor domestic accidents which occur in ordinary homes over a couple of centuries.

Yet this piece of cheap silk, yellowing with age, dark with dust along the line of its age-old folds, has endured, while men and buildings of its time are gone and forgotten.

Mr Alan Hoad turned it up in the course of some shift-round in his house in Fareham. He asked his neighbour, Alan Wassell, the Hampshire cricketer, if he knew anyone who might be interested in it: so, a few weeks ago, it reached me from a man I had never met.

Open out the little square of nondescript material and

there is the printed score of one of the greatest of all early cricket matches – played at Sevenoaks in 1777, when Hampshire beat All England for a purse of a thousand guineas.

Usually when such an item is unearthed it has passed through so many hands that its history cannot be traced. Even here the thread is thin and incomplete. The handkerchief was among some personal odds and ends left to Mr Hoad by his sister who, in 1932, had inherited it from an aunt – a Mrs Harris, formerly Miss Fanny Hoad: she was given it while she was 'in a gentleman's service' in the Fareham-Portsmouth area in 1866: and Mr Hoad, now in his sixties, recalls her telling him 'one handkerchief was given to each member of the Hampshire team.' That piece of hundred-year-old hearsay is all we know of its origin.

The imprint reads: 'Moxon, Printer, Portsea.' Irrespective of the fact that it was probably the nearest printing press to Hambledon, it is not surprising that a cricket match should be celebrated in Portsea. For, in 1765, the following notice appeared in the *Salisbury Journal*: 'To the gentlemen players of the County of Southampton. The Cricket players of the parish of Portsea will play the game of Cricket with any parish in the said County for 20 guineas each match, home and home.' Among the few remaining records of their doings at that time, we find that in 1772 there was a cricket match 'Milton *v.* Portsea Island for 11 gold laced hats and 11 crowns: when after two days smart play, Portsea won'; a week later they won the return 'played upon the same terms'.

Their *Salisbury Journal* challenge, however, was a dangerous one, for only a few miles to the north the first great cricket club, Hambledon, was approaching its zenith. The 'Hampshire' side of the handkerchief, apart from Lord Tankerville, is composed entirely of Hambledon players. But this is one of the first occasions on which a cricket team played under the name of Hampshire. Only three years before the distinction between club and county had been emphasized by a match, on Broad Halfpenny Down, 'The County of Hampshire *v.* the Parish of

Hambledon'; the result cannot be traced, but there can be little doubt that Hampshire won.

Other scores of the Hampshire-England match vary in detail from the handkerchief version which, however, is the one accepted by Haygarth in *Scores and Biographies*. It needs, perhaps, some explanation for those more accustomed to modern score-sheets. For instance, in the manner of the time, a bowler is only credited with a wicket if he bowled the batsman out: otherwise the catcher alone is given the credit. Notice, too, the third – 'total' – column for the England players, in which each man's scores for the two innings are added together; the method of declaring the result – 'won . . . at one innings, by a Majority of 168.' It is important, too, that the players' names are not set down in batting order: the 'backer' is put first and the remainder in some rough order of seniority: in fact, Aylward opened the innings. The date on the score, June 20, is that of the last day: England batted first and were put out on the first day – 18th June – before five o'clock, when Aylward went in; and again after three o'clock on Friday, after he was out.

The 'handkerchief' match was worthy of special commemoration for several reasons. Hampshire's 403 was the first innings of more than 400, and Aylward's 167 the highest individual score recorded until then. Less obvious, but perhaps more important, this was the first time Hambledon had ever beaten the full strength of the Rest of England on even terms. Their four earlier wins were achieved either with the aid of a 'given man' – 'Lumpy', the most accurate bowler in the country – or in the absence from the England team of Minshull, one of the two best bats outside the Hambledon club. Lord Tankerville can hardly be called a 'given man': he was almost certainly in the Hampshire side because he put up the crucial thousand guineas. Haygarth in *Scores and Biographies* says of his lordship, 'most probably he scored best before this book commences, in 1772'. The contemporary, and less charitable, *St James's Chronicle*, described him, in 1774, when he was convicted of assaulting a coachman,

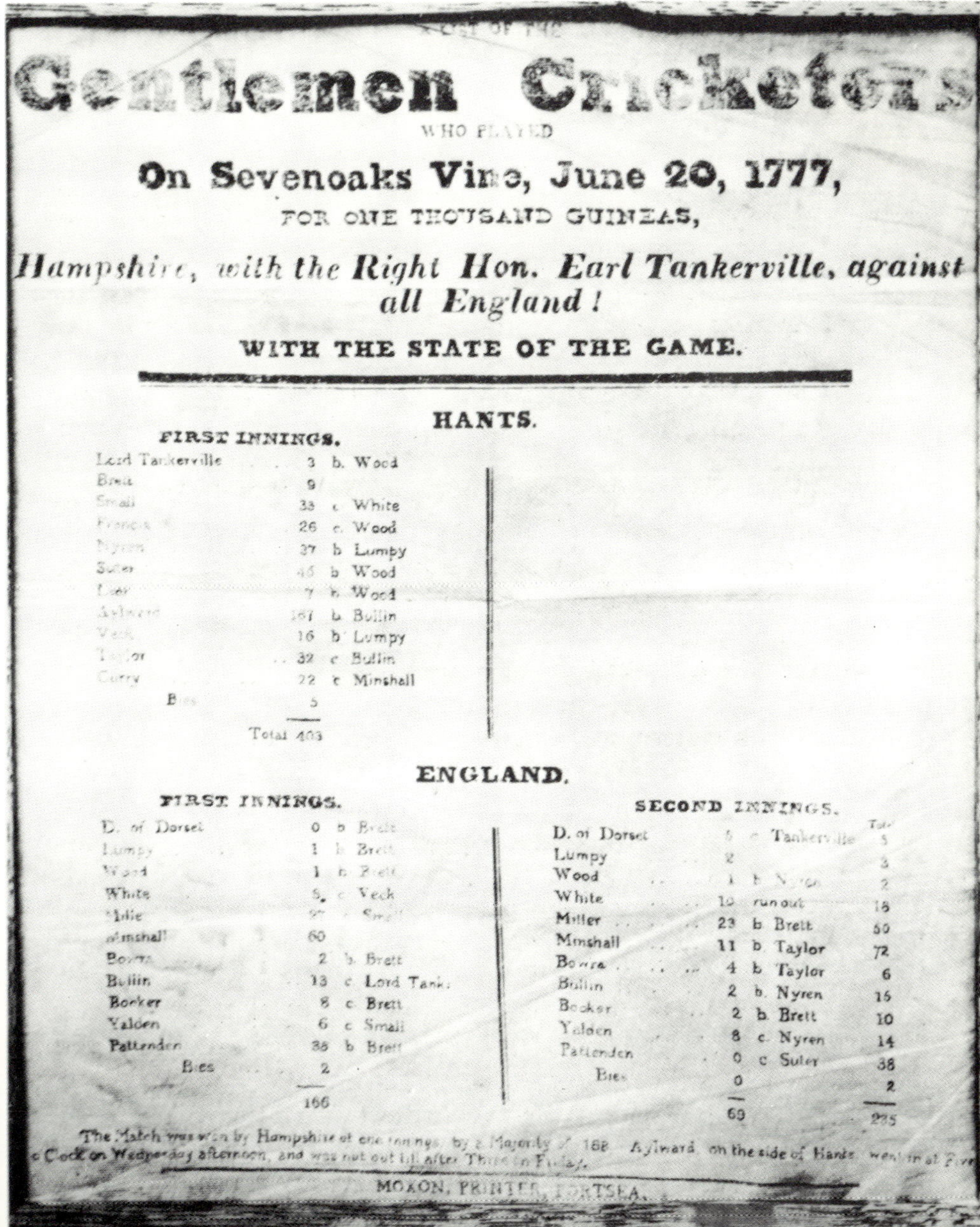

LIST OF THE

Gentlemen Cricketers

WHO PLAYED

On Sevenoaks Vine, June 20, 1777,

FOR ONE THOUSAND GUINEAS,

Hampshire, with the Right Hon. Earl Tankerville, against all England!

WITH THE STATE OF THE GAME.

HANTS.

FIRST INNINGS.

Lord Tankerville	3	b. Wood
Brett	9	
Small	33	c. White
Francis	26	c. Wood
Nyren	37	b. Lumpy
Suter	46	b. Wood
Leer	7	b. Wood
Aylward	167	b. Bullin
Veck	16	b. Lumpy
Taylor	32	c. Bullin
Curry	22	c. Minshall
Byes	5	
Total	403	

ENGLAND.

FIRST INNINGS.

D. of Dorset	0	b. Brett
Lumpy	1	b. Brett
Wood	1	b. Brett
White	5	c. Veck
Miller	27	c. Small
Minshall	60	
Bowra	2	b. Brett
Bullin	13	c. Lord Tank.
Booker	8	c. Brett
Yalden	6	c. Small
Pattenden	38	b. Brett
Byes	2	
	166	

SECOND INNINGS.

			Total
D. of Dorset	5	c. Tankerville	5
Lumpy	2		3
Wood	1	b. Nyren	2
White	10	run out	18
Miller	23	b. Brett	50
Minshall	11	b. Taylor	72
Bowra	4	b. Taylor	6
Bullin	2	b. Nyren	15
Booker	2	b. Brett	10
Yalden	8	c. Nyren	14
Pattenden	0	c. Suter	38
Byes	0		2
	69		235

The Match was won by Hampshire at one innings, by a Majority of 168. Aylward, on the side of Hants, went in at Five o'Clock on Wednesday afternoon, and was not out till after Three on Friday.

MOXON, PRINTER, PORTSEA.

A precious piece of cheap silk.

as 'The Rt. Hon. The Earl of Tankerville, renowned for nothing but cricket playing, bruising and keeping of low company.'

As a player he would barely have balanced the Duke of Dorset, the backer of the England side and an old rival of Hampshire. The *Morning Post* reporting a match between England and Hampshire in 1773, noted – 'The Duke of Dorset played on the part of England, and having run a considerable number of notches from off-strokes, the Hampshire people very unpolitely swarmed round his bat so close as to impede his making a full stroke; his Grace gently expostulated with them on this unfair mode, and pointed out their danger, which have no effect, he, with proper spirit, made full play at a ball and in so doing brought one of the gentlemen to the ground.'

James Aylward's 167 was his greatest triumph in a cricket career which stretched over thirty years. Our acceptance of modern cricket figures makes it hard for us to comprehend what a remarkable performance it was. He scored more runs than a whole team usually made in those days, against the best bowling the Rest of England could muster urged on by the stake, quite vast by the standards of 1777, of a thousand guineas. (Taking the players' social conditions and changing money values into consideration, it might represent £25,000 today.) The two-day duration of his innings, so admirably noted at the foot of the handkerchief, was something more than a nine-days wonder in the world of Georgian cricket.

Aylward, whose descendants still live in East Hampshire, was a strongly built and somewhat clumsy-looking left-handed bat: but John Nyren, the chronicler of Hambledon, called him 'one of the safest hitters I ever knew in the club'.

Aylward was born at the Peak Farm at Warnford, near Droxford, and later lived and farmed at Corhampton. In 1779 Sir Horace Mann persuaded him to become his bailiff at Bishopsbourne, and play for Kent. But he never made many runs against Hambledon (his old colleagues knew his play too well), and he seems to have been no great success as a bailiff. He died in London and was buried in St John's Wood churchyard, close by Lord's ground.

Lord Tankerville apart, this was truly a team of Hampshiremen. Richard Nyren (father of John) was born in Kent, and Francis in Surrey, where Nyren was a farmer and innkeeper, Francis a gamekeeper. George Leer – not Lear as the old score sheets called him – was born and died in Hambledon, though he spent some years as a brewer in Petersfield. 'Curry' was the nickname of Edward Aburrow, the Hambledon shoemaker; Tom Sueter, the wicket-keeper, was a village carpenter and builder in Hambledon. Thomas Brett – 'the fastest as well as the straightest bowler that was ever known' – came from Fines Head Farm at Catherington. John Small, Hampshire-born at Empshott, moved to Petersfield when he was six and gave up shoemaking to become the first great maker of cricket bats and balls. Thomas Taylor, from Ropley, was for many years landlord of 'The Globe Inn' at Alresford, where Richard Veck 'was engaged in mercantile pursuits'.

Which of them all, I wonder – if the story told to Miss Hoad was true – owned this particular handkerchief? It is too much to hope that we shall ever know that. Whoever he was, he must have felt that he had shared in the making of cricket history. But he can hardly have dreamed that, almost two hundred years afterwards, in a day of over-arm bowling, when as many as nine centuries might be recorded in a single day's first-class cricket without undue remark, the newest owner of his handkerchief would be too terrified to watch the creases being ironed out of it for fear the heat might lift his – or any other – name from that simple square of Hampshire history.

Hampshire, the County Magazine, August 1962

36

Champion County

One hundred and eighty-four years on came another historic moment for Hampshire cricket:

Champion County

A TRIBUTE TO HAMPSHIRE COUNTY CRICKET CLUB

ARLOTT: It was about ten minutes past four as far as anybody in Bournemouth can remember at the moment very clearly, when Hampshire for the first time became county champions. We were recording – we'd been recording, in fact, hopefully for the best part of an hour when it happened – and this is the way precisely that it did happen.

ACTUALITY: Derby, 111 for 9 and Sainsbury bowls to Taylor, Taylor goes down the pitch, it's a long catch to Livingstone, he's held it. (*Crowd roar.*) And the boys flock on to the pitch and Hampshire are county champions. They have beaten Derby by 140 runs, and let us add to that, that they've done it, they've bowled Derby out in about 2 hours 25 minutes and the crowd now flocking round the pavilion. Hampshire, champions for the first time in the club's history.

ARLOTT: The crowd wanted a speech, it wanted the captain, Colin Ingleby-Mackenzie, and it got him with eleven players, the dozen happiest cricketers that you've ever seen out on the pavilion balcony and the captain reaching for the microphone. (*Applause.*)

INGLEBY-MACKENZIE: Ladies and gentlemen, this is

obviously the most wonderful occasion for me, of all time, and I would herewith like to toast ten of the greatest men and certainly the luckiest captain of all time.
(*Cheers and applause from crowd.*)
Thank you very much for your magnificent support and when I said ten I completely forgot one of the greatest off-spinners that has ever had the privilege of playing under me, Mr Mervyn Burden.
(*Applause.*)
I must confess, I think you're the best-looking crowd I think I've seen for a long time ... and throughout the year you have supported us magnificently. But all I can say is – I can't say very much I'm afraid, obviously I'm far too excited to really have words to speak – a dream has come true, and I only hope tomorrow morning I won't wake up and we're twelfth in the championship.
(*Laughter from crowd.*)
Thank you very much indeed.
(*Applause.*)

ARLOTT: So it had come true at last. Hampshire were champions. And it hadn't always looked like it in this game, particularly when Derby got a first-innings lead and the bonus points and even this morning the position was pretty tense especially when Marshall was out early on, which might have heralded collapse. But then came those two old comrades in arms, Peter Sainsbury and Mike Barnard to put on 99 in eighty minutes, and with a little bit of odd help, at three minutes to one Colin Ingleby-Mackenzie declared. Hampshire 263 for 8 were setting Derby 252 to get in 192 minutes, and far too often for the comfort of Hampshire men in recent seasons, Derby have reached and bettered the target that Hampshire had set them. But this time, they were never really in the hunt. Derek Shackleton produced probably the finest spell of bowling even of his remarkable career. Because this wicket, technically speaking, was no use to him whatever. But he had Charles Lee caught by Leo Harrison behind the wicket before lunch at 11 for 1, and then he went on in a quite bewildering spell on this slow pitch. Twenty-four overs, 10 maidens, 6 for 39 and he smashed down the real strength of the Derbyshire batting. When he eventually went off, Peter Sainsbury and Alan Wassell carried on. But after lunch in just an hour and six minutes, Hampshire had knocked Derby down to 52 for 8. Victory and the championship seemed right within their grasp. And then came this stand between Taylor and Rhodes, who doubled the score and gradually Hampshire hopes seemed to waver a little until Sainsbury brought off that very nimble caught and bowled to get rid of Rhodes and then as you've heard with the last pair there, Taylor and Jackson, Taylor went for his fifty with a long stroke and was caught by Livingstone in the deep and Hampshire were county champions.

Well, the thing to do then was to go and meet this side, to try to push in to odd corners and get little interviews from men, so happy, at times they seemed almost incoherent. To interrupt one of the best cricket parties there's ever been, just to talk to the men who've made this victory possible.

Colin Ingleby-Mackenzie has skippered the Hampshire side with considerable success ever since he took it over. And he's succeeded, moreover, in being a well-liked skipper not only when he was losing, but also when he was winning. Perhaps you'd better tell us first, Colin, the explanation for that fact.

INGLEBY-MACKENZIE: Well, I think probably, John, I've got the greatest men under me of all time and every single one of them's a gem of gold and I think anybody who was given my job, when I was lucky enough to by Desmond Eagar in 1958, can think themselves very lucky indeed.

ARLOTT: But, all right then, Colin, explain why it is that other sides like you?

INGLEBY-MACKENZIE: Well I don't know, John, but probably because I happened to miss a very straight ball early on, I think.

Hampshire, County Champions. *Back row L to R*: M. D. Burden, H. Horton, D. A. Livingstone, A. R. Wassell, M. Heath, D. W. White, P. J. Sainsbury, D. O. Baldry, N. Drake (scorer). *Front row L to R*: J. R. Gray, D. Shackleton, A. C. Ingleby-Mackenzie (Captain), R. E. Marshall.

ARLOTT: Now tell me, how long do you think you can endure this cricket game?

INGLEBY-MACKENZIE: Well I think it's a fascinating game, I simply love it. I think that it is a game definitely bettered by the good weather which we've certainly had down in Bournemouth this week. I think that 1961 has been a great year for the revival of cricket in its best possible shape. There's been attacking cricket, and that is what I've been trying to play for the last three or four years in Hampshire, and at last and through this great side of mine, we've managed to bear the fruit that we have today.

ARLOTT: Just one other thing. Yesterday, when I was shaking at the knees, you told me Hampshire was certain to win. How did you know?

INGLEBY-MACKENZIE: Well, it's my crystal ball, John. I have a little one stationed at Southampton, and it told me last night that we would collect the points today.

ARLOTT: Eleven to ten, I think you thought the odds were yesterday at four: did you get any money on at that price?

INGLEBY-MACKENZIE: I'm afraid I didn't, I was so confident, I thought it was taking money from the poor, John.

ARLOTT: But from a purely cricketing point of view, when today did you reckon Hampshire were going to win and be champions?

INGLEBY-MACKENZIE: Well, it's a very difficult question, John. I think it was a very exciting day because up till lunchtime it was an even money bet, I thought that Derby had a great chance of winning as soon as they came out after lunch. I also, secretly, thought that we had a great chance of winning, and I think really the turning point to me was when Derek Shackleton came on and bowled Laurie Johnson with yet another of his unplayable balls and I think from then on we were supremely confident. It was just a question of winding old D. Shackleton up for L. Harrison to take all his catches behind the wicket and it really was inevitable from then on I thought.

ARLOTT: Just one thought, tomorrow you play Yorkshire, any feelings about that?

INGLEBY-MACKENZIE: I just sympathise with Yorkshire for losing another match, John.

ARLOTT: On that comment I think we'd better meet the rest of your side and the other people who are behind you. I wonder if first of all, we could have a word with Harry Altham who's the greatest of cricketing after-dinner speakers and the game's greatest historian. The President of Hampshire looks happier than ever today. You'd better go on yourself, sir, I wouldn't presume to question you.

ALTHAM: Well, John, I feel in considerable difficulty you know, because I never could play strokes like Mackenzie; I was never prepared to take quite the risks that he does or get away with them as he does. And as the first Test match I saw was in 1899 I doubt whether I make much sense about the modern game. But one thing I'm certain about is that I couldn't have had a happier day. To see victory for this great team – in all senses of the word because they are a team that enjoy their cricket and who are friends and who never let the game get them down.

ARLOTT: Well now, sir, many of us associate you with that nostalgic golden age of cricket before the 1914 war. Do you suppose that it produced many things much better than this cricket match?

ALTHAM: No, I don't think it did for a moment. I've seen some splendid stroke play, not only by Hampshire 'cos this Derbyshire batsman Johnson played a magnificent innings on a beautiful wicket. I've seen some very good fielding. Not perhaps Hampshire at their best on the first day but they looked all right today, and I've seen a lot of very accurate bowling which I think is a great test of batsmanship and the whole thing was a fascinating balance fluctuating up to a point of almost unbelievable excitement.

ARLOTT: It was twenty-two years ago when I first saw Leo Harrison play for Hampshire on this ground at Bournemouth against Yorkshire, and though he wouldn't like me to remind him of it he's the oldest member of the side today. You'd better say how you feel about that, Leo.

HARRISON: Well, what I am going to say, John, is very short, very sweet because I'm more or less emotionally upset, but I do thank everybody for the magnificent way they fought this year and I cannot think of anything nicer than to say it couldn't happen to a better captain than we have at the moment. That's all I really want to say.

ARLOTT: Could you have believed that you'd be the oldest member of the champions?

HARRISON: No, I couldn't, I really couldn't have believed it but after twenty-two years the unbelievable has happened and I am jolly thankful it has, I really am. Thank you very much.

ARLOTT: Well, now we turn to one of the men who, in the last analysis in this final game, produced a match-winning stroke. Derek Shackleton, when he ran through the early Derbyshire batting. I think everybody knew that their tail might be vulnerable, but nobody surely could possibly have believed that they were going to be knocked down to 52 for 8 and that, of course, was due almost entirely to Derek Shackleton's opening spell. Now Shack, sometimes I think you're never tired. Are you ever tired?

SHACKLETON: Occasionally I get tired, but it's one of those things peculiar to the day. I mean, the skipper put me on that end and I felt that if I could keep going, bowl at the wickets, make the batsmen play, that was my job done.

ARLOTT: Wasn't a very good wicket for you, Derek, was it?

SHACKLETON: Not particularly, but I always say this: if a bowler can bowl straight, make the batsmen play, he's doing his job to the best of his ability.

ARLOTT: But a few of them weren't straight. A few of them missed middle and beat the offstump, didn't they?

SHACKLETON: A few of them went off the wicket, but it happens in cricket, you know.

ARLOTT: How do you reckon that with a not particularly powerful physique you keep going as long as this and as accurately as this?

SHACKLETON: Well, it's just one of those things. The skipper says he winds me up and that's it for the day.

ARLOTT: How do you feel when you come off, relieved or . . .?

SHACKLETON: Well, particularly today, I felt relieved when we'd won. Because it's been a strenuous season. We've all played as a side, we haven't played any individualists. And we've come out on top and it couldn't have come to a nicer chap than we've got as skipper.

ARLOTT: Can you face tomorrow's game with Yorkshire?

SHACKLETON: Of course, head in the air, no worries.

ARLOTT: Roy Marshall, in addition to some sparkling openings, was a hero, though crippled, of the amazing win over Essex against all the odds at Cowes, and he played the innings here in the last match against Derby that steadied Hampshire's second innings and gave them the real chance to win. How do you feel, Roy, about this season?

MARSHALL: Oh, extremely happy about it all. It's all like a dream that suddenly's come true. And it's achieved a very great ambition.

ARLOTT: And has it been worth coming to England for this?

MARSHALL: Oh yes, I don't think we'll get it again, but we'll always try.

ARLOTT: And have you enjoyed it?

MARSHALL: Oh yes, immensely.

ARLOTT: No one in the world is happier at Hampshire's championship win than Desmond Eagar and in a way, without adding to his true age, we might say that he's almost the father of the team that's won the championship. After the war he added direction to their cricket, gave great drive and verve and enthusiasm to their fielding and handed over to a man he was very fond of, and then, as so few people in these circumstances could have done, stood back and didn't worry them, left them alone, suffered sometimes, helped when he could, admired most of the time. Desmond, what are your real feelings about Hampshire county champions?

EAGAR: This is the most wonderful day in my life. I've been working for fifteen years, hoping that one day we would win the championship. I wish we'd done it under me but I'm very proud of those who have done it, and I would like to congratulate Colin for his magnificent leadership. I hope I've never been a nuisance to him or the lads. If ever I have, I'm sorry. They've made me so happy today. Thank you, John.

ARLOTT: Just one thing more, Desmond. I know they

know how much you've done. But tell me what's the special quality you see in this side that enabled them to win the championship?

EAGAR: I should think they were the nicest bunch of chaps that have ever come together in one team. There could be no nicer chaps than the people who've played for Hampshire these last fourteen years.

ARLOTT: Mervyn Burden was twelfth man in the side that actually won the match against Derby to clinch the championship. As he did say to me earlier in the match, they do the playing and I sit back and do the nail-biting and chain-smoking for them. But he took crucial wickets in the early matches of the season which, as much as those that came late, clinched the championship. Probably bowling better this year in fewer matches than he's ever bowled before. But perhaps you can put into words, the thing we both suffered while they were playing in this match, Mervyn?

BURDEN: Well, it was a bit hair-raising, John. I think sitting and watching is worse than being out there playing. At least you've got something to think about when you're bowling, but I would like to say that the boys have turned on the treatment real good and proper this year. I would've liked to have played more, but the wickets have suited the seamers more than the spinners and the boys have done us proud.

ARLOTT: Peter Sainsbury was one of the many who'd take credit out of this particular clinching match for his batting, which on this third morning just gave Hampshire enough runs for the bowlers to feel they'd got something to play with. And then he came in at the end, of course, and took the last two wickets, but I think you might want to take a rather longer view than that, Peter, and tell us, not so much about being champions, but about this season.

SAINSBURY: John, it's been a wonderful season. I'm sure all the boys have thoroughly enjoyed themselves. We played the game under Ingleby-Mackenzie, our captain in a wonderful spirit. He keeps us going when things aren't going very well, and all I can say really is it's nice to be up on the top.

ARLOTT: Just tell me one thing, Peter, how hard has it been to change over from swinging the ball out of sight in all directions to being a responsible old number 5?

SAINSBURY: Well, it's come a bit hard for me, John. I had to pack up the old come-over on several occasions when I used to play it quite a lot. But I thoroughly enjoyed going in five and I really hope that I can stay there for a few more years.

ARLOTT: And catch them at short leg, I trust?

SAINSBURY: I hope so, yes.

ARLOTT: David White, I think the cricket critics would say, gave Hampshire this season that edge of really high pace, that changed them from a tight bowling side to a really attacking side, and his four wickets in one over against Sussex was yet another of the match-winning individual performances that every member of the side produced at some time during the season. The Bournemouth wicket wasn't completely what a fast bowler would ask, but I think he was happy enough not to be bowling while the wickets were falling. Now tell us, David, this is a season that's brought you selection for MCC to India, how do you feel about your cricket just at this moment?

WHITE: Well at the moment, I think we're all so pleased about winning the championship and as far as the Indian tour is concerned, John, it should be very hard work but it must be a wonderful experience and I'm really looking forward to it.

ARLOTT: Now do you reckon you're always bowling as fast as ever you can bowl?

WHITE: Well I don't think so, 'cos with a Hampshire side you always bowl such long spells and I think you bowl three, four quick balls an hour and when the captain comes up to you and says, 'I want everything you've got', and then one produces everything one's got, that's all you're asked of.

ARLOTT: Now just one other thing, they used to say

that you only moved the ball one way. That was in to the batsman. Now do you think you've extended that this year?

WHITE: I think yes, John; I think I learned a great deal from my first full season last year and with the aid of Derek Shackleton, I think I've definitely developed an away-swinger and only hope that with Derek's help again next year I develop a lot more.

ARLOTT: And just one other thing. Are you sorry that you made the shift to Hampshire?

WHITE: I shall never be sorry for that, never.

ARLOTT: Danny Livingstone comes from Antigua, and by way of Warwickshire this was his first full season in the Hampshire side, and he had the privilege, though it may not have seemed a privilege while it was in the air, of making the catch that ended the match that made Hampshire champions. But there are more things than that, that you'd like to talk about at the moment, Danny. What are they?

LIVINGSTONE: Well, I'd like to talk about the honour of being a member of the Hampshire side this year. I mean in every sense of the word it's been a team effort all the way along and I'm greatly honoured.

ARLOTT: Now your own batting has improved a lot, it's a lot sounder, but perhaps you don't score quite so quickly as you did. Do you think you're going to increase your scoring rate, yet again, in the seasons to come?

LIVINGSTONE: Well I hope so, but I find that in first-class cricket it's a lot different from second-class cricket. When I used to play in the second team I used to have to score very quickly. Now I find I've got a little bit more time and I can spend a bit more time building the innings.

ARLOTT: And would you also feel that your defence is sounder than before?

LIVINGSTONE: Well I think my defence is a lot sounder having come up against more accurate bowling.

ARLOTT: And I think we'd all want to say thanks for

that thousand runs in the season of yours that has given the county just that little lift in the middle order that it needed.

LIVINGSTONE: Well, thank you very much, John.

ARLOTT: It seems rather strange, that Jim Gray, who I knew as a lad, is now one of the elder statesmen and a very thoughtful all-rounder. Now he's opened the Hampshire innings for many seasons, never more valuable but in this season, and it can't always be easy batting somewhat in the shadow of Roy Marshall as far as spectators are concerned, but how much have you enjoyed this season, Jim?

GRAY: Well, John, I didn't think I'd live to see us top of the table and success is an easy thing to enjoy and I thoroughly enjoyed this season.

ARLOTT: How about the season on the way up. Did it seem hard?

GRAY: Oh very hard, yes. It's much easier when you're not near the top, when you're around middle having a reasonable season. You don't have the worries of having to win every game, although of course you still try.

ARLOTT: Now, of all the people that talk to you and who think it's just fun to be at the top of the table, is there anything you'd say to them about the strain of it as far as players are concerned?

GRAY: Well, John, a lot of people say it's harder for us at home listening, than for you playing. But we're there, we see more than they do. We know the real problems, and believe me, we're in the most difficult position.

ARLOTT: Now there's one question I'd like to put to you. I suspect that Middlesex, though a good side, cracked partly because they weren't used to this horrible top-of-the-table tension going on week after week. Now Hampshire had it in '55, again in '58. Do you think that hardened the side up temperamentally?

GRAY: Well, John, there's no substitute for experience, and we are a very experienced side. We've got a blend of youth and I think that experience has stood us in good stead in the final struggle, especially the last month. If you remember when we finished second, we won two games at the beginning of August and then never won another one. This time we lost those same two games against Kent, drew with Kent, lost to Essex, and we won every game since.

ARLOTT: And any particular facet of this season's side that made them champions and not nearly champions?

GRAY: Oh yes, yes. I think we've all, all of us have put something into this year. I think all eleven players that have played on one particular day have – when the start of the batting's failed, the middle batting's come off; when the middle batting's come off maybe the start has failed and I think we're a better balanced bowling side than we were when we finished second.

ARLOTT: It seems strange to call Henry Horton anything else but H, and I think all over England they know him as the straightest batsman in the business. But others know him, of course, as a very successful footballer with Blackburn and Southampton and with Hereford. But now what's your feeling about this season, Henry?

HORTON: Well, John, I've been with two relegated football teams, and to be in a winning side as champions is something that I never expected, and it's a great feeling.

ARLOTT: How do you feel about your own batting this year?

HORTON: Well, I'm always a little critical about my own batting, but I'm really quite satisfied as I've reached 2,000. I naturally would've liked to have reached a higher total.

ARLOTT: Now tell me, watching this side over the previous years when they missed the championship, what do you think was the difference this year?

HORTON: Well, I think we've been possibly keener this year, we've sensed that we had a chance. We started off the season very very well. We had about, I think, three wins out of four matches and we went from there on and we kept winning and I think that kept the spirits up and well, here we are as champions and it's the fact that we've had a great spirit that's brought us this achievement.

ARLOTT: Mike Barnard is another one who's just been raked out of the celebrations to say his word or two about this. For years we called him a promising player. My goodness, he redeemed the promise magnificently on the run in. Perhaps indeed his one innings, that century against Warwickshire when Hampshire seemed to be losing, stamped the side as a genuine championship team. Would you like to pick the story up at that point, Mike, and say how your batting's gone since then?

BARNARD: Well, I've had a bit of luck and things have gone rather well the last month I've been in the side. The boys have really been trying their best and the best has turned out to be good enough in the end, John.

ARLOTT: Well now Mike, I think this morning before you went in, you had a few butterflies in the stomach, right?

BARNARD: Yes, I think we all did. I don't know whether I had more or less than others.

ARLOTT: Well, what cleared those before you got 40 at a run a minute?

BARNARD: What cleared those? I think going up to Peter Sainsbury and saying don't take any quick singles. I had a slight pull in the leg muscle, John, and Peter said, 'You're probably quicker than me, anyway.' Somehow it made me settle down, he being there for two hours already, that helped a great deal.

ARLOTT: And then moving on to Alan Wassell; he's the youngest member of the side and I suppose, Derek Shackleton included, he's bowled more overs than anybody else in this match. A slow left-arm bowler. We think in Hampshire that he'll play for England before he's through, but for the moment he's probably more concerned with being a member of a championship side. How does it feel at this very short range, Alan?

WASSELL: It feels great, John, at the moment. I was terribly nervous to start off with today, but after Derek

Shackleton got those first quick wickets I settled down a bit and I didn't do badly, I suppose.

ARLOTT: Well now, the Surrey match was your personal triumph when you as a bowler almost won it; I can't say off your own bat as a bowler, but by yourself. Now do you feel that you've become a better player this season?

WASSELL: Well, I've learnt a lot this season, John. You know, experience and all that. I've had a bit of luck, I suppose, and things are going my way at the moment so, you know, it's not too bad.

ARLOTT: But now, you bowled yesterday, punctuated by the lunch interval, I suppose, for four hours and you hardly bowled a bad ball all that time. How did you manage to do that on relatively limited experience?

WASSELL: Well, I wouldn't say I didn't bowl many bad balls – I got a bit of stick, I suppose, but it's all concentration, you know, and things like that.

ARLOTT: Well you've got twenty years to come. I hope the concentration lasts out.

WASSELL: I hope so, John, yes.

ARLOTT: And even after that we must remember, of course, those very valuable reserves, who gave all that they were asked to give through the season. Dennis Baldry, Malcolm Heath, Brian Timms, Bernard Harrison. Not to forget Arthur Holt, who's coached so many of these young local Hampshire players and made them into first-class cricketers, who's done a magnificent job behind the scenes. And time, too, to remember we're grateful to this side, but we're grateful, too, to those who began the Hampshire cricketing tradition. Four of the great, no longer alive to relish this victory. Lionel, Lord Tennyson, the great Philip Mead, Alec Kennedy that early Shackleton, and Alex Bowell. But of that great early side, George Brown, Jack Newman and Walter Livsey and before them Charlie Llewellyn are still alive to relish the feat their successors have brought off. And so are some of those who helped in the hard hoe between the two wars. Johnnie Arnold, Lofty Herman, Neil McCorkell, Jim Bailey and later still Neville Rogers and Vic Cannings. Yes, this today was a great day for Hampshiremen. Cricketers and their supporters, at last it had come true. Hampshire, County Champions.

BBC Home Service, September 1961

37

Broncho, Badminton, Beer and Skittles

John maintains an interest in all sport. Once asked about his golfing ability, John replied, 'If it goes on improving I may become poor.'

One evening in Brisbane, on the 1954–5 tour of Australia, John was invited to watch the beefy belt 'em brigade in a 'punch-up' on the outskirts of town. His graphic account of the contest contrasts sharply with a cool assessment of badminton in Britain that follows.

Badminton was John's best game. He once played a Hampshire county trial and says that 'the sport gave me up when war broke out'.

He's also played all the games under scrutiny in 'Experts at Beer and Skittles' (below): 'It indicates the amount of time spent in pubs.'

Broncho

Rodrigo Marcos, although a Spaniard of Spain, was clearly unaccustomed to the type of heat that Brisbane calls normal. In his own land, the sun may burn, but there is always escape into the shade. In the hot-house humidity of Queensland, where pineapples grow like weeds, the only corrective to irritability is air-conditioning.

Brisbane, however, is slightly more temperate than the Queensland backblock township of Mareeba on the Atherton Tableland, known – insofar as it is known at all – as the air-base for the Battle of the Coral Sea and the postal address of Donald Johnson. Johnson is known as 'Broncho' to the five thousand observers of boxing who compress themselves, every Friday night, into the Brisbane Stadium. There, under the arc-lamps and the dark weight of ceiling, they conspire with the normal climate of the city to create an atmosphere in which the mere act of breathing acts as a perspiration pump, and all voluntary movement is reduced to a gingerly minimum.

Johnson is not taken entirely seriously by the local spectators. To be sure, he was amateur middleweight boxing champion of Australia before he became a professional to relieve his family's temporary financial difficulties by undertaking five fights, in a booth, for a total 'purse' of five shillings. His training consists largely of tree-felling in intervals of rough-riding, horse-breaking and the staging of rodeos in the sparsely populated areas of North Queensland. His wife is purely of the first Australian people and, when her husband's various employments take him from home, she and their two children travel in the caravan attached to the rear of his car. One of the major difficulties of arranging fights for the Broncho is that from time to time he will decide to 'go walkabout', as the aboriginals call it, so that he cannot be found for several weeks.

In appearance Johnson is more remarkable than impressive. His vast mop of black hair continues down his cheeks in two fan-shaped side-whiskers; the remains of the beard he removes for appearance in the boxing ring. His dressing-gown is decorated with a large picture of a bucking horse and, when he takes it off, his body appears no more than serviceable. His chest is not deep nor his arms thick; his legs look unathletic and the size of his feet gives more promise of balance than suggestion of aesthetically pleasing proportion.

Rodrigo Marcos, undefeated welterweight champion of Spain, has added weight until he fights at 11 stone 4lb, but he looks an athlete. He is powerfully built, with strong shapely legs, firm arms and a sturdy neck; his face has a cast of breeding: it is lively and little marked by his trade. Johnson versus Marcos was the main match of the evening.

The spectator in front of me wore the wide-brimmed trilby hat and the half-sleeved shirt, open at the neck, which mark the Australian on a sporting occasion. Turning round to the rows of faces which shone and steamed back into the darkness of the five-shilling seats, he shouted, with little hope, 'I'll bet five to one.' He had no need to indicate that he was laying odds against Johnson. The appearance of the two boxers in the ring was already enough to promise a one-sided fight.

It was confirmed by the first round, in which the Spaniard gave a skilful demonstration of attacking boxing. It was marred – without discredit to the demonstrator – only by the fact that Johnson would not play his part. Instead of giving ground, he continued to advance, however hard he was hit, in a belligerent shuffle towards his opponent. From time to time, indeed, he came close enough to him to embrace him, and grind his stubbly jaw, with a half-tender roll of the head, into the hollow of Marcos's shoulder while seeming to congratulate him with slaps on the back of the neck and over the kidneys. He had a habit of breaking from clinches with his right hand cupped over his ear as if he were straining to hear some whisper from Marcos. His body reddened under quick, whippy punches and a swing peeled his nose like a tomato.

Yet, as the gong went for the end of the round, Johnson drew himself up and, breathing in the greatest possible volume of the oxygen-starved air his lungs could contain, swaggered with a self-conscious air of mastery to his corner.

For one three-minute round after another, Johnson walked determinedly if ungracefully towards Marcos and Marcos punched him. Perhaps once in a round Johnson landed a punch: Marcos landed a dozen. Four times Johnson's upswinging fist made a strange angular line in the space where Marcos had been a moment before. Tobacco smoke had turned the steam-heat into a swamp mist. Punches landed with the sound of a boot clapped into a puddle. Gloves stamped against Johnson's guarding arms and hands, against his face and ribs.

It was a gladiatorial certainty that he could not last four rounds. Yet he swaggered only a little wearily back to the ice-water and ironic sympathy of his seconds after the seventh round. He had barely moved from his stool for the eighth round when Marcos ran at him and hit him and hit him again and again with a feminine intensity. Johnson could not fall down, the ropes were at his back. He started to walk towards Marcos, through the blows. Then he put his arms round him, pinioning his arms and, resting his gritty chin again on Marcos's shoulder, put out his tongue. 'He's tough,' said an Australian, 'you can't knock him down except with an axe.' 'Johnson's knees is wobbling,' tore a bugle voice in my ear, 'the Broncho's had it, he can't take another punch.' Someone – was it me? – said, 'A pound he doesn't go down.'

In the ninth round, Johnson still walked towards Marcos, and Marcos, in intervals of almost hysterical punching, leant on Johnson. Late in the tenth round Johnson hit Marcos: not very hard, for he was tired. Marcos staggered, partly fell through the ropes. Johnson pressed forward, stumbled, hit Marcos again, off one knee; the gong sounded. Johnson swaggered to his corner, Marcos went slowly to his; the referee followed him. He was jaunty but he was a cold grey colour. He could not come to his feet for the eleventh round. The referee raised Johnson's hand as the winner. Johnson acknowledged the applause with a perfunctory smile and a wave.

Then Johnson, who is used to the Queensland climate, bathed and changed and waited the long three-quarters of an hour until Marcos had recovered from his chilled fatigue. The Broncho's vocabulary and style of speech stem purely from the Bible. He declared himself well pleased with the fight and so valiant an opponent. He received the sum of £400 for the fight. It is said in Brisbane that Broncho Johnson is a showman.

The Spectator, January 1955

Shuttle Service

The badminton season has been at its busiest. It is the only athletic sport, if we except table tennis, widely available on murky, cold, wet nights; and it vies with hockey among British games in being, simultaneously, highly skilled, fast, competitive, satisfying, underestimated, under-publicized and truly amateur. It is not a spectator sport in this country, and the non-playing public tend to hear more of it than they see. The evening thump and thunder of hurrying feet on wooden floors echoing from countless village, church and parish halls – and any other kind of building with room, often only by a hair's breadth, for a court 44 × 20ft – throughout the country, argues the width of its spread. It is played at county, national and international level in more commodious conditions, but its health, if not its strength, lies in the provinces and villages. Three thousand clubs, with 70,000 members, are affiliated to the Badminton Association of England, whose officers cannot guess at the number of unaffiliated clubs who, with schools, may account for half as many more unregistered players.

In the muddled ancestry of the game, an Indian form probably was more paternal than an English battledore and shuttlecock, but it took shape and name on the Duke of Beaufort's estate – Badminton – in the 1860s, and matured in Britain. Every winner of the All-England Championships (begun in 1899, and still the major individual competition) came from England or Ireland until 1939, when Danes won the men's singles and ladies' doubles, and a Canadian the ladies' singles. England were unbeaten in international matches from the first, in 1902–03, until they lost to Denmark in 1948. Since the Second World War, however, the idiom of the game has changed and the power has shifted, first to Denmark, and, latterly, to South-east Asia.

The outstanding British players of the formative period, such as the great J.F. Devlin, were spectacular, extrovert and physical. The coolly concentrating American, Dr

Freeman, unbeaten in singles in his short post-war career, indicated the new way, and the Malayan, Wong Peng Soon, took it, to become the finest individual player in the world. He ghosted about the court, beat internationals without taking off his cardigan or breaking sweat. The badminton smash is one of the fastest and most stirring strokes in any game: Wong's timing and wrist power were such that he seemed to play it with no more than a simple upward stretch of the racquet, while he picked up the same shot from his opponents at sauntering ease. The Malays have inherited from him as by nature.

The world competition for the Thomas Cup – given by Sir George Thomas, father figure of the game – held three-yearly since 1948–9, has been won four times by Malaysia and three by Indonesia. Badminton has become pre-eminently the game of South-east Asia. For this year's Thomas Cup challenge round between Indonesia and Malaysia, in Djakarta, the hall was filled with 12,000 people, and thousands more were turned away. The match was abandoned by the English referee because of the biased and unruly behaviour of the crowd and, when Indonesia did not agree to complete it in New Zealand, the Cup was awarded to Malaysia. This matter, however, will not disturb the surface of English domestic badminton where, for a season's subscription of two or three guineas (shuttlecocks supplied), the social life of the local tennis club continues through the winter. They have their special problems: the ideal court is at least 30ft high, but theirs often is a bare fifteen, so low that games are won by the wily who steer the 'bird' through the spider's web of rafters or girders ('fault on the striker's side of the net, let on the other'); there should be a minimum five feet of space behind the base line, but many a man has played a long clearance at Basingstoke with the stove singeing his shorts.

The real battle, though, is with the Saturday-night dancers who put down French chalk to make the floor slippery. The badminton players retaliate – of old with Vim or a mixture of tea-leaves, sand and water, but latterly with special preparations – to give themselves a secure foothold for fast turning; the dancers, in their turn, execrate and destroy it on the following Saturday. There are other problems. The young man caught in an occasional evening of preponderantly female attendance fumes when he sits out more than the usual hour (for a one-court club) and has to suffer the endless tedium of a ladies' four, in the hope that, if he stays late, he may bribe the caretaker to delay closing the hall to allow a furious men's singles.

The Listener, March 1968

Experts at Beer and Skittles

Pub games have declined considerably since the days when the tavern stood with the parish church as a centre of English social life. Except, perhaps, in a few secret places, legislation has stamped out cock-fighting, dog-fighting, dog-and-rat fights that survived bull-baiting, bear-baiting and thrashing-the-hen as sports of the inn yard. Gaming in taverns was a serious anxiety in Tudor times, but the GAMBLING PROHIBITED notice is now so generally respected that, of card games, only cribbage – played at high speed – has endured to any extent. Of the other table games, dominoes has proved the hardiest.

Trap ball – bat and trap – still survives in some Kentish pub gardens; and knur and spell, its northern counterpart, in some regions of Lancashire and Yorkshire. In the eighteenth century almost every inn, town or country, had a bowling green or alley, but bowls has tended to move away to private clubs and public parks.

In the past thirty years darts has become the most important of all public-house games. Of the several games that can be played on a darts board, the standard form now is 301 up, starting and ending with a double, with the treble settled as a middle belt after experimenting with V set inwards from the outside – or double – ring. Local leagues and national individual championships are firmly established, and the best players will score their two, or even three, treble twenties each time they go to the board, or make their double out with a couple of darts. The darts themselves have changed during the past twenty years, from the comparatively light, wooden-stemmed type with feather flight to a shorter kind with much heavier metal body carrying plastic flights, which are thrown through a lower and faster arc. Boards, too, have developed from solid timber - often dipped in bar slops to prevent them from drying and splitting - to elaborate bristle or rubber.

Casual games of darts - usually in the public bar - are governed by the convention that the winning player or pair continues to play until beaten by one of a series of challengers. Each 'best of three' is understood to be played for a drink which, unless previously varied, should not be more expensive than a half-pint of best ale.

Skittles is firmly established in the West, largely in Somerset and Gloucestershire, and especially in Bristol. The alleys, often in a separate building and sometimes of great age, vary from stone or cement floors, rumbling to the passage of the weighty cheeses of rural Somerset, to the new rinks in Bristol where the smaller ball flies along the highly polished boards as if on ice. Here, too, in numerous leagues, teams from pubs and clubs maintain a remarkably high standard of precise skill. The bar-room form of skittles is a table ninepin game with a ball swinging on a string from a vertical stick, and called 'The Devil Among the Tailors'. This had a brief vogue, but the sets that remain are usually idle and, like the rings thrown on to numbered hooks on a board that flourished in the twenties, seem to be dying for sheer lack of interest.

Shove-ha'penny, if only because of the time taken to play a game, remains a casual amusement, with expert performers few and far between and the boards nowadays more often polished with French chalk or furniture polish than wiped with beer, as was once the custom.

The billiards table in most inns has gone to make more room for people who come to drink. Where it survives it imparts to its setting a more cathedral atmosphere than any other public room in the house. The billiards room is no longer the centre of local raffish life: the once familiar figure of the marker has almost disappeared and even billiards itself has largely given way to snooker.

The licensed house has changed from a place where men drink, talk and play games, to a resort of mixed company for drink, talk and the preliminaries of courtship. Darts and skittles flourish partly because they are encouraged and provided for by brewers and publicans, who recognize that a home match brings a volume of trade that would not otherwise exist in midweek. These games still throw up their experts, though none is comparable at skittles to that legendary all-round sportsman Sammy Woods. In the main, however, the customers of the modern public house prefer the entertainment of the 'telly' to entertaining themselves.

The Times, April 1958

38

Cricketers are always Convivial Companions

The pub on the edge of the village green is, of course, an integral part of the tapestry of cricket.

So many English pubs are called 'The Cricketers Arms' or 'The Bat and Ball' that the game must always have been associated with conviviality. Indeed that cricket classic, *The Young Cricketer's Tutor* has no more lyrical passage than Nyren's entire page devoted to the drinks served at Hambledon – 'Punch – stark! – would make a cat speak' and 'Barleycorn such as would put the souls of three

'Bat and Ball' inn, Hambledon, around the beginning of this century.

Taking tea with the Gloucestershire and New Zealand teams, 1949.

butchers into one weaver. Ale that would flare like turpentine – genuine Boniface – this immortal viand.'

We know, too, that on the first morning of a home match, W.G. Grace used to greet his friends with the cryptic remark, 'She's down the well, she's down the well.' 'She' meant 'The Widow' – Veuve Cliquot champagne – which he had lowered down the well on a string to chill it for dinner that night. W.G.'s drink during a long day's play, however, was the unusual one of a large Irish whiskey with Angostura bitters and soda.

Harold Larwood's first county captain – Arthur Carr – taught him to drink beer because he believed in the old cricketers' adage that a fast bowler needs something to sweat out. Larwood's other – England – captain, Douglas Jardine once told me that when he was in the field throughout a hot day he used to order at teatime a double Scotch in a cup of hot, strong and very sugary tea – the whisky for a quick lift, the sugar to sustain him.

In the dressing room at the same match.

A well-known bowler of my acquaintance, under the impression that he would not have to bat that day, once refreshed himself after a long spell with a number of pints of beer. His side collapsed and, as he left the dressing-room to bat, one of his colleagues said, 'Play the middle ball.' He was bowled first ball and on his return, before anyone else could utter a word, he said, 'There were two middle balls.'

Perhaps cricketers drink less nowadays than they once did, though they remain convivial company. The men of old would have raised at least their eyebrows at the sight of bottles of milk being taken into the dressing-room, though there have been some distinguished teetotallers. Sir Jack Hobbs was virtually a total abstainer and non-smoker during his playing days. He took this stand solely on his estimate of maximum fitness. After he retired he enjoyed an occasional cigar and a glass of wine – especially champagne in the mornings. On the other hand, Frank Tyson once said that all his great Test bowling performances occurred after he had drunk red wine with his dinner of the previous evening.

The Hampshire team were at one time an enthusiastic and critical group of burgundy drinkers while Glamorgan have, on occasions, matched their enthusiasm, if not their criticism. Perhaps the last word may come from an old friend of mine. He had just made a 'King Pair' – out first ball in each innings; and he buried his nose in a pint pot with the words, 'I don't know how teetotallers put up with cricket.'

Jack Bond, the Little Giant (*John Kay*), *1970*

39

THE THREE GREAT C'S – KILKENNY, CLARET, CRICKET

It comes as no great surprise to discover that even in Ireland cricketers like to raise their glasses:

In June, 1832, Lord Ossory inscribed a book to Henry Baker. Then, finding that he had written on the back flyleaf, he turned it round and wrote again, at the front. That book, signed at both ends, is beside me as I write. It is a quarto, of twenty leaves, printed on one side only, and consists of prose, cricket scores and verse. Its title, in the rolling manner of the period, is *A Short Account of the Origin of the Kilkenny Cricket Club and of its Proceedings in the Years 1830–1831*: and it was published in London in 1832.

Apart from play between members, the club had only one game in 1830 – against the Twenty-first Regiment, then stationed at Kilkenny and who were beaten by an innings. In August of that year, the Ballinasloe Club challenged Kilkenny to 'an immediate match'. But, we read, 'An answer was returned by Lord Ossory declining to play at that period of the year, in consequence of the impossibility of making up an eleven. It may not be improper here to state that the meeting of the club is considered at an end on August 1, in consequence of the approach of the shooting season. The Ballinasloe Club, however, claimed it as a victory, and it was entered on their books accordingly.' Now the point of the book emerges with: 'Fortunately for Kilkenny, an opportunity was not long wanting for doing away with any erroneous ideas that might have arisen from this circumstance; for at the beginning of the season in 1831, a second challenge was sent from Ballinasloe.'

Kilkenny accepted: the match was played on their ground at Johnswell, and they won by 16 runs. Walshe, one-eyed, long-legged and long-armed, was their top scorer with 31 in the first innings; and, though the score is given in the old manner which only credits the bowler with wickets actually bowled down, Lord Ossory, with nine clean bowled in the two innings, was clearly most effective.

The return match was played on Lord Dunlo's ground at Garbally. There was a certain amount of 'edge' to the game – the clubs were not only in different counties of Kilkenny and Galway, but in rival kingdoms of Leinster and Connaught; as the verse has it –

Encouraged by their run of luck
  In county matches many,
They took it in their heads to send
  A challenge to KILKENNY:
Not doubting that they'd take the shine
  From out the men of LEINSTER,
For CONNAUGHT had a foolish whim
  That nought could stand against her.

Ballinasloe, batting first, made 97 –

But how can their brief fates be told?
How Clayton caught! and WILLIAM bowled!
How Harry stumped! and 'YARD-AND-A-HALF'
Picked bombs off the point of the bat with a laugh!

In Kilkenny's innings, Butler and Walshe put on 104 for the first wicket.

Next our 'NOVICE' and 'CYCLOPS' went in for the day
With DONLO'S slow lobs hit in sixers away . . .

Walshe retired after a blow on the knee, but resumed his innings at *8 a.m.* on the second day. Kilkenny's 248 was a dispiriting total. Bayly and Harry Baker – the recipient of the book from Lord Ossory, who alternated between wicket-keeper and fast-bowling – put out Ballinasloe for 77 –

> And when the second match was o'er
> And we could count our winnings,
> We found we'd beat by SEVENTY-FOUR,
> And in a SINGLE INNINGS!!

In the prose account of the subsequent celebrations – 'As soon as we had crossed the Shannon we transplanted a few trees on the Stuart principle, attached them to the coach, and having cheered through Leinster, reached Kilkenny at half past one, rending the welkin with our Hurrahs. We determined to steep our laurels at the Club on Tuesday the 27th instant, and expected to have a dropping evening.'

The first of the poetasters expresses it –

> So steep we our laurels till morning's light
> For *bats* have a claim to enjoy the night,
> And sure 'tis but justice, if each jolly soul
> From *bowling* down *bails* turns to *baling* the *bowl*.

But the last word may lie with the second versifier – reputedly Lord Clanricarde –

> And now, my boys, give one cheer more,
> For Bat, Ball, Bails and Wicket,
> While I propose the three great C's,
> KILKENNY, CLARET, CRICKET.

The Cricketer, May 1965

40

BEAUJOLAIS, FIZZ AND ICED COFFEE

For many years now, John has been wine correspondent of the Guardian. *A piece for the paper in 1978 on vigneron Ernest Aujas sealed the coveted Glenfiddich Wine Writer of the Year award for its author.*

You are on the north road out of Julienas when you pass the Coq d'Or and Chez la Rose, next door to each other on your left. Tiny as they are, they are two of the dozen best restaurants in the entire Beaujolais. The road, like any other in Beaujolais, never continues straight for more than a few metres; but soon it runs like a shelf let into the hillside of south-east facing vineyards. After perhaps a kilometre, a stream, less than a yard wide, comes sparkling down the hillside on your right. It crosses the road through a shallow conduit and then leaps into the wall of a grey stone house, of which only a single – windowless – storey shows at road level.

This is the home, press-house, cellar, and bottling shed of the vigneron, Ernest Aujas. There is no footpath; the wide wooden doors at the end of the building give directly on to the narrow road and, when they are opened, the ancient, hand, wine-press can be filled directly from trucks standing in the roadway.

At the other end, the path just wide enough for the family truck, turns, hairpin, quickly down to bottom floor level of the house, while the hill tumbles on steeply away; so steeply indeed that the plough is drawn up the vineyard slope by a winch. The cellar yard is cut deeply into the hill and on the bank rest the carcases of a couple of cars, a dozen or so worn out tractor tyres, a heap of gnarled, grubbed-up vine-roots, and an orderly mountain of empty, green Burgundy bottles waiting to be filled.

The ground floor of the house, its windows looking out across its own hill to others, and the cellar, are one solid, stone-built unit, running far back into the earth. The stream bursts from its under-floor tunnel, across the yard and gushes on, between the rabbit hutches and the dog kennels, through the garden patch and the olive trees, and down the hill.

Ernest Aujas is strongly built, six feet tall, sixty years old; his face weather-beaten to a brick red; a sun-bleached beret partly covers his white hair; the frilly stub of a hand-rolled cigarette clings to his lower lip. No spendthrift of words, he answers questions with the quiet certainty of a man who has worked out his problems.

He shares the labour of a six hectare (ten acre) vineyard with his son. They split the proceeds 3½/2½: the son will inherit. Roughly speaking, the son cultivates the vineyard, the father maintains the cellar, vinifies, bottles and packs. This, though, is a harsh work-load possible only with family help from wives, cousins, even grandparents, at busy times; a team of as many as two dozen Portuguese – mainly students – in the ten to fifteen-day vendage.

The cellar is gravity fed from the press at road level; five vast and four smaller, but still mighty barrels hold the wine. In March 1978, the 1976, big and tannic, was still unbottled. M. Aujas, content that he had a fine vintage did not propose to hurry it. It was safe in his cellar, where the temperature is safely static, and he takes regular samples of all his wines – and allows them to his visitors – in the traditional tastevin which hangs, worn and gleaming, from a tape about his neck. He never fines nor filters; his is a natural wine that throws a natural deposit.

He bottles it himself – as many as 20,000 bottles in a good year – in his primitive one-man bottling machine. His 1976 was still a big tannic wine last spring. As always, he refused to bottle except when the wind was in the north and the moon on the wane.

Now some of that wine has arrived in England, ready to drink; but it will be better yet. Substantially bigger than a normal Beaujolais, almost of the stature of a fine Burgundy, it has the usual Julienas bouquet of summer fields; and, while the taste is fresh, clean and young in the classic Beaujolais fashion, on the palate it is full and round with a perfumed quality which is by no means usual. It is as if it were the essence of Beaujolais.

The Guardian, 1978

As a summer variation, there were tips for holidays and balmy evenings, whether the tipple be champagne, Pimm's, or just iced coffee.

Play It Cool: Open a Bottle of Fizz

If all be right that I do think
There are five reasons we should drink.
Good wine – a friend – or being dry –
Or lest we should be by and by –
Or any other reason why.

Thus – originally in Latin – Henry Aldrich, the interesting seventeenth century divine, scholar, musician, and architect, twenty-one years Dean of Christ Church, Oxford. In addition to learned works, he wrote a catch on smoking 'to be sung by four men smoking their pipes, not more difficult than diverting to hear.' He also drank, and was well liked.

Summer is an appropriate time for drinking; like spring, autumn, and winter. The most refreshing, cooling – and exhilarating – summer (spring, autumn, or winter) drink is, as has been said so often before, champagne. Depressing, but true, the finer the champagne, the higher the price. Happily, France, Spain, Germany (for those of sweet tooth, Italy), and, latterly, Alsace, all produce cheaper sparkling wines, a number of which are quite as good as some cheap champagnes.

The cheaper fizzes are happy in an imitation 'champagne cocktail'. Put a lump of sugar in a flute glass; drench it with Angostura bitters; add a healthy dash of brandy, and top up with the iced sparkler. Or Buck's Fizz; put the juice of a whole orange in a long glass and fill with the iced fizz. It is well worth while using fresh orange juice.

Historically, of course, the drink to wash dust out of British throats, and replace British sweat, is beer; and it remains the country's most popular drink. Its province has been invaded by lemonade and ginger beer in shandy, which some beermen still regard as the root of a heresy swollen by the addition of ice to their traditionally lukewarm beverage. Wine's answer to beer is Beaujolais, the quaffing drink of the bereted boule players of France: best taken chilled.

For some, summer sunshine evokes a vision of lounging in a deckchair imbibing a long, well-iced Pimm's, its flavoured freshness reinforced by the tingle of fizzy lemonade. They mean, of course Pimm's No 1, first created a hundred years ago by James Pimm at his Oyster Bar in Poultry, and bottled at the request of captivated customers. Its fame spread rapidly across the world, and a supply was sent to General Gordon's officers' mess at Omdurman and, before their tragic end, at Khartoum. Basically it is a gin sling; the remaining ingredients are a firm secret: and it is debasement to add more than lemon, borage (mint at a pinch), cucumber, ice, and fizzy lemonade.

The firm, who describe themselves as 'Compounders', used to make six of these 'cups'. No 2 was based on scotch whisky; No 3 on brandy; No 4 the winter warmer, on rum; No 5 on rye whiskey; No 6 on vodka. In 1972 when No 1 accounted for 95 per cent of sales, the other five were abandoned. Although the No 6 has since been revived. No 1 remains the major product, with worldwide sales, and is made under licence in France and Canada.

Those who count eating French oysters a summer delight – with no worry about an 'r' in the month – whether in France or imported, will relish wines to go with them. Chablis, golden green, and, at its best, a great wine, used to be regarded as obligatory. Round about the French oyster beds nowadays; they eat them with those happily rounded Loire wines, such as a Muscadet de Sevre-et-Maine, Fief de la Brie, or Sancerre. Or, ambitiously and somewhat extravagantly, try a Coteaux Champenois – the still champagne, deep and dry and full and powerful.

What with strawberries, raspberries, melon, peaches, apricots? Sauternes or Barsac, luscious as they are, so far from being astronomically dear, are probably the cheapest French wines on the English market. Otherwise, the neighbouring Monbazillac white – called the poor man's Sauternes is similarly and genuinely – by 'the noble rot' – rich and worth searching for.

The faithful will not miss their quota of claret or burgundy in the warm weather. Still, the white wines make the obvious summer appeal; sweet or dry to taste. To do the whites justice, ice – but do not freeze – them; overchilling takes away both bouquet and flavour; and deals the teeth and the roof of the mouth a savage blow. Aim at cool cellar temperature. Say, for a dry white wine, 12 degrees C; rose 12 degrees C; champagne, certainly in the summer, can be 8 degrees C; so can the sweet dessert whites. Chilling in a refrigerator will take best part of a couple of hours from tepid; but use the bottom shelf, wine does not like violent change; an ice bucket does the job in a quarter of an hour.

Sangria is the classic Spanish cup. Take a large jug and slice into it an apple, an orange, a lemon, and a few skinned and seeded grapes: add juice of a lemon add a dash of brandy. Pour in two bottles of (good Spanish) red wine; top up with a bottle of champagne, sparkler, or soda water. Stand it in the refrigerator for an hour before serving.

Kir – named for the French priest, resistance leader, and mayor of Dijon – remains a summer favourite. Simply enough, pour a spoonful of creme de cassis into a wine

The bouquet is eminently satisfactory.

glass and fill up with – for a true Kir – a well chilled Bourgogne Aligote. Others use other white wines; or some a sparkler, when they call it Kir Royale.

For teetotallers the various fruit juices will blend into some colourful glasses. Be ambitious – use passion fruit juice, coconut cream, French sirops like cassis, grenadine, framboise. Tomato juice seasoned to taste with Worcestershire sauce, celery salt, or paprika; yogurt, mixed fifty-fifty with water or soda water and pepped with salt and pepper, are sophisticated non-alcoholics.

For teenagers, try tea or coffee made to double strength and poured over cracked ice, with or without sugar; or strong cafe au lait over ice, with ice cream. For the small children try one of grenadine, two of lemon juice and six of raspberry syrup with a lump of ice, and a few raspberries floating on top. Or – infallible with the really young – one of hot water, one of sugar, four squares bitter chocolate (melted), hint of salt, teaspoon of vanilla. That is the syrup. Take one of syrup to eight of milk: froth up in a blender, pour over ice, and crown with whipped cream.

A fine hock drunk in the garden of an evening will blend its aroma with that of the flowers. A Schloss Vollrads Riesling Kabinett 1979 or young Moselle will enliven the palate. The delightfully clean Alsace wines, especially the Riesling, with its steely freshness, but also the unusual Muscat-raisins on the nose, dry on the palate are unique.

Still, though, that Coteaux Champenois lingers; Berry Brothers & Rudd quote their Binet, accurately, but also beguilingly, as 'vin nature et tranquille'; the huge Chardonnay, Blanc de Blanc, of Ruinart is like being run over by a steam roller with rubber tyres. Refreshing and thirst-quenching during the hot day; the white wines of the world become ruminative pleasure in a summer evening when there is relaxed time for them to titillate the nostrils, flood unhurriedly and savourily over the palate, and leave behind their particular aftertaste. Neither eating nor drinking holds a greater delight.

The Guardian, 1982

41

A Commentary Box of Bamboo and Palm Fronds . . .

A commentator might need iced coffee to sustain him in some pretty and unlikely places:

Idyllic is not a word commonly associated with commentary boxes, but it could be used without great extravagance of the structure that prompted these musings. Gray's Inn, on the north coast of Jamaica, was receiving a visit from an overseas team for the first time. The ground was, in a way, reminiscent of Swansea. On the north side, the road runs along the edge of the fence with the railway and Annotto Bay Station behind it, a couple of lazily swaying palms and then the whole distant sweep of the Caribbean, far bluer than the blue of Swansea Bay. But one nostalgic Welshman – Owen Davies, doyen of Jamaican umpires – muttered, again and again – 'St Helens – yes, yes – St Helens.'

The temporary stands were in place for the first time. More than three thousand people had paid a sum far greater than the club's coffers had ever known before – and to the rapture of the local children the Brigadier had flown in and landed his helicopter on the ground in front of the pavilion to watch the play. Not only was it the first broadcast ever made from Gray's Inn, but the Jamaican Post Office could not offer a lines service nearer than ten miles distant, so some very high frequency indeed was called for – with mixed success. But, for the visiting commentator, it was something of an occasion: the commentary box – or to be precise, squared arch – had walls of

Phew!

still-green bamboo stakes and a roof of even greener palm fronds. What matter that elderly rum-punchers rumbled deeply at our backs, or that their juniors, leaping to their feet in excitement at every local success completely obscured the view of play? A commentary box of bamboo and palms, somehow, completed the circle.

Circles, fortunately, do not start, so this one may be broken at any point. We might come in at the point of no box at all. At the short-lived Ellis Park, which housed Tests at Johannesburg between the two Wanderers grounds, the commentator stood in the narrow strip between the boundary line and the crowd-fence with straps round his shoulders, carrying a board like a muffin man's tray with a microphone standing in the middle.

The roof-top positions at Cardiff Arms Park and St Helens, Swansea, used to be completely enviable when the sun shone, harsh places in the rain: emergency cover has removed the problem.

Immediately after the war, the pre-1939 box still clung to the wall opposite the scoreboard at Old Trafford. Bombing had blown away the hand-rail and most of the steps, and to see C.B. Fry, then in his seventies, swing his way up, monocle firmly fixed, binoculars swinging, was to know genuine admiration for the traditions of athleticism and the Royal Navy. Eventually, as had been threatening for years, a storm blew the old box down into the road behind – and splinters. Thereupon broadcasting was transferred to a hermetically sealed room in the score-box: air has since been introduced mechanically.

Most commentary boxes, however, are one-night stand affairs, sited as a result of compromise between a BBC engineer and the ground secretary, each doing his best to preserve his own people's interests. In the days when a scorer was solely a Test match luxury, commentators were housed in little, green, wooden boxes with just sufficient room for one in comfort, two in acute discomfort. The commentator relied implicitly on the scoreboard and endeavoured, when a wicket fell, to fill in his score-card while talking about something else – or attempting to give the impression of repeating the facts at dictation speed for the listener. In one such arrangement at Bath, the engineer had not appreciated that only one scoreboard maintained the running total and the individual scores of the batsmen. So when the commentary box was set down exactly in line with that board, there was no view at all of its highly relevant data. The scoreboard, built on huge trestles, looked as if it might be movable: at the expense

Now, what's all this about?

of a ricked back and a pulled thigh-muscle it was proved that two men could not move it an inch. After ludicrously elaborate experiments with mirrors, the eventual solution was for a friend to stand fractionally inside the boundary with a sideways view of the score, writing it down and turning it to the commentary box. Memory recalls, too, a weird, green, tarpaulin igloo at Leicester, wide open to the prevailing wind, which always seemed to prevail markedly on match days.

It compared oddly indeed with the present-day carpeted, boardroom air of the box at Trent Bridge: the perfect, lofty view at the Oval: the intimate but roomy box at Edgbaston: the spacious, yet still poorly angled viewpoint at Lord's: and the straight-down-the-pitch aquarium at Headingley.

Yet the engineers themselves are probably proudest of their ingenious, fixed-in a jiffy, outside broadcast vans where, in a few minutes, steering wheel and all controls disappear under desk-tops, windscreens can be raised or closed and kept wiped, and a whole day's broadcasting can be recorded only inches away from the microphone or fed, on the instant of a distant cue into services stretching to five continents.

Science – it's wonderful: but I hope the Leicester igloo has been preserved for the eventual museum of radio.

The Cricketer, March 1965

42

THE WEST INDIES SIDE OF '63

There can be few more popular sides to have visited British shores than the West Indies 'class' of '63. Here, in effect, were the one-time pupils from the islands showing the one-time 'teachers' in the old country how the game should be played. Led by the astute and caring Frank Worrell, the West Indies were a perfectly balanced cricketing unit with their bowling spearheaded by the devastatingly fast Wesley Hall and the fearsome Charlie Griffith.

On the second day of the second Test at Lord's, England had kept their opponent's first innings within reasonable bounds at 301. They then faced an uphill struggle having lost two wickets for 20. Dexter and Barrington came together and Dexter proceeded to bat with superb disdain. John continues with commentary:

It's Hall to bowl now to Dexter. He comes in from the Nursery end at full speed and bowls, and Dexter plays that very calmly back down the pitch off the middle of the bat as if Hall were a medium pacer. There is about Dexter, when he chooses to face fast bowling with determination, a sort of air of command that lifts him, or seems to lift him, above ordinary players. He seems to find time to play the fastest of bowling and still retain dignity, something near majesty, as he does it.

Hall comes in again then. Bowls to Dexter, Dexter goes onto the back foot and hits him square away to third man, he's imposed a third man on the West Indies, it's Butcher, but with the single which takes the total to 35 that third man moves up and becomes a fourth slip for Barrington. So there are two silly mid-ons, a leg slip, three slips. Now he's turned and run out again. So there's a third man for Barrington also. Just Gibbs in front of the wicket on the offside. Another change there and Hunte has come from leg slip to backward short leg. Moved a full ten yards.

Hall comes in, bowls to Barrington and Barrington dabs down on a ball of full length. Gibbs whips it in from cover, carries the stumps and McMorris was backing up and stopped it. A well taken quick single, taking England to 36, Barrington to five, Dexter 23.

Now Hunte has moved back to leg slip, so again we have five men in a row there within a sixth of a circle and very deep indeed and there's no doubt that the ball's going to carry if it's nicked.

Hall bowls, Dexter flicks down the leg side. Another no-ball and Hall hangs his head quite penitently. May well be, I fancy, that English umpires, since the new rules, the front-foot rule, have become altogether more no-ball conscious and find, in fact, watching the back foot easier in terms of quickness of shout than watching the front foot. This is a strange thing, but so it seems to be. The front-foot call comes slower than the back-foot call.

In again comes Hall from the Nursery end. Bowls to Dexter who gets over it and hooks it imperiously downward past McMorris at silly mid-on for two. McMorris turns, to the alarm of an otherwise peaceful pigeon, and throws back. The pigeon takes off and goes straight into the pavilion. 39 for two, five to Barrington, 25 to Dexter. And still this ominous looking field with the men deep for the nick, and up close for the man that plays back to the ball that pops up.

And Hall ruefully flexes and tenses his right foot, sweeps in again. Bowls to Dexter, another no ball, it's cut for four. I am a little sorry to see this and I could wish in fact that the white marker would be produced which was such a help to English pace bowlers in particular in recent seasons. This white metal marker to show the taking-off point. Take the bowler back a few inches and save him bowling a no-ball under the old rule. I feel it'd be a great help to these two because there's little doubt that they're bowling in their normal style and there's no attempt to take an advantage.

Hall comes in bowls to Dexter, who gets over it and turns it magnificently away there down to mid-wicket. It's chased but fruitlessly by McMorris. It's another four. This takes Dexter up to 33 out of 47. Of course he's made bigger scores than 33 in Test matches and he may well do so this time. But I think I've never seen Dexter bat more reassuredly nor more commandingly and the situation he'd have to cope with immediately after lunch would have been a desperate one for any batsman in the world. He's risen to it, quite gloriously.

The dramatic ebb and flow of the game is now cricket lore. England finished four short on the first innings, dismissed the West Indies for 229 and thus were set 234 to win. English hopes were dashed when they lost the first three wickets of their second innings cheaply; then Cowdrey and Barrington led a spirited fight back before Cowdrey retired injured. With five wickets gone and in poor light, Close and Titmus faced an equally inexorable clock and Wes Hall.

England want 43 to win in fifty-five minutes. And Hall – that little shower apparently wetted the outfield and for the first time today a bowler has recourse to the sawdust heap – Hall comes down, dries it – turns at the pavilion end and comes up on his great tigerish run – the leap; he bowls to Titmus. Titmus covers up, it goes off the edge of the bat and hits a single to gully. A single to gully there – the ball didn't travel a third as far as the batsman ran. A very quickly taken single to make England 192 for five. This is where one is almost afraid to breathe for fear of rocking the boat, and these two batsmen now faced with a tactical decision on almost every ball. Two slips, leg slips, silly mid-on for Close.

Hall comes in, bowls to him, and he plays that straight up to silly mid-on, Worrell. Hall turns and walks back, Close again, goes up, prods the pitch. The trees away in the distance heaving under this strong wind which, in fact, would help Hall to swing the ball into Close. The wind is coming in from about cover point, say extra cover. The trees heaving and bending under it, the light murky.

And Hall comes up again, past umpire Phillipson, and Close tries to hook, he's beaten long leg, it's through, it's four runs. Close is 50 and the people here are sorry only that they couldn't make ten times as much noise. An innings of remarkable shrewdness, good judgement, courage and very sound technique. Fifty in three hours 15 minutes, with 5 fours. His first 50 in a Test. His previous best, 42 against the West Indies at Birmingham in 1957.

And now it's Hall again from the pavilion end – in, bowls to Close, oh, tried to cut outside the offstump. Through to the wicket-keeper and about six rows of members down here fidget as if their ants were full of pants, er, pants were full of ants. Absolutely unable to stay still there. This awful moment when you see a batsman play outside the offstump at pace and it goes through. 196 for five, (*more measured*) 196 for five.

And Hall comes in again, bowls to Close. Close tries to turn that on the onside – takes that on the thigh again as he turns, walks away, a little hobble. Still disdaining to run. A very hard man this, and he's been hit a couple of dozen times on the thigh. He's resolutely refused to rub – he was cracked once on the forearm and I would think that was the first time in this innings that Brian Close has flashed outside the offstump, and the reaction amongst the crowd was almost terrifying. 196 for five then, 38 wanted.

And Hall comes in bowls to Close. Close hooks and again he's beaten leg slip, but not long leg. Fielded by Butcher, they take a single, a Constantine-style sprint pick-up and return. It's a 197 for five. Titmus 11, Close 52, England 197 for five. Want 37 to win and there are fifty-two minutes left.

(*Pause*)

Now Gibbs comes in, bowls to Close who goes down the pitch. But checks the stroke, Worrell fields and you can hear the sighs come out of the spectators like punctured bicycle tyres, every time a risk is taken. Everybody walking the tightrope.

Gibbs to Close. Tries to swing it, appeal for LBW, not out. Taken by Sobers at slip and he appeals for a catch. A few brows being mopped, though it's not a warm afternoon.

And Gibbs comes again and bowls to Close, a little short, but Close using his reach goes forward, smothers any turn and plays it out on the offside. 197 for five, and still with this very economical field, eight men saving the one.

Gibbs comes in bowls to Close, Close swings him on the leg side. Four again. Two hundred's up. It's been a long, long road to home this. Now England want 33.

Gibbs bowls to Close and Close plays out on the offside. Two hundred and one for 5, Close 56, Titmus 11, and that grotesque tower away in the distance suddenly catching the sun like a beacon.

The ground in bloom, as Gibbs comes in – bowls, and Close steers him to short third man and takes a quick single. Two hundred and two for 5, Close 57, every Englishman in the ground with him. Every West Indian in the ground after his blood.

The game eventually produced perhaps the most exciting drawn Test match there has ever been, with four different results possible as the last ball was bowled. England won the next encounter at Edgbaston and then went to Headingley where Dexter once again had the unenviable job of trying to restore his side's fortunes after the loss of two early wickets.

In comes Griffith from the Kirkstall Lane end, in, bowls to Dexter and Dexter steers that out on the offside to cover. A quick chip in there by Solomon carries the wicket-keeper, they're going for a second run, a throw to the bowler's end. A little comic act by Worrell there pretending to have missed it. Actually pouched it perfectly safely. That's two more to Dexter.

And Griffith as he comes up – it's hard to describe Griffith as jaunty – he's a mountain of a man – but he comes popping up planting down those big flat feet almost jauntily with the tonic of those early wickets behind him. He comes in once more and from the edge of the crease pushes that in toward Dexter who plays absolutely straight beside his left pad and down toward mid-on where Hall walks slowly in, picks up for Griffith. A little polish on the seat of the pants and Griffith spreading those feet at the end of long thick legs walks back to his mark. Dexter, a little relaxed bend of the shoulders, settles into his stance, bat patting in the crease.

Griffith comes in, bowls to him and Dexter gets over that. Tries to cut, gets a thick under-edge and plays it out bobbing on the offside for Gibbs to come out of the gully and pick it up before it can reach Solomon coming in from cover. 32 for two.

Griffith, a great square back showing to us, walks down to the Kirkstall Lane end, turns at the end of a pitch-length run, comes up ball held in both hands, then just over the last few strides the right arm breaks and then he bowls. (*Roar, applause.*) That was a great big in-slanter right up on a full length; Dexter, I think, just got a touch of it, and it spread the middle and leg stumps and England are 32 for three with Dexter out, bowled Griffith eight.

The West Indies won that fourth Test convincingly and so went to the Oval 2-1 up. In the fifth match England led by 29 runs on the first innings and then struggled hard to consolidate their position. Wickets fell to Griffith, Sobers and Hall.

Back again with Hall. Still a stirring sight to watch as he comes in with these great leaping strides. Turns away, comes to his distant mark. Pulls out of the slouch, furls the right sleeve, absolutely eating up the ground, comes in bowls to Trueman and Trueman edges that and it's caught by Sobers. (*Huge roar.*) And the cheer is so great that every pigeon on the Oval ground heads off. They've settled again now, away in the distance. Trueman is out, caught Sobers bowled Hall, five. England are 196 for seven . . .

. . . Lock coming out to what, I believe, is generally called a mixed reception. 196 for seven, and the sort of position that Lock rather relishes, though it seems of late that since he played those two extremely good innings at Edgbaston and Headingley that Worrell calls up Griffith for him and that Lock is treated, as you might say, like a batsman. That's to say, that he is treated to the bouncer. If treated to is appropriate, perhaps it should be treated with the bouncer. 196 for seven then. Sharpe not out 75.

Hall from the Vauxhall end – comes in great breaking strides, he bowls to Lock and (*roar*) – bowls his middle stump out of the ground. (*Applause.*) And if only you could see the far end of the ground. It's as if the ground is erupting. Cushions thrown in the air, men springing high in the air, arms up, utter pandemonium and joy. I shouldn't think Lock in his entire career has ever given more pleasure. And now England are 196 for eight. And the balance of the day tilted toward the West Indies quite positively. England's lead now worth 225. Hall two wickets with consecutive balls – the hat-trick's on and Brian Statham, the man faced with the task of stopping him. And he isn't here yet, presumably still bustling into his pads. There's the applause, he's moved down the pavilion steps . . .

. . . the left-handed Statham. Two leg slips, a forward short leg, silly mid-on, silly mid-off, three slips, gully, wicket-keeper standing back. This is nine men close round the bat, ten men round the bat. Only Hall outside it and he'll complete the circle as he follows through.

Statham looking fairly phlegmatic faces Hall and Hall races in from the Vauxhall end, bowls to Statham, but he's got four. Four brings the 200 up.

England were dismissed for 223 and then with Trueman unable to bowl because of a damaged ankle, the West Indies scored the required runs easily, helped by two fine innings from Conrad Hunte and Rohan Kanhai.

After the game, John took the microphone to the teams:

(*Crowd roaring; calypso music:*)

ARLOTT: That was the sound of cricket in England 1963. A great season for cricket. So great indeed that it was never dimmed by the weather. Surprisingly bad even for an English summer, bad enough to have blighted the game in an ordinary year. This was the season that refuted the Jeremiahs who insisted that the game was dying. The West Indians, as many had hoped, but few had dared to be sure, repeated their triumph. A triumph, greater in long term impact, than winning a Test series. The triumph they'd achieved in 1960–61 in Australia, when they lifted public interest in cricket to heights they hadn't known there since the heyday of Bradman. This West Indian tour produced a revolution, not the usual revolution of establishing something fresh. But the much harder revolution of restoring old glories in the public mind.

Some of their appeal lay in the fact that they were a winning side. But how did they play? The first man on that subject ought to be the England captain, Ted Dexter speaking at the Oval at the end of the last Test.

DEXTER: I congratulate Frank on a wonderful series. We've all enjoyed it tremendously. I've just been talking to Tony Lock down in the dressing-room. Now he's an old warrior, and he says he's enjoyed every minute of it, and he's enjoyed it more than any other series. Now that, coming from Lock, is a pretty good comment on a wonderful series.

ARLOTT: The second question is more important. Why did the West Indians make such an impact on the English people? Not only on the regular cricket followers: but listeners, viewers, the man in the street, the man arguing in the pub, the club, or the café. Some may say because their batsmen played so attractively, and certainly in some county and festival games they showed off a bewildering array of strokes. But in fact, and this may surprise some people, they didn't score as fast as England in the Tests. The figures, produced by Arthur Wrigley, and no mere commentator would venture to doubt, showed that throughout the Tests England scored at a rate of 43.5 runs per hundred balls bowled to them, and the West Indies at 42.2 per hundred. They didn't even bowl their overs so quickly as England. Eighteen an hour to England's 19. So, Arthur Wrigley goes on in his letter, you will have great difficulty in proving by figures what we all know, that this was the finest Test series we've ever seen. That question is, I'm sure, one of feeling. They were essentially a happy side. As we thought you'd best sense if we brought a group of them round a table, relaxed, after the season was ended. There we asked Frank Worrell for his wide view of the tour.

WORRELL: On arrival here, my ambition was to establish the group as an international side to warrant frequent returns to this country. We had the nucleus of a

The West Indies team, 1963. *Back row L to R*: G. Duckworth (scorer), B. F. Butcher, M. C. Carew, L. A. King, A. W. White, C. C. Griffith, L. R. Gibbs, S. M. Nurse, E. D. A. St J. McMorris, D. Pye (masseur). *Middle row L to R*: B. Gaskin (manager), W. V. Rodriguez, R. B. Kanhai, A. L. Valentine, F. M. M. Worrell (Captain), C. C. Hunte, G. St A. Sobers, W. W. Hall, H. Burnett (assistant manager). *Front row L to R*: D. L. Murray, D. W. Allan, J. S. Solomon.

side in Australia where we established not only a way of life, a pattern of behaviour and approach to the game, and it was only left to us to get the new members into the fold. There was no difficulty at all in doing such a thing. The series has been won and lost. I feel that had we won by a 3-2 margin it would have been a more fitting end than the 3-1 margin, because 3-1 suggests that we were that much better than the England team. I don't think that we were. I thought that the result should have been, West Indies victorious at Manchester, Leeds and the Oval. And England victorious at Birmingham and Lord's.

ARLOTT: Do you think it's the best West Indies side you've ever been in?

WORRELL: Yes, it's the best balanced team, balanced on the cricket field and off the cricket field. And I'm proud to say that at no stage has there been any rift at all.

ARLOTT: This general air of happiness in the side was reflected in their cricket. But no one pretends their cricket wasn't competitive. Fast bowling's a major tradition in West Indian cricket .... How did the West Indies seem to an opposing bowler? Fred Trueman:

TRUEMAN: They're a good bunch of boys, they're always laughing and I got on tremendously well with them. But looking at them from a bowling point of view, after the first Test at Manchester I realised very quickly that if I could bowl round about the off stick or just outside, I might get some of these people out. And as you see through the series, it's paid off. I got 34 Test wickets against them. Looking back over the series two innings stand out in my mind. Basil Butcher played a very, very good knock indeed, at Lord's and then the onslaught that Rohan Kanhai brought against the England team in the last Test at the Oval. In the second innings that was another innings that will stand out as well. I only hope that they will come back here very quickly, because I think in this country they've done cricket a tremendous power of good.

ARLOTT: Another Yorkshireman, Brian Close, almost

won the Lord's Test with his great second innings. How did he feel about playing against the West Indies?

CLOSE: I've enjoyed playing against them tremendously, and there's nothing I like better than a real hard, give-nothing-away tussle, as it were. And believe me, it's been a wonderful thrill for me to play in these Tests. As far as tension, and giving nothing away, well, there's one thing about these West Indies bowlers – they never give anything away, they really make you struggle for every single run as I had to in the Lord's Test against Hall and Griffith. Believe me. It was some fight.

ARLOTT: There is no doubt that that pair of fast bowlers captured the imagination of everyone who watched them. But most of us have a few questions that we would like to ask them. What happened for instance at Lord's, when Brian Close started to walk down the wicket towards Wesley Hall? Wesley?

HALL: I thought he was mad, to be honest, because I've bowled a few thousand balls in my career and I have never seen it happen before. The skipper had asked me not to bowl a no ball, so I was going to make sure that I wasn't going to bowl a no ball, and in my delivery stride, actually when a fast bowler is at his maximum speed, I looked up and I saw Brian four or five yards down the wicket, my immediate reaction was that he must have been picking something off the wicket. I've been trying unsuccessfully to tell the boys this all along, and I was very glad today when Charles Griffith who had been fielding at mid-on thought the same. And immediately, rather than bowl the ball and hit him or anything, I tried to stop which is nearly impossible at full speed, and I hurt my back a bit.

ARLOTT: But if you'd realised he was walking down the pitch to you . . .

HALL: I would have bowled . . . yeah, sure . . . I would have bowled the ball, yeah.

ARLOTT: What would you have bowled?

HALL: Well I don't know, but I would have bowled it for sure.

ARLOTT: And what about Charlie Griffith bowling the bouncer to Tony Lock coming in at number 9?

GRIFFITH: I think that Tony was becoming a batsman. He made fifty something so I saw him playing the rising ball pretty well, getting across the wicket and hitting them down to square leg and so I said I'll try one and see if you'll be able to hit it, too. So I did, but unfortunately he didn't hit it ... Just one of those days it happened.

ARLOTT: Frank Worrell always seemed to have a fast bowler ready and fresh to throw in against any stand made for England. Was this carefully planned?

WORRELL: Oh, I think this is because we had Sobers who would fill in the odd hour in order to provide the other fast bowlers with a rest that was necessary.

ARLOTT: There was never a major stand made against you in the series, was there?

WORRELL: I don't recollect it.

ARLOTT: Where does the Captain feel that the strength in his side lay?

WORRELL: That's a rather awkward question to answer because I think in all departments the boys equipped themselves really well. Sobers performed magnificently. This is individual, because if I was going to single out anybody it would be Garfield, because this is a chap who's got the ability to bowl the Chinaman, and he can bowl seam stuff, he can bowl the orthodox stuff. But what I liked about Garfield in this series is that he seemed to have matured so much. He buckled down, he played each ball on merit. But apart from Sobers' contribution, I think that the fast bowlers gave a hundred per cent. I recollect Charlie Griffith at the Oval with one foot in the grave and one on a banana skin; he decided, 'I've got to keep going. Because this is the final Test match and I've got to contribute.' Wes Hall came on to save old Charlie from the sack cloth and ashes and he turned in a magnificent performance. Well, these are our best bowlers. Lance Gibbs, a man who was always in the game, never relaxes; to him cricket is a game that's gotta be won and he's there in the middle. And then the tremendous performances of the batsmen up front. And then we've got a young man by the name of Deryck Murray, again with both feet firmly on the ground.

ARLOTT: So we come then to Deryck Murray. Brought over straight from school for experience. But he suddenly found himself first wicket-keeper and broke the record for the number of victims for a wicket-keeper in a Test series. What did the tour seem like to him?

MURRAY: Well, I was very apprehensive about it at the start. But I was fortunate enough to have such a great captain as Frank Worrell, who immediately made me feel I was no longer a boy and I was one of the Test team, and he kept encouraging me, giving me hints and making me feel at home on the Test field even though I was feeling like I was in the lion's den. And then these chaps who I have been with all the time immediately accepted me as one of them and I couldn't hope to make a better Test debut than with these chaps who I have been with for the past six months.

ARLOTT: And now Frank Worrell's announced his retirement from Test cricket. The only possible reaction to that is, why?

WORRELL: Well, I've got a bad knee to begin with; and on top of this, I've been around for twenty-six years, been playing international cricket from 1948 and having come on this tour when I realised that we've got young Deryck Murray here, for instance, who was born two years after I'd been playing international cricket, I thought it was time to get out of this game. (*Laughter.*)

ARLOTT: You couldn't have picked a much better note to quit on, could you?

WORRELL: Well, this was pre-planned. It just happened that the results evolved. But I'd planned to retire at the end of this tour irrespective of what became of the series.

ARLOTT: And what are you going to do?

WORRELL: I shall go back to this very mundane job of

mine in Jamaica, and try to exist to the best of my ability, watching these boys perform internationally for the next, in some instances, five years, and others, ten.

ARLOTT: But was there another extra ingredient to this tour that was completely new? Surely there was. For the first time in the history of Test cricket the two teams, at least at Edgbaston, Lord's and the Oval, were equally supported. In fact, it sometimes seemed that the West Indies had more backing than England, but that may have been because of vocal volume. Sometimes I went round there amongst the West Indian supporters. It wasn't easy to push a way through. Once a West Indian turned round to me, I'm only six-feet-one tall and said languidly, 'Like to come in front of me, man, I can see over you.' He must have been six foot five, but it was no good, those in front of him were nearly as tall. How did the players on the England side feel about the West Indian supporters? Philip Sharpe.

SHARPE: Ah, the West Indian spectators, they add greatly to the atmosphere. I love playing in front of a large crowd. I think it does a great deal. I think it sets the English fans going as well and that brings the crowds in.

ARLOTT: And Brian Close?

CLOSE: The atmosphere about the cricket – well, that's really made these Tests into what they have been for cricket.

ARLOTT: Knowledge, enthusiasm, enjoyment, happiness, fun. You may feel that we've stressed facets of cricket that can't be proved by statistics. But surely these human qualities made this tour such a success. Such a human success. The happiness of a team reflected in their play and reflected back from those who watched them in a perpetual give and take that perhaps in our sophistication some of us here had forgotten. These West Indians, players and supporters, were determined to have their day of enjoyment. Sometimes to be sure, the spectators booed umpires' decisions, but I thought that grew less as the series progressed. The essential aspect of their attitude to cricket was, it seemed to me, not just that they enjoyed it, but they were quite determined to enjoy it. They never set up the noise of hate, the slow handclap which is also usually the voice of lack of understanding, they were never spiteful to a cricketer on either side. When any orchestra produces a great performance we congratulate the conductor: the tributes to Frank Worrell were genuine, not overdone. His leading performers, obviously, were the players, Conrad Hunte, Basil Butcher, Garfield Sobers, Easton McMorris, Joe Solomon and so on. But the chorus, the West Indian supporters reminded English spectators how to enjoy their cricket, too boisterously perhaps by some of our standards, but never grudgingly. Today, you may call these men who were given, or took, a day off from conducting buses, collecting tube tickets, sweeping streets, washing dishes, portering on railway platforms, you may call them West Indians. It's important that they're British. In twenty years, perhaps less, their children will be playing cricket in England, playing by right, for English counties; let's hope with the same gusto as the earlier generation, whether playing or watching. Perhaps indeed, this was the greatest reason why this summer was so remarkable, that a fresh section of the English cricketing community spoke out loud and clear for the first time. We watched a great West Indian team, but we heard cheering them on the fathers of the cricketers who in a few years' time will follow Ron Headley, Danny Livingstone, Rudy Webster to share English cricket with the descendants of the men of Hambledon and Nottingham, Canterbury and Leeds, Lord's and Manchester. We heard the history of English cricket changed. Events will soon prove it. Listen again to the sound of English cricket in 1963, alive, different, but as we may note with gratitude, certainly not dying . . .

Actuality of cricket match faded into Calypso Music.

BBC Home Service, September 1963

43

TRIBUTE TO SYDNEY BARNES

In the spring of the year that the West Indies made such a vivid impression, 1963, John compiled a radio tribute to the great Sydney Barnes who had reached the age of ninety. He found Barnes far more forthcoming than usual: 'Willing to talk on and on. Poor old boy! I think he thought he was being paid by the minute on the amount we recorded rather than that used.'

ARLOTT: Cricket grants the title of the greatest only rarely and on grounds of conclusive evidence. In fact, you'll find some dispute about all the superlatives except perhaps one, this one: who was the greatest bowler that ever lived? Here first of all is the opinion of Sir Jack Hobbs, England's master batsman of this century.

HOBBS: I don't think, even now, there's anybody better than Syd Barnes. I've seen him on mat in Africa and Australia, then in England and I put him the tops still.

ARLOTT: E.J. Smith, 'Tiger' Smith, kept wicket to Barnes in four Test series. Where does he put him?

SMITH: Honestly, in my own mind, I believe he's the greatest bowler that I've seen.

ARLOTT: Then Wilfred Rhodes, that legendary Yorkshireman and as shrewd a judge of the game that ever lived?

RHODES: Sydney Barnes was the greatest bowler I ever played with.

ARLOTT: Sir Learie Constantine played against Barnes for the West Indies and in League cricket over a period of fifteen years.

CONSTANTINE: No bowler could have bowled better

than Sydney Barnes. I don't care what part of the world you go to. He was the best bowler I have ever played against and often I have played on his side.

ARLOTT: The late Sir Pelham Warner, who in more than seventy years played in and saw more first-class cricket than anyone else whoever lived, declared that S.F. Barnes had never been equalled in his style in any period of English cricket. And A.G. Steel called him 'the greatest bowler the game of cricket has ever produced'. This is a degree of unanimity from different generations of opponents and colleagues that must carry great weight, yet Barnes is somehow the least known, the least recognized, certainly the least seen of all the great players. Why, he barely made a hundred appearances on the first-class grounds of England and of those all but about a dozen were more than sixty years ago, so while in his native Staffordshire he's still a lively, known and respected character, to the rest of the world he's something of a dim legend, the legend of a tall, dark, forbidding, relentless cricketer. Now what was there about Sydney Barnes's bowling that made it so outstanding? 'Tiger' Smith watched him from behind the stumps:

SMITH: I believe he always weighed the striker up before he delivered the ball. His arm action was close to his head which gave him every advantage a bowler could wish for. He also had that which is necessary for any bowler to be a success – an immaculate length. His lift off the pitch came from the height of his delivery. He bowled anything. He could bowl the off-spinner, he could bowl the outward-swinger, he could bowl the inward-swinger, he could bowl the ducker. The leg-break he could bowl with leg-spin, or he could bowl it with the cutter.

ARLOTT: That's fairly complete, isn't it? Now, again Sir Jack Hobbs, the batsman's point of view:

HOBBS: Well, he seemed to me to have it all, this leg-break and the off-break, he was fast, he was tall and made the ball get up to unpleasant heights. On the matting he was wonderful. In those days they had these higher stumps – he was absolutely fabulous – he beat the bat sometimes four or five times an over without getting a wicket.

ARLOTT: Sir Learie Constantine, again from the other end of the pitch:

CONSTANTINE: At the particular time I met him, he was fifty years old when he had finished in the Lancashire League. He went to Staffordshire League – he was in his sixties – and at that time Syd Barnes set his same silly gully and his silly slip, his silly short-leg and his silly mid-on; he bowled at sixty-five with that field set just as he set it in 1923. It means he had absolute control of length, he had not lost it between 1923 and 1936 or '37. So that, if anybody can do that, then I would pay the same tribute to them that I would pay to Barnes, but I don't believe anybody has done it other than Sydney Barnes and he is therefore the greatest bowler that I have ever played against.

ARLOTT: And that craftsman with an acute eye for cricketers and men – Wilfred Rhodes:

RHODES: He was tall, six feet high and with a very high action, a long arm and a high action. He's all the attributes a bowler should have, he's a very strong character – a man with a very strong character. He fancies his chances against any batsman.

ARLOTT: And that of course is said to be the bowler's basic asset. Now A.C. MacLaren, 'Archie' MacLaren, the Lancashire and England Captain, is usually said to have discovered Sydney Barnes. In 1901, when MacLaren on his own initiative picked Barnes to go to Australia, he was choosing a League bowler, a man who had taken altogether just thirteen wickets in first-class cricket and they had been spread over seven years; yet from that tour onwards Barnes was unmistakably a great bowler. Twenty-odd years afterwards, MacLaren wrote:

The bowler who is great under all conditions is naturally a *rara avis*. Such a bowler was Barnes who could bowl on any type of wicket against the highest class of

Sydney Barnes not to be denied.

batsman with astonishing success. Indeed, it has always been my opinion that relatively speaking he showed greater genius when conditions were favourable to run-getting and when the ball came faster off the pitch than when everything was in favour of the bowler. Barnes had the most extraordinary natural gifts, he made full use of his height, his length was perfect, he came very fast off the pitch, he could spin the ball, he could swing it away and also dip into the batsman. Such a combination sounds almost too good to be true and undoubtedly is so rare that one might almost be justified in calling him unique.

And now, the thought of the man himself – Sydney Barnes speaking at the age of ninety:

BARNES: There was a ball bowled down, that could worry the batsman and that's the ball I wanted to bowl. And to bowl that ball you've got to get direction and length. And I was always told, straight balls never get wickets so I always tried to do a little bit. Every ball that I bowled down, I had to spin – fast, slow or medium, I spun the ball, and I thought at that time I was at a disadvantage, because I had seen fellers bowling the swingers, they simply pointed the ball which way they wanted it to go and it went. Whereas if I bowl an outward swinger to a right-hand man, I had to put the off-break on. The only time I was tired of bowling was when I wasn't. I remember one match we played in and Frank Woolley went to the Captain. He said, 'For God's sake put Barney on,' he said, 'he's looking miserable not bowling.' Oh, it was nothing for me to bowl three to four hours without a rest.

ARLOTT: His was quite a unique cricket career. He played his first first-class match in 1895 and his last in 1930, a span of thirty-five years, but two championship matches for Warwickshire in 1895, and one in 1896, two for Lancashire in 1899 and one in 1901, and four seasons with Lancashire in 1902 and 1903 were the full extent of the county cricket he ever played. The rest of his first-class play was in Tests for English teams on tour in Australia and South Africa, or the Players against the Gentlemen, for Wales or Staffordshire usually against the touring sides. He was a Test match bowler.

BARNES: The last fourteen matches that I played in Test

cricket I took 120-odd wickets for about 16 runs a wicket. That's against Australia and Africa.

ARLOTT: He took some 720 wickets in first-class cricket, not many by comparison with a number of the great bowlers, but of those wickets 189, more than a third, were taken in Test matches. And another 155 on three tours of Australia and one of South Africa. That means with Gentlemen-Players and Test trials, more than half his first-class wickets were taken in representative matches. Why did he play so little county cricket?

BARNES: They wanted me to play with Lancashire and I agreed to play with them, but from the time I went with them, it was always a question of £sd. I hadn't been with them long, we were playing Warwickshire and word came down that I wasn't chosen for that particular match. So of course up I went to the committee room and I said, 'What game are you playing now?' 'Well, we don't think it's your wicket.' It had been raining, looked like being a sticky wicket. 'Well that just shows how much you know about the game,' I said. 'The first time that I've ever heard that a man who can spin the ball, can't bowl on a sticky wicket,' I said. 'But still, that's all right with me, if you're going to rest me, you can rest me all the season if you like,' I said, 'but if you're not paying me, I've finished with you now, straight away.' I said, 'I can go anywhere in England and get my living, or get more than I'm getting here, so it's up to you.' Jimmy Lancaster, he was Treasurer, he said, 'I'll see your money's right.' 'Well,' I said, 'you'd better, because I mean what I say: if I walk out of here, I can get a job anywhere in England.' But anyway, they didn't leave me out again.

ARLOTT: He did mean what he said and the end of his county cricket was close at hand, but if he had his time all over again:

BARNES: The way present-day county cricket is played and paid for, I might be inclined to go for county cricket. When I was with Lancashire, I went up to the committee room one day and I said, 'You can keep your winter pay, I'll work for it, so that I've got something to look forward to when I finish cricket.' And their reply was, 'Oh, we can't be bothered to find any work.' I said, 'All right,' I said, 'well, it's up to me then.' And that was the end of Lancashire.

ARLOTT: So he went away to become a professional in League cricket and for Staffordshire in the minor counties. There his record was staggering. In League cricket, and every club he ever played for won its competition; in League cricket he took over 4,000 wickets at seven runs apiece. For Staffordshire, who had in fact the toughest of minor-county fixture lists, he bowled until 1935 when he was sixty-two and took over 1,400 wickets at a fraction of eight runs apiece. But this was the man who was at his best against the best. It was against a great Australian batting side that in 1912 he produced what must still be the finest opening spell in any Test match on an absolutely flawless Melbourne wicket. Does he still recall it?

BARNES: Quite well. Things like that, you know, they only happen once or so in our lifetime and they are sure to stick. The first one was Warren Bardsley. I bowled to him and one that swung into him and he hit it onto the wicket. Kelleway is number two, I believe. He was letting the ball go by, which appeared to be about a foot outside his legs, when suddenly it dipped into him and it was LBW. Clem Hill – I bowled one exactly the same to him, I bowled him the leg-break to a right hander, you know, one coming into him. He played it and I bowled one that pitched on his leg stick, it was an off-spinner. He paid me a compliment, he said, 'I've never had such an opener in my life.' Warwick Armstrong, he was a right-hand batsman, I forget now how many I bowled at him, but one pitched on his leg stick – 'Tiger' Smith caught him behind the wicket.

ARLOTT: Yes, of course, his old fellow black-countryman 'Tiger' Smith was keeping wicket.

SMITH: He varied not only the length of the ball but the width of the ball trying to get the striker to feel for the ball. He got Bardsley out, bowled off his pads, the ball hit his leg stump. He got Hill bowled, Kelleway leg before wicket, Armstrong was caught at the wicket by myself which gave me confidence which, I hope, I continued with throughout the innings. It didn't remain there. Syd kept them quiet for about an hour and twenty minutes and if I remember rightly, his score analysis was about four wickets for about one run, then five for about six runs.

ARLOTT: That was it, 4 wickets for one run in the first spell and by lunch bowling on his figures were 11 overs, 7 maidens, 6 runs and 5 wickets on a perfect batting wicket. That was his most historic feat, but what of his beginnings?

BARNES: My dad, he used to play a little, not much. I had two brothers, they never had a bat in their hand. The only coaching that ever I had, was a feller, oh, when I was about sixteen, told me how to hold the ball for an off-break. The others I taught myself, by watching others.

ARLOTT: Well what about those early days with Warwickshire?

BARNES: When they asked me to play, they wanted one that was ready made and I know very well that I wasn't, I showed promise and they couldn't afford to wait.

ARLOTT: Oh, but what a return it would have been to wait for. Now, how did he bowl, a thirteen-yard run with a leap just before he delivered. His model . . . ?

BARNES: Tom Richardson. I liked his run up to the wicket and his run up to the wicket fitted in with mine; and I liked his body action and his left shoulder was always down the wicket.

ARLOTT: And his pace, Tiger Smith?

SMITH: His pace could only be anything from medium to slow and he always had what could be a real fast one and I should say he could bowl that slow ball almost as equally as any slow bowler bowling today.

ARLOTT: Now what was his best ball? That famous fast leg-break?

SMITH: It isn't one particular ball. It's a ball that comes along with others. It might be an off-break, it might be a leg-break, it might be a swinger, according to which one takes your pick.

ARLOTT: Six foot one inch, he's still to this day as straight as a guardsman, with high rugged shoulders, a really tough piece of black countryman for his native Smethwick to be proud of and he had an antagonistically high action.

BARNES: I once said to a batsman that we were playing against, 'When I deliver the ball, I want to be eight feet.' 'By God,' he said, 'you look ten feet when you deliver the ball.'

ARLOTT: Oh, his bowling mattered to him, mattered deeply to him, more than anything else in the world. As you may gather from this memory of Wilfred Rhodes:

RHODES: Sydney Barnes was playing against Constantine in a charity match on a ground near Oldham. Barnes was bowling – he got him caught at the wicket in his first over and the umpire gave him not out. So at the end of the over Barnes said to the umpire, he said, 'He hit that, didn't he?' He said, 'Oh yes, he hit it all right, but the spectators want to see Constantine bat a bit.' 'Well,' he said, 'you'd better give me my sweater and let somebody else bowl. I've got a reputation as well as Constantine.'

ARLOTT: A reputation, a legend and the legend is strongly rooted that Sydney Barnes was the most terrifying of bowlers for a batsman to see. Tiger Smith:

SMITH: Well, possibly it was a batsman's vision because he was rather dour in everything he'd done. There's no argument in my opinion, he was out to get the striker out.

ARLOTT: Barnes is a legend as a hater of batsmen. One of the classic cricket stories is of the occasion when two tail-end batsmen were nicking and edging him everywhere except where they were aiming and he stamped off at the end of an over with the words, 'They're not batting well enough to get out.' But did he really hate batsmen so much?

BARNES: (*Laughs.*) We're very, very friendly, but I wanted to see the back of them.

ARLOTT: And he did see the back of them, quickly. He took his 189 wickets in twenty-seven Tests, that's a rate of seven a match; but probably equally important, he took them at the amazing rate of one every seven overs. In South Africa, where he was virtually unplayable on the matting, he took 49 wickets in the first four Tests of the 1913–14 series, then because of a dispute he didn't play in the fifth Test, where he would have surely have set up an unapproachable record. Now it's often asked, was Sydney Barnes simply a natural or was he a thinking cricketer?

BARNES: When I placed the field, I very, very rarely wanted it altered. If I'd been bowling three hours I was still an attacking bowler at the end of that time. I wanted the fielder where I wanted him – I didn't want a fielder for a bad ball to be bowled down.

ARLOTT: In that connection, who was the best captain you ever played under?

BARNES: They were all good captains because they let me do as I liked. When I was bowling I was captain and that's a funny thing to say. MacLaren said, 'He was the easiest man that I ever had to captain – I simply tossed him the ball, he placed the fielders where he liked and bowled as he liked.' That was a compliment.

ARLOTT: Feared on the top level of cricket, it's little wonder that he was deadly in minor county matches, and an utter destroyer in League cricket. But he took those more than 4,000 wickets at a frequency of about one every three overs and at seven runs apiece, less than four in some seasons. And I'll always cherish this story of his. Real Syd Barnes – about one League match:

BARNES: O yes, yes. Scored a run off me the first ball I bowled down, and when the tenth man came in, that was the only run they'd scored off me. And this fellow came to me and said, 'For God's sake, bowl him out, Syd,' he said, 'if he hits one to me I'm sure to drop it,' and sure enough he did. But I got the ten wickets.

ARLOTT: And, not for the only time. For years we find

returns against the strongest minor county sides, like 14 wickets for 13 runs against Cheshire, all ten in an innings for 36 against a powerful Yorkshire second eleven, the first four Durham wickets with consecutive balls. Again in a Durham match he began with 7 wickets for two runs, for Staffordshire against the All India Touring side of 1911, five for 14 and nine for 15 in a single day. In 1908, when the minor counties competition was divided into four groups and played off between the four group leaders on a knock-out basis, Barnes won the championship for Staffordshire. In the semi-final and final he bowled 60 overs and took 24 wickets for 78 runs, an average of three and a quarter runs a wicket against the next two best sides in the competition. Against Lincolnshire, when he was fifty-three years old, he took eight for 17 and six for 14. Against Durham, his favourite victims it seems, in one match he took nine for 37 and eight for 46 and scored a chanceless 136. Oh yes, he could bat a bit.

BARNES: If I'd been out for records, I could have made a lot more runs.

ARLOTT: And he did make runs when they were wanted. In the second Test in the 1907–08 tour of Australia, England with only two wickets left wanted 73 to win and it was, in fact, numbers nine, ten and eleven who were left to get them. Barnes, who was number nine, put on 33 with Humphries and the remaining 39 to win the match with Fielder. Barnes with 38 not out, his highest Test score, made the winning hit. On the same tour, against Western Australia:

BARNES: We were hard put to get a side together, injuries and such like. A.O. Jones came and said, 'I'm going to play you for your batting.' Well, of course, that was a bit of a joke. I told him, 'Well, I think you know very well that I haven't had a bat in my hand all the tour except for practice.' 'I know,' he said, 'but you can do it.' The result was, when I went in to bat I joined George Gunn and we put 200 and odd on for that wicket.

ARLOTT: Still batsmen feared him, still at an age when

he could draw the old age pension there was this tall, upright man, bowling, no not at his old great, great pace, still from time to time making the ball snarl up off the pitch against the fingers. Still bowling that old leg-break and the off-cutter, still bowling an immaculate length, still bowling 'em out, still desperately, desperately proud to be a professional cricketer and earning his money with bat and ball and with all his heart, still giving everything he'd got in his dry, rather hostile, unbending way. Two years later, 1940, sixty-seven years old, and he was playing for Stone in wartime Staffordshire League cricket – five for 22 against Caverswall, six for 32 against Great Shell, bowling average for the season 8.2 and batting at number three. It seemed that he would never end. But five weeks of no cricket, he stiffened up – a little of the enthusiasm went and that was the end of Sydney Barnes's cricket. Fifty-two years of active cricket, it's almost unbelievable. When was he at his best?

BARNES: Well, according to results, I should say from about 1906 to the end of my career. (*Laughs.*)

ARLOTT: Oh dear, oh dear. (*Laughs.*) That is to me the most staggering statement of all. Four and five years before his first date on the 1901–2 tour before he broke down with a knee injury, in two Tests against Australia he took 19 wickets for 300 runs. When he talks about to the end of my career, he's talking about a span of thirty-four years until he was sixty-seven years old. How was he bowling at the very end?

BARNES: Well, truthfully speaking, I wasn't getting the nip out of the wicket at the finish that I used to do, but I'd always got a good length which made them have to watch me.

ARLOTT: In 1953, when he was eighty years old, there was a match in honour of Sydney Barnes's eightieth birthday.

BARNES: And that, I think, was one of the greatest compliments ever paid to an unknown player. There were about sixteen Test players, four or five England captains and for them to come down and play a testimonial game for me was, in my opinion, one of the greatest compliments that could be paid. I said I'd bowl the first ball – instead of the first ball I bowled the first over. Denis Compton was fielding mid-off; he said, 'How are you going on, Syd?' 'Oh,' I said, 'I shall be all right about four o'clock this afternoon.'

ARLOTT: Now Jack Ikin, who played that first over of the match, said that every ball in it would have hit the stumps if he hadn't have stopped it. Appropriately enough it was a maiden over, the last over bowled by the man to whom cricket without qualification has given the title of, 'the greatest bowler that ever lived'. A bowler who was never collared, who gave no batsman and no other bowler best.

BARNES: Well, I believe I got ten wickets, twelve times, but this I can say, that when I've been bowling there's no one from the other end got ten wickets.

BBC Home Service, April 1963

44

Record Commentaries

We are fortunate in finding the senior commentator 'on duty' when some historic moments of cricket chose to arrive.

England *v.* Australia

FOURTH TEST MATCH, OLD TRAFFORD, 1956

And now it's Lock to bowl to Johnston. In – bowls to him – Johnston covers up again, going right back and pushes out to May at forward short leg, who flings it back to Lock. And again Lock comes in to bowl to Johnston.

He's decided now to bowl over the wicket. And Johnston takes fresh guard. Now then, Lock to bowl to Johnston, bowls to him, Johnston again covers up, stabs out on the onside and that's the end of the over.

Laker coming over, peeling off his sweater as he comes, handing it over to umpire Lee. To bowl to Lindwall – the close field gathers, but there's a deep field, Richardson out on the deep square leg boundary. Statham at mid-on. Cowdrey at slip. Oakman forward short leg, Shepherd just back of square, and Lock inevitably at fine short leg. In comes Laker, bowls, and Lindwall plays that with a free flow of the bat back to the bowler. Two hundred and three for 8 Australia, 203 for 8, Lindwall 8, Johnston one. And Laker comes in again to Lindwall. In – bowls, and it's played on the leg side and he's caught. There's an appeal and he's out. Caught Lock, bowled Laker. Lindwall, caught Lock, bowled Laker 8. Well, that's 18 wickets, the most ever taken by a bowler in a Test match, 18 wickets to Laker. Johnston not out one. Lindwall caught Lock, bowled Laker, 8.

Jim Laker on his way to a record breaking 19 wickets in the 4th Test *v.* Australia at Old Trafford in 1956.

(*A little later:*)

Once more, Lock comes back with that customary lick of the fingers. In, bowls, quickish one, Johnston shuffling across covers the break and it was a fair amount because it was a bit short. And Lock turned it quite a bit, Johnston moved with it, and we can see from the point he's patting now just how short that was dropped.

Lock now to bowl to Johnston, with England on the brink of victory. Lock to Johnston, he drops that out on the onside, and that's the end of the over. Arthur Wrigley tells me it was 1905 when England last won a Test at Old Trafford. They haven't won this one yet of course, but now their problem is to take one wicket in 63 minutes. Go on, Arthur.

(*Murmuring off mike.*)

Well, you said since they won a Test. You mean, against Australia. In fact, it's 1905 since any game was finished. The Australians haven't won one either.

Now Laker comes in, bowls and Maddocks drives to cover. Well, Old Trafford has redeemed itself with the last hour of flawless sunshine. And Laker comes in again, hair flopping. Bowls, turns it on to Maddocks (*Shout – applause.*) he's out lbw. And Laker's taken all ten. The first man to congratulate him is Ian Johnson. And England have won by an innings and 170 and Laker has taken all ten wickets for 53 in the second innings. Now, for statistical necessity, if I may use the phrase, I'm going to read you today's score card. They started at twenty minutes to twelve with Australia 84 for two, then McDonald caught Oakman bowled Laker 89. Craig lbw Laker 38. Mackay caught Oakman bowled Laker nought. (*Prolonged applause.*) Now, here's the avenue forming up for Laker there as May pushes him ahead to go in first into the pavilion. All the members standing, waving their score cards, standing up on the balcony, leaning down and applauding him, as he runs up the pavilion steps in through that crowd and is followed into the pavilion, and there's friends of mine who said they weren't going to come today, they thought it might rain. Well, I admit it did look as if it was going to rain. They missed a very great piece of bowling.

England v. West Indies

FOURTH TEST MATCH, HEADINGLEY, 1957

Loader to Johnny Goddard faced yet again with an innings collapsing about his ears. He settles, the close field fit themselves round. Loader comes in, bowls ... (*Roar from crowd.*) ... moving down the line of what was to him an outswinger. (*Applause from crowd.*) The stump leaning drunkenly back, West Indies are 142 for 8 and the possibility, I think, is now not to be precluded that England may bat tonight. And sample themselves the effect of a new ball in this light and in this atmosphere. The bowler's now very much on top – these two pace bowlers who've done a very fine job on a wicket that has never been very fast. I think the experts thought it might give them a little bit of help before lunch, but these two are finding this atmosphere encouraging all day long. Well now once again there is, unless my eyes deceive me, rain in the air, a sort of Scotch mist, but nothing like that ever seems to deter these West Indies players. They pass one another, the outgoing batsman passing the incoming and they've shown every disposition, always to get on with the game whether it's going in their favour or not.

And now as Ramadhin comes in, walking at a brisk military gait to be joined by Alexander who must have a few butterflies under the bottom ring of his sweater, the thought of his first Test innings, as close fieldsmen group up. Graveney, Cowdrey second, Shepherd third, Smith in the gully, Lock leg slip, Trueman backward short leg. Evans standing back, seven of them in a half circle round the back as Loader from the pavilion end comes in, bowls to Ramadhin (*Roar from crowd*) and Ramadhin's skied it and Trueman's under it and he's caught it just by the square leg umpire. And West Indies are 142 for 9. Ramadhin caught Trueman, bowled Loader, swinging, nought. 142 for 9 and for Loader a hat trick is on. Well, Fred Trueman can't catch him in this innings now for all his late acceleration. Come in, if you will, Norman Yardley.

YARDLEY: Well, there's no doubt about it, these two really have made this new ball move about in this heavy atmosphere. The wicket's had nothing to do at all with any of the wickets that have fallen today. It is purely the heavy atmosphere and the ball has moved about through the air. There may have been slight movement from time to time off the seam off the wicket. But generally it has been the atmosphere that has made this ball move about. Loader particularly has made it go both ways. To give you an idea when Smith was out the ball started outside the leg stump, he went across to glide it, but the ball came back through the air and just flicked his leg stump en route. Now, of course, the excitement is boiling up, everyone wondering if Loader is going to get his hat trick. I can't quite remember, can you John, when a hat trick was last done in a Test match?

ARLOTT: I can't, Norman.

YARDLEY: I can't, offhand.

ARLOTT: I know a man called Matthews did it in a Triangular series in 1912, if that's any help to anyone, but I don't remember one since then.

YARDLEY: You've set a problem here for Jack Price – he's searching among his library now.

ARLOTT: I think you will find it was Matthews in the Triangular. May have been one since. Now it is the luckless Gilchrist to face Loader and again those seven close fieldsmen grouped round the bat and three up out in the defensive positions. And Loader from the pavilion end comes in, bowls to him and he's bowled him all over the place, it's a hat trick and Loader is jumping about like a monkey on a stick. And everyone's coming up, Fred Trueman, bless him, flung both arms round Loader, and Lock coming up to pat him on the back and now I'm afraid, Jack Price, the question is irrelevant – who did the hat trick last in a Test match?

ENGLAND *v.* NEW ZEALAND

THIRD TEST, HEADINGLEY, 1965

ARLOTT: And now it's Titmus who comes in, bowls to Yuille and Yuille is caught at slip. It went with the arm, went forward, got an edge and Cowdrey got it as easily as shelling peas. 158 for 6. Yuille caught Cowdrey, bowled Titmus.

YARDLEY: Well, that's a pretty sorry blow now for New Zealand with only four wickets to go and still an hour and thirty-five minutes to see this day through. Two attacking batsmen to come in, Taylor and Motz – I don't think we'll see much pushing and prodding and sitting on the splice from these two. They both like to go out for their shots and of course if they're so doing they're always giving the bowler a chance.

ARLOTT: And I do hear, Norman, that it's not certain that Ward will bat . . .

YARDLEY: Was that from the blow he got on the hand from Loader in the first innings?

ARLOTT: I think it may have been. Certainly it's Taylor coming now, the tall left-hander to replace Yuille with New Zealand 158 for six. And, as a matter of mathematics, Arthur, what is now the deficiency? Five off 200 – 195. It's the first time I've ever beaten you to it, you might chalk it up. 158 for six and Taylor looking taller than ever in this long and well-stretched pullover that comes right down and over the hips, a left-hander of course, though he bowls right arm, coming to face Titmus who is asking for a change in his field. No short leg to the left-hander, a slip and it looks as if Barrington is going to silly mid-off and with four men saving the one on the offside . . . Titmus to Taylor. Forward defensive stroke, back to the bowler, looking very competent and easy about it. He settles back in his stance, back curved, a very bent sort of stance, shoulders round a bit. Titmus bowls, he lofts it, he's out, caught and bowled. Taylor caught and bowled Titmus, nought, New Zealand 158 for seven, and Titmus two wickets in three balls. He had played one in between, hadn't he, Arthur? Taylor's second innings nought in consecutive Test matches and he got nought in the second innings at Lord's.

And now it's Motz and one wonders quite what he'll do. In the first innings we thought he played rather doggedly, back-to-the-wall stuff and wasn't quite true to his own nature. On the other hand, I'd think that any one of these New Zealand tail-enders would hope to be able to stay with Pollard until Pollard got his fifty. Motz takes guard. Titmus asks for some considerable changes in the field. A backward short leg. Now Barrington comes from silly mid-on to square short leg, a mid-wicket and mid-on and now with two men up close on the leg side and a slip and Titmus to bowl to Motz. Titmus now three wickets. Three for 14 in fact. He comes in, bowls to Motz, and Motz goes forward (*Roar.*) and is caught by Smith at forward short leg. A superb gliding catch – I couldn't tell for the moment. No, Barrington – whether he'd grasped it as he took it, must just have turned his hand as he dived because the hand hit the ground but he must have turned it as he dived – his body was screening it from me. So that's Motz playing a feeble little defensive push as in the first innings – much out of character – that's cost him his wickets. New Zealand are 158 for eight, they've lost three wickets in less than five minutes and surely enough Ward is not going to bat. Collinge is coming out, Ward is going to bat number eleven, and Titmus's figures now must be, Arthur, four for 14 – a remarkable number in twenty-one overs. At least he hasn't quite completed twenty-one overs and now he is on a hat-trick. Now Smith is setting a very hostile field, silly point, slip, two slips. Well, the last hat-trick here for England was of course Loader against the West Indies in '57. Two short legs, two slips and a silly point up close, a wide mid-off, a deep mid-on, a mid deep-wicket and a deep square leg and Titmus comes in, bowls to Collinge and he gets an edge to it, but it bounces to

Barrington at forward short leg and the fieldsmen stay up close . . .

Titmus comes in, bowls, and he bowls Collinge off the inside edge. (*Roar.*) My goodness, what an over! Four wickets in the over, and Collinge turns and walks away bowled Titmus nought. One wicket to fall, that's if Ward comes out and we've seen an amazing transformation in this over from 158 for five to 158 for nine – a complete transformation.

ENGLAND *v.* WEST INDIES

FIFTH TEST, THE OVAL, 1966

ARLOTT: It's going to be Holford to Higgs from the Vauxhall end and remember this is a real last wicket partnership. It's not a recognized batsman on number eleven, it's numbers ten and eleven, in fact when they're at home they're both number eleven. And it's Holford to Higgs and Higgs pushes him very sensibly on the onside – there are three men saving the one on the off, three men saving the one on the on, a leg slip, a long leg and in comes Holford, bowls to Higgs. He tries to swing him, it takes him on the pad and bounces ahead of him down the pitch. A man on the mid-wicket boundary, a man on the long leg boundary. Six saving the one and only one man near to the stumps and Higgs and Snow two runs short of the Test last wicket record.

And Holford bowls to Higgs and again he lets that pop up off his pad and bounce out on to the onside and Hendricks comes out and retrieves it. A few defiant shouts from the Caribbean corner over on the right and Holford comes in again, bowls to Higgs, he tries to swing him, fails and it runs off his pad down to Gibbs at leg slip. And now in again comes Holford, pitches up and Higgs drives it (*Shout.*) – back to him and he's out. Caught and bowled Holford, 63, John Snow not out 59 and 128 for the last wicket. A little pat on the back for

John Snow from Lance Gibbs and the West Indies fieldsmen standing back and applauding the batsmen in. And smiles on the faces of a few of the West Indians as they applaud the batsmen in and the applause in fact a crescendo of amazement and admiration. The last wicket stand has made 128.

The 1977 Gillette Cup final at Lord's between Middlesex and Glamorgan could not by any stretch of imaginative licence be termed historic, but there were high spots.

ARLOTT: One hundred and fifty-three for 5 and Llewellyn really looking for runs and Glamorgan need them now and need them quickly. And they're not going to hit them hard, I would imagine, off Daniel. They've got to try to get after the slower or medium-pace bowlers – and Emburey comes in and bowls. And that's tucked away by Eifion Jones down to long leg – a single only and that's really what they want, anything that will give Llewellyn the bowling. He's not a consistent player, he's rather an erratic one, but when he's going he does hit the ball very hard indeed.

Emburey then goes round the wicket to the left-handed Llewellyn who goes down (*voice rises*) and hits him a sky-high (*shout from crowd*) and that's six into the front of the pavilion (*sound of ball hitting roof*). No, on top of the commentary box. (*Excited laughter and chatter in background.*) And that's a very, very big hit indeed. (*Applause.*) Now, that was a prodigious blow and that was as high as the roof of the pavilion and only fifteen yards short and we've made signs of surrender (*laughter*) asking not to be bombarded, but that was a mighty stroke. Albert Trott once hit one over the top of this pavilion and Frank Mann, I believe, landed on the roof – but that only wanted another ten yards carry and it would have cleared it. As Fred Trueman got up, I thought he was going to try to catch it. (*Laugh.*) I now realize, he was taking cover.

45

QUOTES FROM AND ABOUT

At the Prudential Cup match at Lord's between England and Australia in 1979, scorer Bill Frindall had been indulging in rather elaborate mathematics with his figures for the run-rate.

ARLOTT: Ah, I see that Bill Frindall has done a piece of mental arithmetic with his calculator. Thanks, Bill, for restricting the figure to two decimal places. I did find five decimal places rather wearing. What I really want to know, Bill, is if England bowl their overs at the same rate as Australia did and Brearley and Boycott survive the opening spell and that the number of no balls is limited to ten in the innings and assuming my car does 33.8 miles per gallon and my home is 67.3 miles from the ground, what time does my wife have to put the casserole in?

*

ARLOTT: Cricket is a game of the most terrifying stresses with more luck about it than any other game I know. They call it a team game, but in fact it is the loneliest game of all.

Take the player on a bad trot, desperately needing to come good again. He goes out to bat and gets the only ball that lifts all day. Or the worst fielder who throws out a hand to a ball he hasn't even seen to take what everyone has to regard as a magnificent catch.

The truth is that many of us do not know enough to be profoundly critical. To understand that playing forward when you should be back, or back when you should be forward, can mean a snick, a catch and out. It is a brutal, one-error only game.

*

ARLOTT: I talk about what I see. A lot of commentators tend to talk about what they are thinking rather than what they are watching.

*

DENZIL BATCHELOR: His special gift is that he invites the public to see the whole picture through his eyes. The scoreboard and the strokes are not enough. He sees (let us suppose) Keith Miller, heroic sized, lion-maned, with a disposition that is a cross between that of a Viking and that of an irresponsible schoolboy. He establishes this picture with the public before he tells us that Miller has hit a cover drive or been yorked first ball. He peoples his drama not with the names of cricketers, but with living characters who happen to be playing cricket.

*

ARLOTT: (*after South Africa's 'Tufty' Mann had baffled England's George Mann with three successive deliveries*): It is a clear case of Mann's inhumanity to Mann.

*

ARLOTT: (*describing a bowler with crab-like run and bent knees*): He approaches the wicket like Groucho Marx chasing a pretty waitress.

*

ARLOTT: The umpire signals a bye with the air of a weary stork.

*

ARLOTT: Umpire Alley, the solitary dissident.

*

Tony Lewis's favourite Arlott phrase:
Butcher drops his head, both hands behind the back and looks sheepishly down the wicket like a small boy stealing jam.

*

TREVOR BAILEY (*as quoted by Alan Gibson*): Here come the umpires, wearing their new short coats, looking rather like dentists. Over to John Arlott –

ARLOTT: It occurs to me, Trevor, that it is rather suitable for the umpires to look like dentists, since one of their duties is to draw stumps.

*

ARLOTT: And now it is, in the words of that Oxford poet of the '30s – 'waiting for the end boys, waiting for the end'.

*

Twenty Questions: The object was, What the butler saw.
ANONA WINN: Is it a bit of fluff?
ARLOTT: In its most interesting form, yes.

*

ARLOTT (*discoursing on Jim Laker*): ... very English looking, six feet tall, firmly built, fair-haired, fresh-faced, quiet in demeanour, coming up to the bowler's end with his shoulders hunched, cap at a jaunty angle. He moved to his bowling mark at a constabular stroll and with the laconic air of one with his tongue in his cheek, pattered along a run of artfully varied short strides. Then, wrist and arm cocked, from a good sideways-on beginning, he swung through a model high delivery-arc into the positive follow-through which generated so much spin and life.

*

CARDUS: Hazlitt on his loved jugglers was not more vividly graphic in words than this –

*

ARLOTT (*on Hazlitt*): He has been the greatest influence. Apart from the detail, there is the perfect length, structure and shape –

*

ARLOTT (*on the books in my life, 1957*):

William Hazlitt *The Spirit of the Age*
John Betjeman *New Bats in Old Belfries*
Havelock Ellis *The Dance of Life*
John Stuart Mill *On Liberty*
Michel de Montaigne *Essays*
John Nyren *The Young Cricketer's Tutor*
Lawrence Sterne *Tristram Shandy*
Andrew Young *Collected Poems*

Today, John's choice would be the same and he would wish to extend his desert island reading by adding Beyond a Boundary *by C.L.R. James, Betjeman's* Collected Poems, *and* Death of a Hero *by Richard Aldington.*

*

MICHAEL CAREY (*in the* Daily Telegraph *reporting on a match in the 1984–5 Indian tour and quoted in* Wisden Cricket Monthly):

What appeared to be the familiar voice of John Arlott could be heard joining in the radio commentary from hundreds of transistors. Heads in the press tent turned. Then it was revealed that the voice belonged to Pat Pocock, doing a Yarwood rather than a Larwood.

*

GEORGE SCOTT (*writing about* Cricket on Three *in* The Listener): For myself, whenever John Arlott is off the air, I am waiting for his return. Impersonators have captured his voice, but they have never captured the craft or the imagination of the man. The greatest tribute I can pay to Arlott is that he never sounds like a caricature of himself; it would be so easy for him to do so. It would be easy for him to sound like that, if he ever reached, lazily, for the cliché, or even for the second-hand, reach-me-down phrase that would allow him to get by without extending himself. The astonishing thing about John Arlott is that he seems ever to be seeking the fresh image, the image that will light up his own perception of style or character, even at the most soporific moments of the day. To listen to him is to hear the poet chipping away at the language in public, sometimes failing to carve the scene sharply enough – and he must be conscious himself of the occasions when that happens – but never failing to try to pass on to the rest of us his individual vision.

*

Someone once wrote that John's voice 'has become as satisfying to the cricket lover as the bouquet of matured Burgundy is to the Voice'. In the Evening News, *thirty years ago, he commented on his imitators:* I had just heard Jonathan Miller – in 'Out of the Blue' – give an impression of one of my commentaries. I was wiping the perspiration away when someone asked me: 'Did you think it was a good imitation?'

I do not know. I realize that Jonathan Miller is that rare combination of gifted clown and pretty wit. But I cannot say whether his 'Arlott voice' is like mine because, although I've had the old thing since it was a whimper, I have only rarely heard my 'real' voice, in a few recordings. One's voice as heard from the inside is a very different matter.

One of my first broadcasts – as compère in *Country Magazine* – was recorded and broadcast again, overseas, in the small hours of one Tuesday morning. My wife and I made our sleepy – but for my part, at least, excited – way downstairs, tuned in, and pressed our ears closely to the loudspeaker to catch the faint emanation.

After three or four minutes I said, 'There, I knew I did it badly.'

'What do you mean?'

'Well, it's the same script but they've had to get this country chap in to do it again.' The country chap was myself. I had heard my voice for the first time.

*

DENZIL BATCHELOR: ... before even that brown velvet, or if you like gravelly, voice became known on the air ... remember that someone once remarked to William Barnes, the Dorset poet, 'Why don't you speak the King's English?' – to be told, 'I do: the first King's English: the one that was crowned in Winchester.'

46

On His Seventieth Birthday

In his final season commentating on cricket in 1980, John was besieged at every turn by the media. After his farewell at the Warwickshire v. *Somerset, John Player League fixture at Edgbaston, Russell Davies, in the* Sunday Times, *noted that 'John Arlott, excused from commentary, and almost militantly glass-in-hand, said a last goodbye during the tea interval, thus bringing to an end the most exhausting cycle of interviews any man has undergone since Rudolf Hess landed in Scotland.'*

John had sold most of his cricket book collection shortly before, though that did not signify divorce from the game as a whole, and then moved to Alderney where he enjoys going out in the morning, as he says, 'to have my coughing practice in sight of France'. Immediately, he proceeded to lead almost as busy and active a life as he had ever done – articles for magazines, pieces for the papers, talks and interviews on radio and television, wine-tasting trips to the Continent and Eastern Europe and, oh yes, a solitary well-earned holiday in Tokyo, where son Tim was opening the bowling for Yokohama. He even made a film acting debut as a grandfather in a comedy written by Elisabeth Beresford of 'The Wombles of Wimbledon' fame, that was part of the festivities for the 1984 Alderney Week. Incredibly, it was a silent movie.

At one of the interviews on his 'retirement from the box', John had said,

> *'I am the son of a poor man who has been paid to watch what, as a sixteen-year-old I used to have to save to see. I can look back on conversations with marvellous cricketers, like Maurice Tate and Jack Hobbs, who were schoolboy*

heroes. I can reflect on a game I love taking me way beyond the abstract into the company of marvellous people. And I can, I suppose, liken myself a little to the young lady Oscar Wilde once described thus: "She knew nothing at all about music, but was very fond of musicians".'

That fondness has been reciprocated by practically everyone with whom John has had contact. Examples of his generosity and kindness in dealings with fellow man are legion. Writer and broadcaster, Alan Gibson, phrased it aptly when he wrote: 'John Arlott ... a source of happiness to a great many'.

Just before his seventieth birthday in 1984, John talked with former England captain, current commentator, Tony Lewis:

I think when you're seventy you realize you've probably had the best of life – you've reached the allotted span. I'm lucky – I've got to seventy without – so far as I know and the doctors have not disillusioned me – without any trouble except my wheezy old chest which does sometimes sound like a pair of bagpipes full of dust, but – I get by ...

To John Arlott On His Seventieth Birthday

25th FEBRUARY 1984

Does threescore years and ten
Confer the wisdom of a Solomon?
Well, you were always wise in cricket lore
And, under tranquil skies, your garnered store
Spilled from the treasure chest of memory
To share with us the things that used to be –
Beauty and wit, supremacy or sorrow,
Momentous yesterday, anticipant tomorrow,
Some rustic hit, a bowler spinning spells,
Impassive umpiring, pavilion bells,
Ducks on the pitch, a six, a century,
Groundsmen, Hambledon, the county scores at tea,
Woven in green and white within a hedge
of Tests; good humour pulsing round the edge.
Emeritus professor of the game
With cricket heroes in the hall of fame,
At slippered ease, a connoisseur of wine,
A book, a pipe, old friends to talk and dine,
And cherished memories to muse upon.
Salve maestro! Vive, valeque, John!

by Imogen Grosberg from A Few Quick Singles

Index